SNAKES

of North America

Western Region

SNAKES of North America

Western Region

R. D. Bartlett
Alan Tennant

Maps by Patricia Bartlett

GULF PUBLISHING
Lanham • New York • Oxford

SNAKES

of North America

Western Region

Published by Gulf Publishing
An Imprint of the Rowman & Littlefield Publishing Group
4720 Boston Way
Lanham, Maryland 20706

Distributed by National Book Network

Library of Congress Cataloging-in-Publication Data

Bartlett, Richard D., 1938–
A field guide to snakes of North America—Western region / Richard D. Bartlett, Alan Tennant ; maps by Patricia Bartlett.
p. cm — (Gulf Publishing field guide series)
Includes bibliographical references.
ISBN 0-87719-312-6 (alk. paper)
1. Snakes—West (U.S.) Identification. I. Tennant, Alan, 1943– II. Title. III. Series.
QL666.O6 B3295 1999
597.96′00978—dc21 99-32825
CIP

Printed the United States of America.
Printed on acid-free paper (∞).

Book design by Roxann L. Combs.

Contents

COLUBRIDAE

Racers and Whipsnakes, 39

Vine Snakes, 55

Patch-nosed Snakes, 57

Lyre Snakes, 64

Sand Snakes, 67

Shovel-nosed Snakes, 69

Hook-nosed Snakes, 73

Leaf-nosed Snakes, 77

Ground Snakes, 81

Black-headed Snakes, 84

Night Snakes, 91

Glossy Snakes, 96

Rat Snakes, 101

Kingsnakes and Milk Snakes, 109

Gopher Snakes and Bullsnakes, 126

Long-nosed Snakes, 132

Garter Snakes, Water Snakes, and Allies, 137

Lined Snakes, 171

Problematic Colubrines—Sharp-tailed and Ring-necked Snakes, 173

ACKNOWLEDGMENTS

There are many persons who helped with the compilation of facts and photos for this book. We offer our sincerest thanks to

- Abe Blank, Dennis Cathcart, Fred Gehlbach, Gerald Keown, Ken King, Randy Limberg, Sean McKeown, Dennie Miller, Regis Opferman, Gus Rentfro, Buzz Ross, and Mike Souza, for field companionship and hospitality during our travels;
- Randy Babb, Paul Moler, and Wayne VanDevender, who provided us with encouragement and challenges—encouragement for the task at hand, and challenges of finding some of the better field locations that they so generously shared and at which we photographed;
- John Cadle, Herndon Dowling, Jim Harding, Al Holman, Hobart Smith, and Wayne VanDevender, who all shared thoughts on classifications and/or taxonomy;
- Bob Espinosa, Michael Dunkelberger, Kevin Emmerich, Robert Fisher, Alex Heindl, Randy Limberg, and Louis Porras, for suggestions made;
- Chuck Hurt, Craig McIntyre, Bill Love, Chris McQuade, Rob MacInnes, Mike Stuhlman, and Eric Thiss, who extended to us the privilege of photographing snakes in their respective collections;
- Breck Bartholomew, Chris Brown, Jim Harding, Bob Hansen, Bill Leonard, Gerold and Cindy Merker, Cecil Schwalbe, Chris Scott, Phil Medica, Karl Switak, Tom VanDevender, Wayne VanDevender, and Steve Zimmerman, who provided us with many wonderful photos that have added so much to this volume;
- Kenny Wray, often my field companion on long and, at times, unproductive field trips, and to his wife Maria;
- My wife, Patti Bartlett, who not only persevered through the rather rocky preparation of this book but, through default, undertook the execution of the range maps;
- The late Gordy Johnston who introduced me (RDB) to the wonders of the Chiricahuas more than 40 years ago;

- And finally to Wade and Emily Sherbrooke, of the Southwestern Research Station in Portal, Arizona, who keep alive the feeling of awe and wonderment that was mine when first I saw these mountains.

Thanks again to all.

R.D.B.

Preface

In 1985, the first edition of Alan Tennant's profusely illustrated *A Field Guide to Texas Snakes* was published. It was a runaway hit with herpetologists, herpetoculturists, and laymen alike. Expanding on this theme, in 1997 Gulf Publishing added two snake identification books to their line, Tennant's *A Field Guide to Snakes of Florida* and Philip Brown's *A Field Guide to Snakes of California.* Together these three books discussed the snake fauna of the three states with most species. All were well received.

With *Snakes of North America: Eastern and Central Regions,* which I had the good fortune to co-author with Tennant in 1999, and this, its western counterpart, we have completed the coverage of the snakes of North America.

There is more interest today in the reptiles and amphibians with which we share our world than ever before, and of these creatures, it is the snakes that are foremost in everyone's mind. They may be revered, they may be only tolerated, or they may be disliked; but interest exists, and fortunately, tolerance for this important group of animals seems to be increasing daily. Perhaps the most encouraging thing is that the interest exists at all levels, from the most basic to the most advanced. Interpretive programs are presented regularly in many grade schools. Programs and assemblies and studies continue through middle schools, into high school and there is now a proliferation of undergraduate and postgraduate college courses offering insights to our ophidian neighbors.

Besides academic interests, snakes have become popular pet items, the target subjects of ecotours, and of interest to gardeners and backyard naturalists. Herpetological clubs, and reptile and amphibian expos (always heavy on snakes), are springing up across the country—across the world, in fact. Internet chats and various "on-line" pet forums are readily available to anyone with Internet access. Accurate information about the private lives of many of the more popular snake species is now available to anyone who wants it.

Unlike the Internet and other information sources, in these pages we have provided you with accurate information about not only the popular snakes of the North American West, but about all snakes from that region—from the tiniest burrower, to the big constricting gopher snakes, to venomous species that seek safe haven in remote mountain seclusion. We find all of the 158 species and subspecies in western North America of immense interest, and sincerely hope that you do also.

Dick Bartlett
Gainesville, Florida

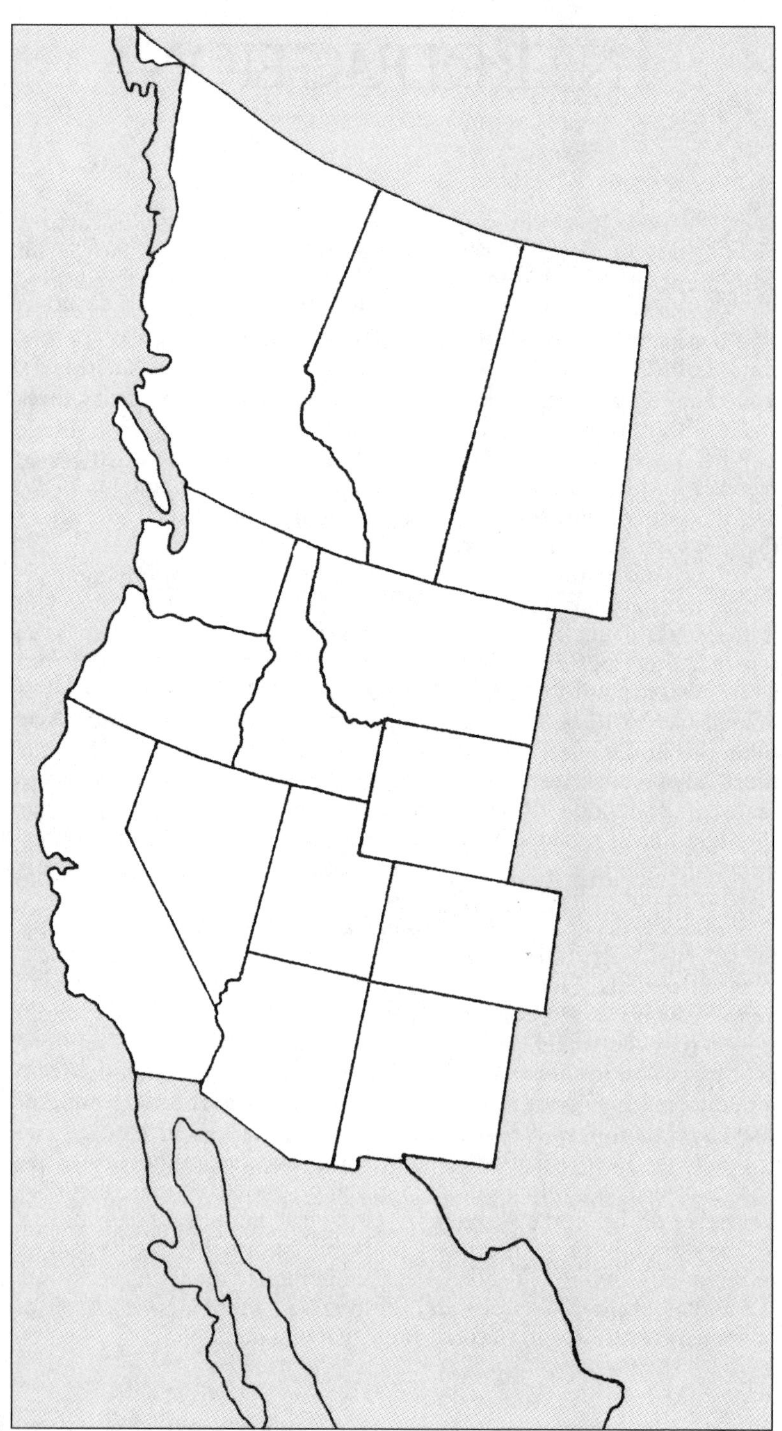

Introduction

Western North America boasts varied topography, varied climate, varied environments, and despite seriously fragmented habitats, a wonderfully varied fauna. The variations are remarkable in many ways. There are forests and deserts, below-sea-level valleys and mountains that are truly worthy of the term "towering," and a climate that varies from hot in northern Mexico to one that comes close to fulfilling the meaning of the word frigid in Canada. Nestled among these many and varied habitats are a wondrous variety of fauna. One can find bison, cougars, and Douglas' squirrels; condors, ravens, and lazuli buntings; and an immense diversity of reptiles, amphibians, and invertebrates. Among the reptiles, there are, of course, the snakes—158 species and subspecies of them, as a matter of fact, and they live in almost every ecological niche. Some are secretive woodland dwellers, some virtually "swim" beneath the surface of hot desert sands, and others inhabit cold montane streams. There is even one that has adapted to life in the ocean. You will meet them all in this book.

Western North America, as defined in this book, is the vast region west of and including the states of New Mexico, Colorado, Wyoming, and Montana, and the Canadian province of Manitoba. We have included the non-contiguous states of Alaska (which has only a single snake species at its southernmost tip), and the mid-Pacific Islands of Hawaii, which, despite their tropical lushness, are home to only two snake species. One, the pelagic, ocean-going, yellow-bellied sea snake, occurs naturally in Hawaiian waters, while the second, the tiny, burrowing, introduced Asian species called the Brahminy blind snake, has been present since at least 1930. There is a possibility, and more than a slight concern, that a third species, the very adaptable, large, highly predaceous, rear-fanged, brown tree snake, a snake that would prove to be an ecological disaster to the islands, will eventually become established.

The two western states harboring the greater diversity of snakes are Arizona and California. Arizona has about 66 species and subspecies of snakes, and California has 76. There are several dangerously venomous snakes in each of these states.

How do you go about finding snakes? The finding of many can be defined in one word—*luck!*—good luck if you're trying to find them and succeed, bad luck if you're trying to avoid them and don't succeed.

Some species may be rather easily found basking on, or crossing, sun-warmed roadways, most often from shortly before dusk when temperatures begin to moderate, to well after darkness has enveloped the land. Some secretive species are surface active *only* after dark, and even then may be only rarely encountered. You may find some snakes by turning surface rocks or discarded construction debris. Some, like the brown vine snake, are not only rare in North America, but are so well camouflaged that unless they happen to be moving, you may look directly at one and still not be aware of its presence.

There is a tendency to classify snakes as harmless, mildly venomous, or dangerously venomous. These terms are actually a simplification of a complex subject. Many of the snakes called harmless, the garter and hog-nosed snakes among them, have complex salivas that may produce a startling (but usually not medically significant) reaction at the bite site. Lividity and edema are two of the symptoms. A bite from some of the smaller snake species termed mildly-venomous (such as the rear-fanged black-headed and night snakes) produces fewer symptoms than a bite from some "harmless species." Because many are reluctant to bite, the significance of a bite from some of the larger rear-fanged species remains unknown. Those snakes termed dangerously venomous are just that, and include the pitvipers, sea snakes, and coral snakes. Steer well clear of all snakes included in these three latter groups. If bitten by any seek medical assistance as quickly as possible (see the chapter on venom poisoning).

Because they are immensely interesting, snakes are often kept as captives. Be aware that many states have laws regulating the capture and/or keeping of (indigenous) snakes. Familiarize yourself with the laws, and be aware that if a snake is collected in violation of a state law, and then taken across a state line, the violation becomes a *federal offense*. Additionally, the Endangered Species Act of 1973 provides federal protection for a few snake species that are now considered endangered or threatened.

How to Use this Book

In these pages we discuss 158 species and subspecies of snakes. While many are of very dissimilar appearance, some are confusingly alike. To add to identification problems, some of these species have two or more color phases. Because of this it is difficult to categorize these creatures by color or pattern. Therefore, we opted to list and discuss all in a traditional manner, divided by families, subfamilies, genera, species, and subspecies.

We do not believe that a guide of this sort is the place to attempt to justify or decry "cutting-edge" taxonomy; we have opted, for the most part, to use the tried-and-true traditional names—common and scientific. Future changes in *both* may occur.

The numerical listing of all species and subspecies in the contents coincides with the numbers in the text and photographs. If you know, or have a good idea what the species is you are researching, begin with the contents listing.

We have listed each major group, genus, species, and subspecies alphabetically by scientific names. Therefore, you may have to search if you know only the common name of a species. Also, check the photo and range map provided for each species.

Scientific names are of Latin or Greek derivation. They can be binomial (two names) or trinomial (three names). Examples of each are:

- Western diamond-backed rattlesnake, *Crotalus* (croat-ah-lus) *atrox* (a-trox). This large and common rattlesnake has not subspeciated; thus it is identified by only a binomial.
- Red-spotted garter snake, *Thamnophis* (tham-know-fis) *sirtalis* (sir-tal-iss) *concinnus* (con-sin-us). The trinomial indicates that this garter snake <u>has</u> subspeciated.

Identification Process

Let's work our way through the identification of a rattlesnake as an example:

While driving a desert road in southcentral Arizona, we've just encountered a small snake lying quietly at the very edge of the pavement. It's reddish-tan and its tail is tipped with a small rattle, easily seen from a distance in the beam of a bright flashlight. The rattle is a giveaway. Turn to the section of pertinent pictures, and you can eliminate those rattlesnakes with dorsal diamonds or strong cross-bands, those with gray or black ground color, and so on.

What we're left with are three races of sidewinder and the south-western speckled rattlesnake.

We look again at the snake and notice that above its eyes there are hornlike projections. That eliminates the speckled rattler.

Suddenly the snake moves from the road and proceeds across the desert sand in a series of loops, its head pointed differently from the direction of travel, an additional confirmation suggested by the common name of sidewinder.

By now the numbered pictures have directed us to account numbers **137, 138, 139** (sidewinders), and we have confirmed our identification.

Now a quick look at the range map will show that only the Sonoran sidewinder occurs in this area, and rechecking the photo will allow us to reconfirm this identification.

While the process of elimination is certainly not scientific, it often will lead us to the same conclusion that scale counts and other more formal procedures will.

A Comment About Snake-like Lizards

Observers occasionally mistake fast-moving, short-legged lizards for snakes. In western North America there are lizards of two genera that look more like snakes than most others. These are the alligator lizards of the genus *Elgaria* (four species that are often referred to the genus *Gerrhonotus*) and the California legless lizard of the genus *Anniella* (one species).

The alligator lizards often exceed a foot in length, and may attain 16 in. They have a distinctly broadened head, a long, easily autotomized but semi-prehensile, tail, an expandable, longitudinal lateral fold separating the dorsal scales from the ventral scales, keeled scales, and short legs, which they use in typical fashion when moving slowly. However, when frightened, the alligator lizards fold their legs back against the body and move in a sinuous, snake-like, fashion. The presence of legs, ear-openings, and eyelids will immediately distinguish these creatures from any snake. Alligator lizards are secretive, woodland, scrubland, and backyard creatures that, when conditions are optimum, can be present in heavy densities. As a genus, these lizards occur from western Montana to southern British Columbia, then southward through much of Oregon, most of California, to northern Baja (three species), with the fourth occurring from southeastern Arizona and southwestern New Mexico, well southward into Latin America.

The California legless lizard is a small (to 9 in.) burrowing lizard that is seldom seen. It searches for its insect repast beneath the surface of sand dunes and gravelly-areas, or beneath surface vegetation. These lizards lack external legs and feet and also lack external ear openings. They do, however, have functional eyelids. They are sharp-nosed, and the tail is blunt. There are two subspecies. One has a silvery dorsum, the other a nearly black dorsum. Both have yellow bellies. As a species, the legless lizard occurs southward along the coast from the vicinity of San Francisco Bay to northern Baja.

A Note on Taxonomy

The science of classification is called taxonomy.

As in any other discipline, there are diverging beliefs, techniques, and applications. Two such different applications are traditional systematics and cladistics. The proponents of either often vociferously decry the suggestions of the other.

Sadly, there is also a current school of thought that allopatrism (non-contiguous populations) equates, in all cases, to speciation. We feel that this is an incorrect assumption, especially because many breaks in range are artificial, and have been caused by the ministrations of humans since the turn of this century. We suggest that every species/subspecies must be evaluated on its own merit.

Because traditional systematics has "worked well" over the years and because we feel that a field guide is not the proper forum for arguing taxonomic principles, we have continued to take this comfortable and conservative approach in these pages. There will be time for changes, if pertinent, later, when agreement is more general.

Wherever we felt it possible, both the common and scientific names used in this book are those suggested in the publication entitled *Standard Common and Scientific Names for North American Amphibians and Reptiles (Fourth Edition)* by Joseph T. Collins.

However, we have diverged on some aspects. We do not advocate the use of "simplified" names when the simplification advocates bad grammar. Thus, instead of the proposed "patchnose snake" for example, we have used "patch-nosed snake."

In time, taxonomy may again become more standardized. We can at least hope so.

The taxonomic scheme for snakes is as follows:

Reptiles

Kingdom: Animalia
 Phylum: Chordata
  Subphylum: Vertebrata
   Class: Reptilia
    Order: Squamata
     Suborders: Serpentes (Snakes)

Despite their singularity of form, snakes are sufficiently variable structurally to allow taxonomists to group them into several different families. Further, within several of the families are small groupings termed subfamilies, followed by the now familiar genera (singular, genus), species, and subspecies.

There are about 2,400 species of snakes in the world, which range in size from the enormity of 30-foot boids (constrictors, such as the Asian reticulated python and neotropical green anaconda) to the few inches of some of the smaller blind snakes of the family Typhlopidae.

In western North America, snakes range in size from the hefty 7 ft of the western diamond-backed rattlesnake to the slender 6–10 in. of the western blind snake.

About the Range Maps

When an area the size of western North America is reduced to a range map of some 1.5 × 1.5 in., there is little hope for complete accuracy. This is especially true when, within a region, a particular snake may be found only in isolated patches of loose sand, along montane streams, or in other localized and specific habitats. The maps should be used only as guides, a way to make you aware that you are somewhere close to the range of a given species or subspecies and to help you eliminate noncontending look-alikes.

What Is a Snake?

Reptiles, as a group, arose from the amphibians, but current thoughts regarding their evolution vary widely. It is rather generally thought that the earliest reptiles appeared about 315 million years ago, in the early Upper Carboniferous period. It is from these reptiles, which were quite lizard-like in characteristics, that modern-day reptiles are thought to have evolved. Snakes are thought to have evolved, about 135 million years ago (during the Lower Cretaceous), from lizards, and through the ensuing eons, and have proven immensely successful. Snakes of some primitive families still retain vestiges of pelvic girdles (boas and pythons even retain external remnants of hind limbs referred to as pelvic spurs) that indicate their relationship to lizards. Today, the extant families (which, varying by authority, may be as few as 11 or as many as 19) contain about 435 genera, and 2,400 (or more) species. Of these, there are 6 families, 35 genera, and 77 species in the North American West.

Predation

All snakes are predatory creatures. Some, because of immense size or virulent venom, are very near the top of the food chain. Others are so small and innocuous that small perching birds, and even toads and frogs often eat them. To an even greater extent than most reptiles, healthy snakes can go for a very long time between meals without ill effects.

Some snakes actively hunt their prey, depending primarily on their acute vision (racers and whipsnakes), gliding sinuously and essentially silently along through the leaves and grasses, head elevated ("periscoped"), or they may find prey by following scent trails. Other snakes are "wait and ambush" hunters, positioning themselves along rodent trails or in other strategic locations, and patiently waiting, for hours, or days, for a prey animal to pass.

Snakes overcome their prey in one or more of several ways. Constriction and envenomation are the two best known methods. Other methods include grasping a prey animal and immobilizing it by throwing a loop of body over it, or simply swallowing the prey animal alive.

When envenomation is employed, snakes with fixed (non-movable) fangs, like the coral snake, usually grasp the prey and retain their grip while the venom does its work. However, the pit vipers, which have long, movable fangs and deliver the venom in a fast strike, allow their prey to run off, then follow the scent trail (the tongue carries scent particles left by the prey to the Jacobson's Organ in the palate for analysis) to the dead or dying animal and eat it, usually only after death has occurred. Likewise, when constriction is used (among others, rat snakes, gopher snakes, and kingsnakes employ this method), the prey is often not swallowed until after it is dead. Constriction does not break bones, but does tighten until respiration is impossible. Burrowing snakes may rely on earth vibrations and scent, more than sight, to locate prey. Indeed, some snakes (blind snakes) rely on their eyes so little that these organs, so important to most species, have become non-functional. Some snakes have developed labial (lip) pits (boas and pythons) or loreal pits (pits on the side of the face between, but lower than, the eye and nostril [rattlesnakes]), which are sensitive to minute temperature changes, such as those produced by the approach of an endothermic (warm-blooded) animal.

Snakes swallow their prey whole. Because a snake's skin is capable of considerable stretching and the jawbones are connected to the skull with muscles and ligaments rather than bone, and because the lower jaw consists of two unconnected bones, snakes can swallow comparatively large prey items. The snake usually swallows the prey nose first, moving first one side of both jaws forward, easing the prey slowly down the throat, then repeating the process with the other side, and doing this again and again. Once into the throat, the swallowing process is assisted by muscular contractions and body curves anterior to the prey that slowly work the prey into the stomach.

Scalation

The scales with which a snake is covered are merely intricate folds of skin. The finished product may be smooth and shiny, be dull and bear a keel, be roughened and rasp-like like the scales of a sea snake, or be lengthened and have a free edge like the belly scales of most snakes. The scales may be of one or more than one color, and the interstitial skin (the skin between the scales) may be colored similarly or differently. When a snake's body is distended, such as with a meal or when a female is heavily gravid, the interstitial skin may be visible, adding to a color scheme hues not normally seen. A snake sheds its skin at strategic times during its life. The causative agents are many and complex. Shedding is associated with growth, with the replenishment of the moisture-impervious lipid barrier, and with pheromone dispersal, but occurs at some rather well defined times in the life of a snake. Among these are following emergence from dormancy, prior to parturition, following an injury, or following periods of climatic change. Young, fast-growing snakes shed more frequently than old adults. For a few days prior to shedding, colors and patterns are dulled and a bluish cast is noticeable, especially clouding the eyes. When the newly formed skin is suitably developed, the old epidermis is nudged free of the lips, and as the snake crawls forward, pushing against irregularities, rocks, and vegetation, it inverts and crawls free of the old skin. Everything, including the transparent brille, is shed. This process is referred to as ecdysis. (See pages 23–24 for scalation diagrams.)

Locomotion

Snakes may move sinuously, pressing the outer edges of body curves against substrate irregularities, or may move straight ahead while paired muscles move their belly scales forward, then rearward, in rhythmic waves. The sharpened trailing edge of each belly scale presses against substrate irregularities, moving the snake forward. When not frightened, heavy-bodied rattlesnakes often employ this method of slow forward movement. Sidewinders, of course, are notorious for their looping method of progression, which moves them in a direction different from that in which the head is directed. Snakes may climb in one or more of three ways. They may simply proceed upward through a thicket by draping their body over various branches. Some snakes may climb a trunk by grasping it with a partial looping of the anterior body, then draw the rear of the body upwards, anchoring it, and pushing the anterior upwards again. Other snakes, like the rat snakes, have belly scales that are angled sharply upwards at their outer edges, forming corners that can catch nearly any irregularity in a tree's bark. These snakes can progress nearly straight up a trunk.

By using a side-to-side sculling motion, most snakes can swim well. Some are surface swimmers that have difficulty submerging while others swim easily well below the surface and may seek prey such as fish, frogs, or invertebrates, while underwater.

Reproduction

Some snakes lay eggs, others birth live young. Not all females breed annually. Males may indulge in ritualized fights to establish breeding rights and territorial dominance. Reproductively receptive females emit pheromones that allow males to trail them, sometimes over long distances. Breeding may involve a male holding a female immobile with loops of his body and/or by biting her on the nape. Prior to breeding some stylized courtship may be indulged in. This may vary from cloacal region stimulation of the female by the spurs of the males, to body vibrations, to the rubbing of the female's nape by the male's chin. Actual breeding may occur while the male and female snakes have their tails entwined or when that of the male is positioned beneath that of the female. If the female finds her suitor suitable, she will lift her tail and open her cloaca, allowing the intromission by one of the male's two hemipenes. Copulation may last from minutes to hours, depending on the circumstances and species involved.

A month or so following a successful breeding, a female of an oviparous species will lay a clutch of eggs in a protected, moisture-retaining area. Some females may produce a second clutch a month or so later. The eggs take 2 weeks (smooth green snakes) to 10 weeks (rat snakes, kingsnakes), or sometimes longer, to hatch. The incubation duration for most species is 55–70 days. It may take the females of live bearing species 3–4 months following breeding to produce their clutch. Live bearing species seldom multi-clutch.

Venom and Envenomation

With their bright, unblinking eyes that reflect an apparently preternatural serenity, an ability to seemingly rejuvenate themselves by casting off their aged skins, and uncanny agility—"the way of the serpent upon the rock"—snakes are clearly different from other animals. For millennia, men have perceived in them intimations of immortality (the serpent that tempted Eve was but one of a long historical line of supernatural snakes), but more often these animals have fascinated men because of their power.

No culture placed more emphasis on serpents' ability to kill than the Toltec-Aztec-Maya civilizations of Middle America, where the early rattlesnake god—ultimately evolved into the feathered serpent Quetzalcoatl—became the deity whose potency sanctified the priesthood's control over every aspect of the peoples' daily lives. The same, seemingly transcendent power of venomous snakes was called upon by the Egyptian priesthood, and by the earliest years of the dynasties the serpent's ability to kill with a pinprick was taken as such a sign of celestial potency that serpent-god, Uraeus, personified by the Egyptian cobra, *Naja haje,* rose among the celestial pantheon to a position second only to that of Ra, the sun king. *Naja haje* thus became the symbol of imperial authority, and the bejeweled face of a cobra glared from the brow of every royal headdress—whose flared neckpiece was itself designed to emulate the snake's spreading hood.

The priesthood, maintaining that the lethal virulence of mortal cobras derived from Uraeus himself, sometimes cut open the limbs of bitten individuals to release the supernatural vapors thought to have been implanted by the reptile's fangs . . . which did no therapeutic good but probably served to further terrorize the populace. Because there was simply no other reasonable explanation for the destructive power of venomous snakebite, however, this supernatural-vapors-theory held sway for hundreds of years after the demise of the last pharaoh, and characterized even the logical Roman approach to medicine. The belief was not challenged in fact until, in one of the lesser-known scientific confrontations of the Renaissance, Francesco Redi opposed the physicians of seventeenth-century Florence (who believed that the virulent symptoms of envenomation were caused by the rage of the serpent, somehow passed, like the madness of a rabid dog, into its victim by the otherwise innocuous saliva), by maintaining, instead, that the "direful effects" of snakebite were the result of a lethal poison held in the snake's "great glands."

There was little to support this point of view, though, for even with the advent of chemical analysis researchers found that those reptilian glands did not hold poison—at least not any substance, such as the toxic alkaloids or burning acids, known to poison. Snake venom, it turned out, was an apparently commonplace protein, so nearly indistinguishable from egg white in structure that in 1886 R. Norris Wolfenden, speaking for the Commission on Indian and Australian Snake Poisoning reported:

> *"It is quite impossible to draw any deductions as to the nature of the poison. It is merely a mixture of albuminous principles."*

The first real clue to how this particular assemblage of reptilian body fluids could bring about the immediate physical deterioration of other animals came six years later, with French physician John de Lacerda's conceptualization of the tissue-disintegrating biological catalysts he termed enzymes.

Much like the enzymes of stomach acid, harmless in the gut but able to break down devoured flesh into its constituent amino acids, the venom of North American pitvipers like the rattlesnakes, copperheads and cottonmouth kills by enzymatically disintegrating its victim. For contemporary victims of envenomation this is a major problem since few but toxicologists have gotten far into unraveling these complex biological sequences, mostly because snake envenomation is a rare injury even in Texas—where more bites occur than in any other state.[1]

Treatment and Toxicology

W.C. Fields liked to tell people he always kept some whiskey handy in case he saw a snake—which he also kept handy. Some people are still drawn to Fields' remedy, but almost no one is aware that following conventional first aid practices is just about as dangerous. Without question, trying to cut open a snakebite wound in the field

---

[1]The vast majority of the several thousand snakebites that occur annually in North America involve non-venomous serpents and require nothing more than reassurance and a tetanus shot. Of the few true envenomations, most occur in the southwestern United States, and less than a dozen a year are fatal.

is far more dangerous than doing nothing at all for, even under the best of circumstances, attempting to suck out the venom from an open wound causes harm and bestows no benefits.

Fortunately, as a practical matter it's also usually out of the question because getting bitten by a venomous snake is such a terrifying experience that subsequently being able to execute this classically prescribed quasi-surgical procedure is simply impossible for most people. It's much better to spend one's efforts getting proper medical management than to try and fumble through ill-advised therapy in the field, and all one need remember is to immobilize the envenomated extremity, remove rings or shoes before swelling makes that difficult, then wrap the limb firmly but not tightly in a splinted elastic bandage. The most important part is promptly getting the victim to a good hospital.

Binding the limb with thin, circulation-cutting cords, packing it in ice for long periods, or cutting open the punctures are dangerous procedures that go awry because they are founded on a basic misunderstanding of the complex process that begins when a venomous snake bites a human being. The scariest misconception is that a strike by one of these animals results in the injection of a dollop of lethal fluid which then oozes through the veins toward the heart. If this were the case one would probably do whatever possible to arrest its progress, but that isn't what happens at all.[2] Once venom enters the body it almost instantly incorporates itself into the body's tissues, where it is no more removable than is ink dripped on a wet sponge. This immediate bonding to tissues doesn't leave venom free to go anywhere else in the body very rapidly either, though, which means that temporarily localizing it in one area is easily accomplished with the mild pressure of an elastic bandage. This simply doesn't call for the radical, invasive techniques of most traditionally-espoused therapies, whose goal is either to drain the venom away or prevent its transit through the circulatory system, neither of which is possible in the hospital, much less in the field.

Why it is not possible—a thought at great odds with the popular concept of snake bite poisoning—is the result of the predatory role venom occupies in a serpent's life. The venom of North American pitvipers is not designed to kill large animals; for example, its primary function is to digest small, mostly rodent prey. Therefore pitviper venom only gradually disperses through the body, methodically

---

[2]Envenomation doesn't always accompany either a coral snake or pitviper bite, and superficial punctures by pitvipers are free of toxins about 15% of the time, while no more than 40% of coral snake bites result in severe reactions. Superficial envenomation is also much more common, and unless heavy envenomation has been established it is irresponsible to destroy irreplaceable nerve and muscle tissue by following invasive first aid measures.

digesting tissues as it goes, using most of its 12 to 30 separate peptides and enzymes for various digestive functions.

Like all digestive processes, this one is complicated, because most of venom's diverse proteases and kinases have different metabolic functions, often a different target organ, and frequently a different way of getting there. These toxins include hyaluronidase, collagenase, thrombin-like enzymes, L-amino oxidase (which gives venom its amber tint), phosphomonoesterase, phosphodiesterase, two kinds of kinases (which are both similar to pancreatic secretions and which prepare soft tissue for more extensive breakdown by analogous solutions in the reptile's stomach), nucleotidase, at least one phospholipase, arginine ester hydrolase, and various proteolytic enzymes.[3]

Within the bodies of human beings bitten by pitvipers these enzymes simply disintegrate the living tissues just as in the snakes' rodent prey—where this sort of pre-ingestion enzymatic breakdown of the prey's internal structure renders large lumpy bodies into softer, more easily swallowed bites. Hyaluronidase, for example, breaks down connective fibers in the muscle matrix, allowing various proteases and trypsin-like enzymes to penetrate the limbs directly.[4]

---

[3]Many of these venom enzymes operate most powerfully in complementary combinations.

[4]Quite different are the deadliest venom fractions, the neurotoxically-active polypeptides. These are the primary venom components of elapids such as the Florida and Texas coral snakes, which are used to paralyze the other snakes on which these elapids feed, but which are often potentially dangerous to the coral snakes themselves. Similar neurotoxically-destructive proteins are present in smaller proportions in all snake venom, even that of ostensibly hematoxic, or blood-targeted venoms, but in the peptide-based venom of elapids these enzymes are targeted toward the neural membranes branching from the upper spinal cord. Here, such peptides block acetylcholine receptor sites in the junctions between adjoining nuchal ganglia, impairing neuromuscular transmission and, by shutting down the autonomic triggering of respiration, can sometimes cause death by suffocation.

Other components of elapid venom are hemolytic, or blood- and circulatory-system directed. While generally less potent than its neurotoxic elements, these cardiotoxic venom components can be lethal in high doses. Wyeth's equine-derived coral snake antivenin (Antivenin, *Micrurus fulvius,* Drug Circular, Wyeth, 1983) does not neutralize these hemolytic elements, however.

Only in fairly high doses does it have any effect against the neurotoxic components of coral snake venom, either, with a median dose 6.5 vials. At this level, 35% of patients experience side-effects; in 50% of those cases, side-effects are severe, resulting in anaphylactic shock or serum sickness.

Another coral snake antivenin, with about the same dosage requirement, effectiveness, and problematic side effects, is manufactured by the Instituto Butantan in Sao Paulo, Brazil, from antibodies generated by a mixture of the venom of two South American coral snake species, *M. corallinus* and *M. frontalis*. Only the new, ovine-based *Micrurus* antivenin currently under development at St. Bartholomew's Hospital, Medical College, London, and the Liverpool School of Tropical Medicine, Liverpool, U.K., neutralizes both neurotoxic and cardiotoxic components of *Micrurus* venom. In preliminary trials during 1993, it has done so with a fourfold reduction in dosage, and because this antivenin is derived from sheep antibodies, the negative side-effects of prior sensitization to equine-based serums used in previous inoculations are largely absent.

In concert with several endothelial cell-specific thrombin-like enzymes, other peptides simultaneously perforate the vascular capillary walls, allowing the seepage of plasma thinned by the simultaneous assault of another set of venom enzymes: phospholipase A combines with lipids in the blood to inhibit their coagulatory function, toxic fibrinolytic and thrombin-like enzymes disintegrate the hematic fibrinogen also required for clotting, and a pair of related hemolysins, specifically keyed to the destruction of red blood cells, attack the erythrocytes directly.[5]

All this begins to occur very quickly moreover, for venom's proteins are so structurally similar to those of its victim that within seconds of injection its toxic enzymes have thoroughly incorporated themselves into the blood and tissues of their recipient.[6]

This affinity of snake venom for living protoplasm was widely recognized among primitive peoples, and stood as the rationale behind the most common American Indian antidote for snakebite, which was to slice through the fang marks and press the freshly opened body of a bird against the wound in the hope that some of the still unbonded serum within might be drawn up into the unsaturated avian tissues. Although venom was never actually sucked out in this way the approach seemed rational enough for variations to have been recommended by frontier medical officers looking for a better means of

---

[5]Circulating lymphatic fluid is the major dispersive avenue of most venom components, but the neurotoxically-targeted peptide components of elapid venoms, including those of the Texas coral snake, disperse primarily through the bloodstream, where they are not subject to any mechanical constraint short of a total tourniquet.

Only antivenin is effective in treating this sort of envenomation, and only in poisoning by such peptide-based venoms is employing a temporary total arterial tourniquet appropriate because, cinched down for more than few minutes a tourniquet is likely to cause permanent injury to the limb, sometimes severe enough to require amputation.

[6]The relative proportion of these elements in the venom mix varies considerably. Determined by the varying output cycles of each of more than a dozen secretory cells that release their separate toxins into a viper's paired storage bladders, or lumens, the venom's composition varies from day to day. This makes venom one of the most complex of biological substances and to some extent accounts for the disparity in potency observed between similarly sized snakes of the same species taken from the wild at the same time. (Since different venom ingredients are present in variable concentrations at any given time, their relative effect on each of a victim's organs may also be somewhat different.)

Outside the lumen, venom will even digest itself, for catalytic agents pumped into the serum from secondary secretory glands located downstream from the primary storage bladder metabolically break down venom's peptide components—which are themselves easily digested proteins.

extraction than the dangerous and ineffective cut-and-suck regimen. Except for the inclusion in some army snakebite kits of thin sheets of latex to place between mouth and wound, however, no improvement on the old method was developed until the 1920's, when Dudley Jackson (1929) slightly refined the extraction approach by placing a series of heat-transfer suction cups over incisions both across the fang marks and around the perimeter of the expanding mound of edema that surrounds most serious pitviper envenomations.[7]

More recently, sophisticated surgical techniques for dealing with the most pernicious type of deep pitviper envenomation were developed by the late Dr. Thomas G. Glass, professor of surgery at the University of Texas Medical School in San Antonio. Although most pitviper toxins reach only subcutaneous levels, occasionally a large rattlesnake accomplishes a much deeper penetration, sinking its fangs through skin, subcutaneous fatty layers, and the outer muscle fascia to deposit an infusion of venom within the muscle belly. While a rattler's toxins are much more destructive here, even a large amount of venom this far below the surface may produce few external symptoms because such areas are poorly supplied with nerve endings. (In subcutaneous tissues great pain, swelling, and discoloration accompany venom poisoning, but at great depth the venom's proteolytic enzymes may be temporarily encapsulated within the underlying layers of muscle, and give few symptomatic indications of how severe the bite actually is. The trick, of course, is being able to tell a real subfascial poisoning of this sort from the far more common, largely symptomless superficial snakebite in which little or no envenomation has occurred, and being able to do it in a hurry. If such a bite is diagnosed, a considerable amount of the infusion can sometimes be removed by deep incision and debridement, although only in this unusual sort of poisoning is a major surgical campaign generally advisable—and then only if it is executed by one of the handful of those experienced in the delicate excision of this sort of deep-lying lacunae.)

Most of the time, however, even under ideal laboratory conditions there is not much to be gained from surgery. In experiments with cats and rabbits, F. M. Allen (1939) demonstrated that no benefit resulted even from removing within five minutes a large volume of tissue surrounding an injection of either western diamondback rattlesnake or eastern cottonmouth venom. Because during this brief time the ani-

[7]Although probably the best of the incision therapies, Jackson's approach was unable to prevent the disabling tissue necrosis associated with severe crotalid envenomation and was entirely useless against the peptide-based venom of the coral snake.

mals had already absorbed the venom's most lethal peptide components, all the victims that received a large enough dose to kill a surgically untreated control also died, leading Allen to conclude that large infusions of crotalid venom spread so quickly throughout a large mass of tissue that even when a large excision follows, the seemingly normal tissue outside the excised area still contains enough venom to cause the animal's death.

Other properties of snake venom also weigh heavily against a cutting into the fang marks after a bite. One of these is the tendency of reptilian toxins to suppress the body's bactericidal and immune responses, particularly the action of its white blood cells, for without the leukocytes' prophylactic intervention, an exceptionally receptive environment awaits the host of pathogens introduced by every deep field incision. Moreover, the rapid dispersal of these infective agents is ensured by the seepage of contaminated plasma and lymphatic fluid that, following envenomation, is suffused through tissues made more permeable by the fiber-dissolving effect of hyaluronidase. It is also almost unbearable to be cut open after a pitviper bite because the digestive dissolution of blood within the subcutaneous tissue releases bradykinin from its disintegrating plasma and serotonin from its serum platelets, and both substances produce burning pain that makes the skin so sensitive that the prospect of crude pocketknife incisions becomes nearly unthinkable.[8]

An even more pressing reason to avoid incision is that the anticoagulant effect of pitviper venom on plasma fibrinogen so impairs the blood's ability to clot that opening an envenomated limb is likely to produce much more profuse bleeding than one would expect. It is always dangerous to risk bleeding in patients with low levels of fibrinogen, and following severe envenomation this is particularly chancy because when people die of snakebite (which happens in less than one percent of poisonings inflicted by native species) loss of circulating blood volume is what kills them.[9] Therefore maintaining suf-

[8]In poisoning by most pitvipers (although envenomations by western (Type A venom) populations of the Mojave rattlesnake, *Crotalus scutulatus,* may entail a large complement of neurotoxically-active peptides) the venom's ultimate target is not the heart, which almost invariably performs perfectly throughout the ordeal, but the lungs. Among snakebite's few fatalities, pulmonary embolism is a nearly universal finding postmortem, but congestive pooling of blood in the lungs seldom has time to accumulate enough fluid to interfere with respiration before fatal shock from loss of circulating blood volume has occurred.

[9]In treating some 200 venomous snakebites, Ken Mattox and his team at Houston's Ben Taub Hospital have used fasciotomy to relieve hydraulic tourniqueting less than a half-dozen times, while Russell, in treating more ophidian envenomations than anyone in North America, has never had to perform a fasciotomy due to excessive intracompartmental pressure.

ficient circulating blood volume is the key to initial management of critical snakebite poisoning, and cutting open a limb which may bleed profusely is not the way to go about maintaining blood volume.

After severe envenomation, internal bleeding of course takes place but, except for the most severe poisonings, it takes hours to lose much blood internally because leakage through enzyme-perforated arterioles and venules only very gradually allows the vascular fluids to pool in the interstitial spaces of an envenomated limb. (Eventually, however, a seemingly minimal amount of such swelling—Findlay E. Russell, the country's leading authority on the subject, estimates as little as a two-centimeter increase in the circumference of a thigh—can account for the loss into the tissue spaces of nearly a third of the body's circulating blood volume, dropping vascular pressure enough to put the patient into shock.)

Ironically, though, the swelling of edema seldom threatens the limb itself. Though huge serosanguinous blisters may bulge up around pitviper bites, the distension is usually soft and limited to the epidermal and outer cutaneous layers. As this fact has become widely known the common practice of surgically opening such swollen limbs—a technique formerly thought to relieve hydraulic pressure built up by the swelling which might cause necrosis due to restricted circulation—is rarely employed, even in the most severe envenomations.[9] (What may help, however, is a mild cooling of the limb, which can offer a slight numbing of the pain. An icepack on the forehead can also mitigate the intense nausea often associated with venom poisoning, and because toxin-induced intestinal spasms have sometimes been violent enough to provoke hemorrhage of the trachea, any reduction in their severity is of importance).

Severely chilling a bitten limb, however, is deadly to it. While the cell-disintegrating action of enzymes is slowed by extreme cold, it would take freezing a limb to achieve sufficient chilling to deactivate its infused venom enzymes.[10]

---

[10]The worst of the cold-treatment therapies was ligature-cryotherapy. This regimen received popular attention during the 1950's as a way to avoid the obvious perils of incision and suction, but it instead combined two extremely destructive procedures: putting tourniquets around a limb or extremity, then radically chilling the constricted part by immersing it in ice, sometimes for hours. As might be expected, tissue deprived of the oxygen exchange and waste dispersal of normal blood flow and subjected to the cell membrane-cracking effect of lengthy chilling—while simultaneously being exposed to a concentrated dose of corrosive venom enzymes—died so frequently that amputations following ligature-cryotherapy became almost routine. Though this procedure is no longer followed in medical circles, a legacy of its erroneous concepts remains, and some public service print materials as well as television commercials still refer to packing envenomated limbs in ice.

By taking the conservative approach of simply wrapping the bitten limb or digit in an elastic bandage, splinting it to keep it immobile, then rewrapping the entire area, one allows essential oxygen exchange while the broad pressure of the elastic bandage (which gently compresses the lymph vessels) slows the largely muscular-contraction-pumped flow of venom-saturated lymphatic fluid (and enzymatic venom fractions, the most numerous components of pitviper toxins, are dispersed primarily through the lymph system).

This singularly safe and effective field treatment dovetails with the medical consensus that now prevails concerning subsequent hospital management of severe reptile envenomation—an approach that relies heavily on the intravenous administration of antivenin combined with antihistamines to stifle allergic reaction. Proponents of this approach maintain that not only are the life-threatening systemic failures that may follow heavy ophidian envenomation best offset by antivenin antibodies, but that the serum offers the only significant means of mitigating the often extensive local necrosis caused by pitviper toxins.

Antivenin

Nearly as biologically complex as the venom it is cultured to neutralize, antivenin is still viewed with suspicion by both doctors and laymen, largely as a result of the poor reputation of earlier, less well-prepared serums. (In particular, the old Institute Pasteur globulin often caused adverse responses because so much was asked of it by European doctors using it under primitive conditions in the bush to treat the devastatingly toxic bites of African cobras, mambas, and vipers.) Administered by an experienced physician with immediate access to intensive care facilities, however, Wyeth's current North American *Crotalinae* and *Elapid* antivenins are fairly safe, although they must be administered with extreme care. Since antivenin can trigger allergic histamine shock, or anaphylaxis—a much more serious manifestation of the ordinary allergic response elicited by sensitizing agents from feathers to pollen—it should never be used outside a hospital.

This is because, like any other immunization, antivenin therapy depends on establishing a protective titer of antibodies in the entire bloodstream.[11] But, unlike other immunizations, to help the victim of

[11]This is why antivenin must never be injected directly into an envenomated extremity: you can't build up immunity in a finger alone.

snake venom poisoning, antivenin therapy must establish this titer in a very short time. That calls for the rapid, massive infusion of the foreign proteins which make up antivenin, but which heavily impact the chemistry of the body's blood supply. (Moreover, if a severe allergic reaction such as serum anaphylaxis occurs, the offending substance obviously cannot be removed. Unmoderated, this allergic response can result in enough swelling to obstruct the respiratory passages, and even coronary attacks have occurred.)[12]

Yet administered by an experienced physician with immediate access to intensive care facilities, both Wyeth's current North American *Crotalinae* and *Elapid* antivenins can save lives. The most critical aspect of their use lies in the need for immediate intervention, usually with antihistamines, to offset the coronary or respiratory difficulties that may be provoked. (Before antivenin can be administered each patient's sensitivity to equine proteins must be determined, which is done by a standard allergic-reaction skin test trial.)

---

[12]Anaphylaxis could probably be avoided altogether if animals other than horses were used to make antivenin, but historically only horses—the traditional source animals for all types of immunization vaccines—have been bled for the serum antibodies they produce in response to small, periodic injections of snake venom. These antibodies are so nearly the same for all North American pitvipers that Wyeth distributes a single antivenin, *Crotalinae*, for use against the bites of copperheads, cottonmouths, and all indigenous rattlesnake species; for coral snake envenomation, Wyeth has a separate antivenin, Micrurus.

The problem is that horses have been used to produce so many antigen-bearing vaccines that people who have been inoculated against typhoid, tetanus, and diphtheria bacilli have often become sensitized to equine cellular matter. This does not create a problem when they receive the very small dose of foreign protein involved in subsequent immunizations, but when a large volume of equine proteins is suddenly dumped into their systems (as happens during emergency antivenin therapy), they sometimes experience allergic anaphylaxis.

Other experimental animals have also been used to produce plasma antigens, but only on a small scale: pitviper antivenin prepared from both sheep and goat blood has produced milder reactions than the equine vaccines because few people have been sensitized to sheep and goat proteins. Antivenin has even been derived from western diamondback rattlesnake blood—to which no one is pre-sensitized. This antivenin has afforded laboratory animals a high level of protection from the effects of pitviper envenomation, especially when combined with goat antibodies.

Human beings could also generate reaction-free antibodies if anyone were willing to undergo the misery of periodic minimal venom poisoning. Understandably, no commercial human-globulin antivenin has ever been produced, but William E. Haast, who for many years operated the Miami Serpentarium, has injected small, antigen-producing amounts of elapid venom into himself for decades. As a probable result, he has survived a number of what in all likelihood would otherwise have been fatal cobra bites and has even transfused his own presumably antigen-bearing blood into other victims of elapid poisoning, perhaps mitigating the effects of their envenomations. (Haast, incidentally, is now in his mid-eighties and remains amazingly vigorous.)

Individuals vary so widely in their sensitivity to antivenin infusion that some people need nearly twice as long as others to build up the same blood level of antibodies, but if it can be tolerated, several vials of the vaccine may be given during the first hour. Infusion is then maintained at two or three vials per hour until an adequate plasma titer is established, after which a marked decrease in the discomfort of the poisoning is normally evident.

The reason for this dramatic improvement lies in the way antivenin acts to prevent the proteolytic, fibrinolytic, and hemolytic action of snake venom. Introduced into the bloodstream, its equine antibody clusters are drawn to the venom's large, variably-shaped toxic peptides and enzymes. (Enzymes are usually spherical; peptides may be tubular, coiled, or globular, but all are spiked externally with sharp-edged, key-like protuberances that penetrate the venom's target cells and disintegrate their structure.) Antivenin antibodies physically encrust these protrusions so thickly that the toxins can no longer penetrate their target cells, eventually building up enough protective frosting to attract the body's particle-devouring macrophagocytes—cleaner cells which, like giant amoebas eventually engulf and digest most of the conglomerate specks of alien protein.

But they don't do it without problems. As the last of the deactivated antibody-antigen complexes precipitate out of the blood 6 to 10 days after treatment, they may lodge in vascular vessel walls throughout the body, causing the skin rashes, hives, and temporary kidney impairment that collectively are known as serum sickness. Moreover, long after recovery a small cadre of the body's own antigens (spawned both by the venom and by the antivenin's equally foreign horse serum antibodies) typically remains in the bloodstream, sensitizing the individual to any subsequently encountered equine globulins—or to another snakebite.

Although both *Crotalinae* and *Micrurus* antivenin are kept by major hospitals, an emergency source is the producer, Wyeth Laboratories of Philadelphia (610 688-4400). Another option is to contact the Antivenin Index, compiled by the Arizona Poison Center, which offers a comprehensive array of data on venomous snakebite and a list of all the antivenins currently stored in the United States, including those for foreign species. Their 24-hour emergency number is 602 626-6016.

Finally, some authorities on envenomation by both native and exotic reptiles are:

Arizona Poison Control System
Coagulation Research Laboratory
Department of Pediatrics,
University of Arizona Health Sciences Center
Tucson, Arizona

James L. Glenn, M.D.
Western Institute for Biomedical Research
Salt Lake City, Utah

L.H.S. Van Mierop, M.D.
Department of Pediatrics (Cardiology)
University of Florida Medical School
Gainesville, Florida 32611

Damon C. Smith
Therapeutic Antibodies, Inc.
St. Bartholomew's Hospital Medical College
Charterhouse Square
London, EC1, U.K.
(New Coral Snake Antivenin)

Venom Potency Table

The following comparative values for the relative venom toxicities of some of the venomous snakes of western North America are based on the widely accepted standard known as the LD50. This stands for the Lethal Dosage, or amount of venom required to kill, within 24 hours, 50% of the laboratory mice injected with it. Used in slightly varying interpretations since the 1930s, it is the standard set (using the Spearman-Karber injection method and employing genetically-uniform Swiss-Webster laboratory mice) by the World Health Organization in 1981.

Species	High	Low	Mean
Western Diamond-backed Rattlesnake, *Crotalus atrox*	4.07	8.42	6.25
Western (Prairie) Rattlesnake, *Crotalus viridis*	2.0	2.37	2.19
Mojave Rattlesnake, *Crotalus scutulatus* (type A) Yuma, Arizona	0.13	0.54	0.34
Mojave Rattlesnake, *Crotalus scutulatus* (type B) Eastern New Mexico/Western Texas	2.29	3.8	3.05

As a comparative measure of venom potency, the numbers used here are a compilation of 13 major studies of venom potency conducted over the last 63 years on snakes from many different parts of the U.S.[13]

Such collective averaging is valid only as an approximation of the general relative toxicity of the venoms of these species because of the great variability that exists in the make-up and potency of toxins taken from the same snake species. (Venom samples obtained from adult individuals of the same species, taken at the same time of year, are often found to be radically different in the relative proportions of their various hematoxic/neurotoxic venom components.) This variability is compounded by the slightly to highly variable differences between regional snake populations.

The venom potency numbers cited here therefore include the highest and lowest potency values (0 being the most toxic) recorded by any of these studies, as well as the mean.

[13]Compiled from: Githens and Wolff (1939), Gingrich and Hohenadel (1956), Minton (1956), Russell and Emery (1959), Hall and Genarro (1961), Weinstein et al. (1962), Russell (1967), Cohen et al. (1971), Kocholaty (1971), Minton (1974), Glenn and Straight (1977), Glenn and Straight (1978), Russell (1980).

Scalation

Head Scales:
Nonvenomous Snake

Head Scales:
Pitviper

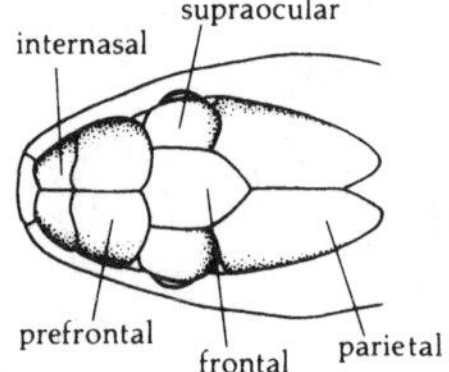

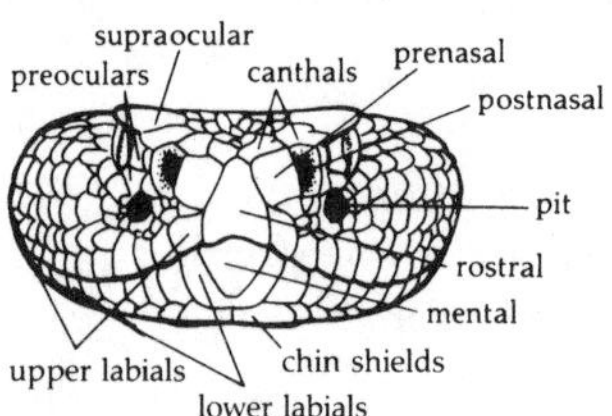

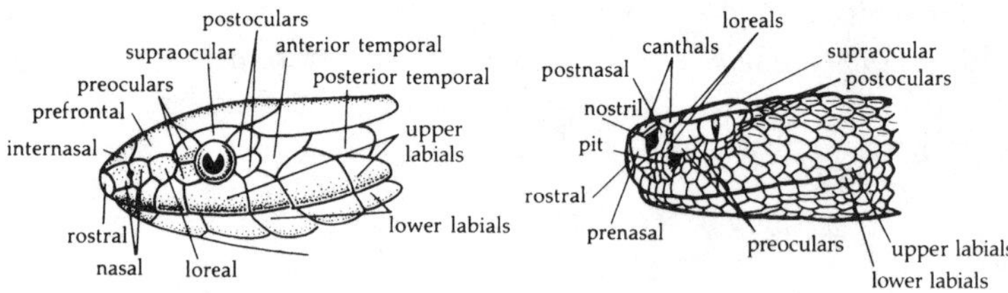

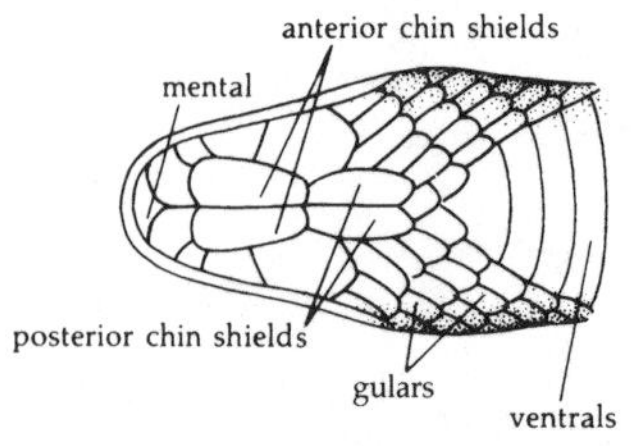

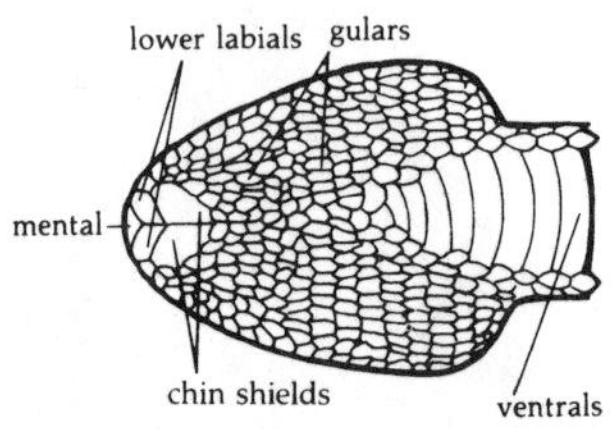

Undertail:
Nonvenomous Snake

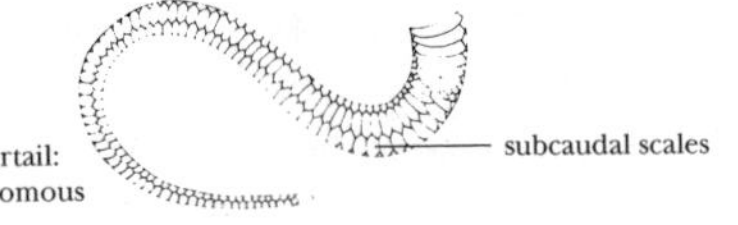

Note: The nonvenomous Texas longnose snake has a single row of subcaudal scales.

Undertail:
Pitviper

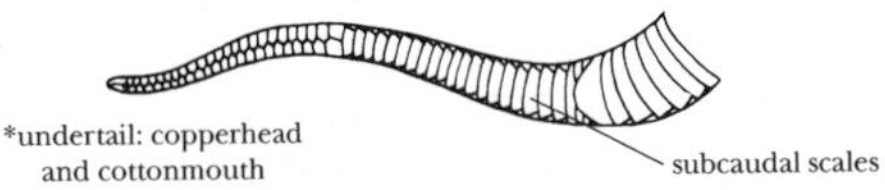

Note: The venomous coral snake has a double row of subcaudal scales.

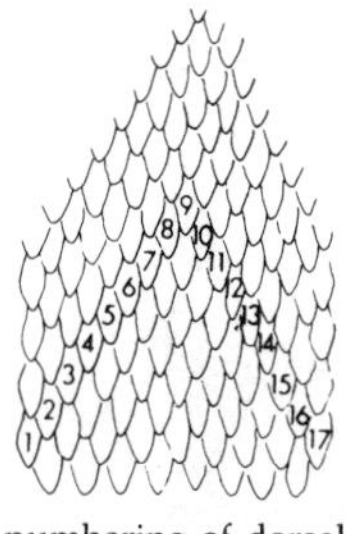

numbering of dorsal scale rows

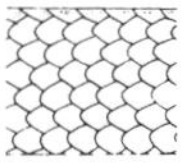

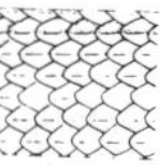

smooth scales

keeled scales

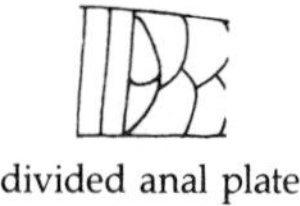

divided anal plate

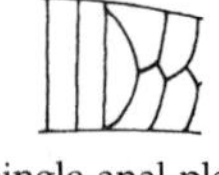

single anal plate

SLENDER BLIND SNAKES
Family Leptotyphlopidae

Within this family are nearly 80 species contained in 2 genera. Of these, only 2 species in a single genus, *Leptotyphlops,* occur in the United States. Both species occur west of the Mississippi River. The blind snakes in this family have teeth only in their lower jaw and have the untoothed maxillary bones fused solidly to the skull.

Slender blind snakes lack enlarged ventral scutes and functional eyes. They are persistent burrowers that surface occasionally in the spring and autumn and when summer rains flood their burrows. It is thought that these snakes feed largely on the larvae and pupae of ants, but subterranean termites and the burrowing larvae of some beetles are also accepted. The snakes in this family are oviparous.

The 2 species are distinguished by the number of scales between the ocular scales.

These snakes may tip the body scales slightly upward when handled or frightened, then appearing silvery in color.

Trans-Pecos blind snake
(L. h. segregus)

Plains and New Mexico blind snakes
(L. dulcis)

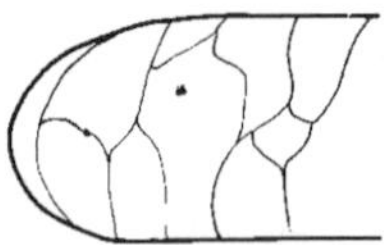

Plains blind snake
(L. d. dulcis)

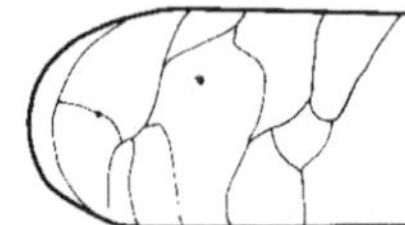

New Mexico blind snake
(L. d. dissectus)

1 New Mexico Blind Snake

Leptotyphlops dulcis dissectus 

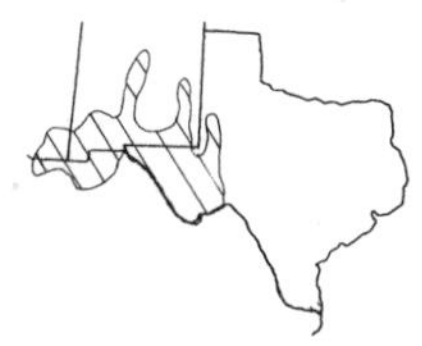

Nonvenomous This diminutive burrower is entirely without venom.

Abundance This is a common to abundant species in suitable habitats. At times, more than a half dozen individuals may be found under a single piece of suitable debris.

Size Only rarely does the New Mexico blind snake attain a size of more than 9.5 in. (10.75 in. is the record size). Most specimens are between 5–8 in. long. Hatchlings are said to be about 2.75 in. long (Behler and King, 1979).

Range This snake occurs to the north and the south of the international boundary from southeastern Arizona, eastward to Val Verde County in western Texas, then northward to southwestern Kansas and extreme southeastern Colorado. A possibly disjunct population exists in central New Mexico.

Habitat This snake burrows persistently, thus is seldom seen. It may be surface active in the evening in warm weather, or during or after heavy rains. It occurs in sandy, yielding soils, where it is most frequently found beneath moisture-retaining natural and human-generated ground-surface debris. Rocks, discarded newspaper, and construction debris, lying on sandy soil, are favored hiding areas. At least a small amount of soil moisture is necessary for the long-term well-being of this blind snake.

Prey Tiny insects—principally ants and their pupae, and termites—are the preferred food of these snakes.

Reproduction Little is known about the reproductive biology of these snakes. Up to 6 eggs may be laid. Eggs, and gravid females, have been found in July as much as 2.5 ft underground in communal chambers.

Coloring/scale form Although lacking annulations, this little snake looks superficially like an earthworm. It is a shiny, but pale, brown to pinkish-brown dorsally, and paler below. This snake has a blunt nose, and a spine- (albeit a *tiny* spine) tipped, blunt tail. There are no enlarged belly plates and the head, neck, and body are all the same diameter. The eyes are present, but are buried beneath a translucent scale and are basically non-functional. There are three scales between the ocular scales and the supralabial (the scale between the scale that covers the eye and the one that contains the nostril) scale is divided in two. The jaw is countersunk, and the anal plate is not divided.

These snakes have a very reduced head scalation. Species and subspecies are distinguished by the number of labial scales and interocular scales. It may be necessary to use a magnifying glass to determine the distinctive characteristics.

Similar snakes *Leptotyphlops humilis* ssp. has only one scale separating the ocular scales; see the account below.

Behavior The New Mexico blind snake is entirely fossorial. Heavy rains may induce surface activity. When attacked by ants, or other predators, the tiny snake writhes and smears repellent cloacal fluids on its body.

Additional subspecies The **Texas Blind Snake,** *Leptotyphlops dulcis dulcis,* occurs east of this area and is described in Tennant and Bartlett's "eastern-and-central-regions" counterpart to this guide.

2 Desert Blind Snake

Leptotyphlops humilis cahuilae

Nonvenomous This diminutive burrower is entirely without venom.

Abundance This is an abundant, but easily overlooked snake.

Size The record size for this snake, the largest subspecies by an inch or two, is 15.5 in. Most are considerably smaller, however, normally measuring 6–12 in. long.

Range This subspecies occurs in southeastern California and southwestern Arizona.

Habitat Although an aridland form, like others in this genus, to thrive, the desert blind snake must have a little moisture in the soil. It is most often found beneath moisture-retaining surface debris, but is fully capable of digging deeply in its search for moist environs.

Prey Although ants, their pupae, and termites figure prominently in the diet of this snake, other arthropods, including surface-dwelling species, are also opportunistically eaten.

Reproduction This is an oviparous species. A clutch can contain up to 6 elongate eggs. It has been speculated that the young are 4–5 in. long at hatching.

Coloring/scale form This is a small, shiny, purplish-brown snake with a paler belly. There is only a single scale separating the ocular scales. The eyes are visible as dark spots beneath the translucent ocular plates. The head, neck, and body are of similar girth. The lower jaw is noticeably countersunk. Both head and tail are blunt; the tail is tipped with a tiny spine. The belly plates are not enlarged. There are 12 rows of scales ringing the tail. This race has 5 weakly pigmented (purplish) dorsal scale rows.

Similar snakes ***Leptotyphlops dulcis*** ssp. has 3 scales between the ocular scales; see the previous account. The silvery legless lizard has eyelids.

Collectively, the 4 subspecies of this little snake are called "western blind snakes." Many researchers do not recognize the various subspecies. The characteristics that distinguish the subspecies are relatively minuscule, and can be difficult to ascertain. Rely heavily on range for identification purposes.

Behavior This snake is rather frequently surface-active after darkness has fallen. When frightened, it will coil tightly and, while writhing, smear itself with pungent cloacal fluids, which apparently act as a predator repellent. This ploy is also used when the snake is attacked by the ants on which it feeds, and even successfully wards off the attacks of introduced fire ants while the snake feeds on their pupae. If grasped, the snake will press its tail tip spine against the hand of its captor, a startling, but, nevertheless, innocuous ploy.

3 SOUTHWESTERN BLIND SNAKE

Leptotyphlops humilis humilis 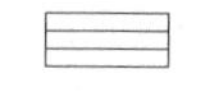

This, the nominate race, ranges widely over much of southern and central Arizona, northward to the southernmost tip of Nevada, westward to the coast of southern California, and southward along the Pacific coast of Baja to mid-peninsula. It has 12 rows of scales ringing the tail and 7–9 strongly pigmented (purplish) rows of dorsal scales.

4 TRANS-PECOS BLIND SNAKE

Leptotyphlops humilis segregus 

This is the easternmost representative of this species. It ranges westward along the Rio Grande, from Val Verde County, Texas to Santa Cruz County, Arizona. This race has only 10 rows of scales ringing the tail.

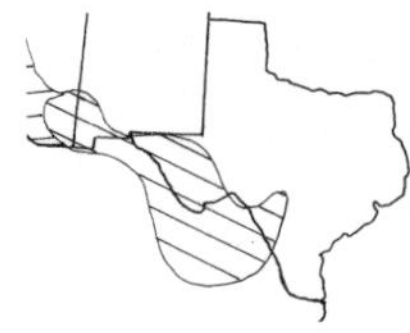

5 UTAH BLIND SNAKE

Leptotyphlops humilis utahensis 

Found in southwestern Utah and adjacent Arizona and Nevada, this race has 12 rows of scales ringing the tail and 7 purplish (pigmented) dorsal scale rows.

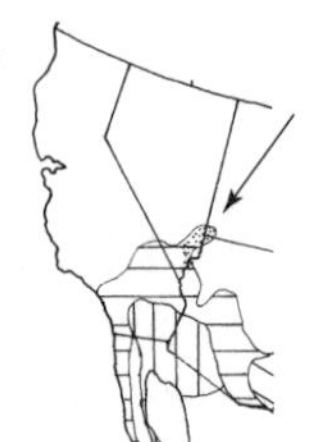

TYPICAL BLIND SNAKES

Family Typhlopidae

The 3 genera in this primarily tropical family contain more than 160 species. All are persistent burrowers. None are native to North America, but one, the Braminy blind snake, has been introduced to the southern half of peninsula Florida, has now been found in the Lower Rio Grande Valley of Texas, and is also firmly established on most of the islands in the Hawaiian chain. In this family the maxillary bones are toothed and are <u>not</u> fused solidly to the skull. The lower jawbones bear no teeth.

6 Brahminy Blind Snake

Ramphotyphlops braminus 

Nonvenomous This snake is entirely devoid of venom.

Abundance Population densities are difficult to assess. In suitable habitats these snakes appear to be extraordinarily abundant.

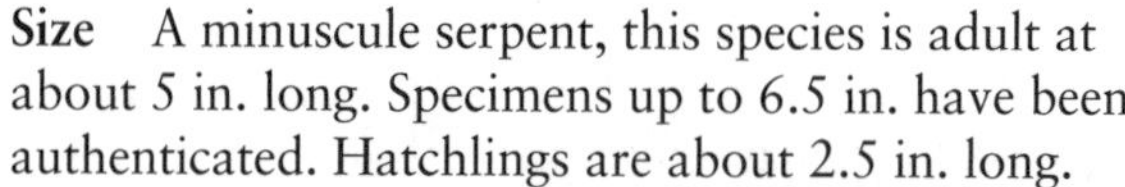

Size A minuscule serpent, this species is adult at about 5 in. long. Specimens up to 6.5 in. have been authenticated. Hatchlings are about 2.5 in. long.

Range Within the scope of this book, this species is known to occur on most of the principal Hawaiian Islands. It also occurs in Australia, Asia, Latin America, and elsewhere in tropical and subtropical regions of the world.

Habitat This burrowing snake is found in areas where the soil is rather loose and retains at least vestiges of moisture. However, the snake is most common in irrigated areas such as lawns and gardens, in naturally moist, often shaded, areas, and is often found in the soil of potted plants. They are often found beneath all manner of moisture-preserving natural and human-generated surface debris.

Prey It would seem that termites figure most prominently in the diet of this snake, but ant pupae, and small, soft-bodied insect larvae are also eaten. After grasping a termite, the snake rubs the insect along the dirt confines of the burrow to break the insect's hard jaws (and sometimes the head) off before swallowing the body.

Reproduction The Brahminy blind snake is a unisexual, parthenogenetic, oviparous, all-female, species. Males are unknown. Each snake is, therefore, potentially capable of producing eggs. Gravid snakes have been found throughout most warm months of the year, and may breed year round. Each clutch contains 2–8 (usually 2–4) eggs.

Occasional mention has been made of this species bearing live young (Tennant, 1997). However, in all cases, specimens in my (Bartlett's) possession have had elongate eggs. It is possible that, as presently understood, this is a complex of species, rather than a single species. This fact would well account for certain discrepancies in authority's statements regarding the reproductive biology of the Brahminy blind snake. Because of one of its favored habitats, the tiny Brahminy blind snake is often referred to as the flowerpot snake.

Coloring/scale form This little snake has smooth, shiny, scales of dark gray to black (silvery-blue immediately prior to ecdysis) dorsally. The belly is lighter. The chin, throat, anal region, and underside of the tail tip are often particularly pale. The ventral scales are not enlarged. Both head and tail are blunt, but a tiny spine tips the tail. The eyes are rudimentary and are covered by a large, translucent scale. The lower jaw is countersunk, an adaptation found in many burrowing snakes. Body, neck and head are of similar girth. There are 18–20 rows of scales at midbody. There is no enlarged anal plate.

Similar Snakes None in Hawaii.

Behavior This tiny snake is persistently fossorial. They may crawl about the surface of the ground following heavy rains but are seemingly uneasy and are jerky and spastic in their motions. When suddenly uncovered, such as when a rock or log is lifted, these snakes disappear into their system of burrows in a literal blink of an eye.

BOAS AND PYTHONS

Family Boidae

Subfamily Erycinae

Today, the boas of the American southwest are steeped in taxonomic uncertainty. An argument has been made that not only are the rubber and the rosy boas congeneric and in the genus *Charina,* but that the West African snake long known as the burrowing python is also a member of that genus. These suggestions have not been widely accepted.

Earlier, an effort to redefine the subspecies of the rosy boas was attempted. The proposed changes were well researched, but they, too, have met with resistance.

Additionally, taxonomists differ in their opinion of whether the 3 races into which the rubber boa is traditionally broken are valid.

We reiterate here what we have stated elsewhere: We do not believe that a field guide is the forum for arguing the validity of controversial taxonomic proposals. Realizing that there is no such thing as a "middle of the road stance" here, we have, nonetheless, chosen to treat the taxonomy of the North American members of this family in the manner that we feel they will be best recognized by the casual observer and by hobbyists. We have diverged from the taxonomic course suggested in *Standard Common and Current Scientific Names for North American Amphibians and Reptiles* by recognizing the genus *Charina* (rubber boa) with 3 races and the genus *Lichanura* (rosy boas) also with 3 races in North America.

The boas are considered primitive snakes. Those of North America are of stocky build and small size but are powerful constrictors. Vestiges of the pelvic girdle remain. Additionally, a tiny movable spur on each side of the vent—a vestige of a hind limb—is present. These are most visible on males; those of the females may be actually hidden in a pocket of skin. A coronoid bone is present in the lower jaw. Rubber boas have large plate-like scales on the top of their head; the scales on top of the rosy boa's head are small and fragmented. Both genera of our boas have vertical pupils; both lack enlarged chinshields. The subcaudal scales are not divided. The body scales are tiny and non-keeled.

7 Coastal Rubber Boa

Charina bottae bottae 

Nonvenomous Rubber boas are entirely nonvenomous.

Abundance Although it is secretive and very easily overlooked, the coastal rubber boa can be present in suitable habitat in considerable numbers. This subspecies does not seem to be in serious decline at any point in its extensive range.

Size This small constrictor is adult at 15–25 in. The very occasional specimen may attain 30 in., and the record size is 33 in. Neonates are 7.5–9 in. long.

Range This race of the rubber boa ranges northward, to the east and the west of California's central valleys, from central California through western Oregon and Washington to extreme southwestern British Columbia.

Habitat The rubber boa may be encountered in several diverse habitats. Look for this little snake beneath decomposing logs or beneath other moisture retaining surface debris, including that generated by humans. It can be particularly common in coniferous forests, but also occurs in mountain meadows, suitable grassland habitats (especially at woodland edges and beneath streamside debris). It also seeks refuge under the loosened bark of standing and fallen trees and in burrows, both those of small mammals and those of its own making. It occurs from sea level to elevations of more than 10,000 ft.

Prey Small rodents (especially nestling mice), an occasional shrew, nestlings of ground dwelling birds, lizards, smaller snakes, salamanders, and possibly, anurans are opportunistically eaten by rubber boas. These snakes are powerful constrictors, but may not actually kill small prey items before eating them. Rubber boas are capable of forming more than a single constricting coil at one time. If rodents are encountered in a burrow where constriction is difficult or impossible, they may be merely pressed against the wall of the burrow to immobilize them.

Reproduction In the manner characteristic of all New World (and most Old World) boas, the rubber boa gives birth to live young. Parturition occurs late in the year, and 1–9 babies are produced.

Coloring/scale form Dorsally, rubber boas are a unicolored tan, brown, olive-brown, or olive-green. The lower sides may have a dusting of slightly darker pigment. The body skin appears loose and may fold into accordion-pleats when the snake coils or turns tightly or constricts. Most males bear prominent cloacal spurs. The tail is thick and blunt and may be rather easily mistaken for the head. Scars from rodent bites or other injuries are darker than the ground color and may make old specimens appear sparingly patterned. The scars are often most prevalent posteriorly, and especially so on the tail. The belly may vary from cream to yellow or olive-yellow and may be marked with patches or smudges of dark pigment. The ventral scutes are well developed, but proportionately narrow. The eyes are small, but fully functional, and have vertically elliptical pupils. The top of the head bears several large plates arranged in a rather unique manner. The babies are more brilliantly colored than the adults, often being an orange-brown to salmon. This brilliance fades quickly with growth. The scales of this race are usually in 45 or more rows. The anal plate is not divided. The parietal scale is usually mostly or entirely divided longitudinally. The upper labials reach the eye.

Similar snakes There is no other snake species in the North American west that could be easily mistaken for a rubber boa. However, the 3 subspecies of rubber boa are very difficult to distinguish from each other. The differences, if valid, are based on the number of rows of body scales, the number of ventral scutes, and whether or not the parietal scale (the rearmost large scale on the top of their head) is single or divided longitudinally into two.

Behavior The rubber boa may be particularly active as storms or frontal systems lower the barometric pressure. This little snake can be surface-active at 55–65°F, temperatures sufficiently cool to render many other snake species inactive. During the hot days and nights of mid-summer, rubber boas may burrow deeply below the ground or into a shady, decomposing stump and aestivate. Rubber boas are largely crepuscular and nocturnal, but may be active by day during the breeding season. These snakes ball tightly when frightened, often elevating their blunt tail above the level of the body. The often heavy scarring on the tail of the rubber boa is usually credited to the supposition that the rubber boa uses that member to fend off the bites of adult mice or shrews while it is raiding their nests of young. Although this is a possibility, no captive that I (RDB) have had has shown such an inclination.

Comments If in the pet trade, it is conceivable that the Indian sand boa could be mistaken for a rubber boa. Despite the Indian sand boa being much larger, the two share the same suite of characteristics, including the blunt, and often scarred, tail. However, the Indian sand boa has a large, wedge-shaped, horizontally oriented, rostral scale, with a very sharp anterior keel.

8 Southern Rubber Boa

Charina bottae umbratica 

This subspecies occurs only in 3 small disjunct ranges in southern California where it is considered a threatened species by that state. It tends towards a smaller size (breeding adults may be only 11–15 in. long), often retains a somewhat brighter ground color, and has 44 or fewer rows of body scales, 191 or fewer ventral scutes, and an undivided parietal scale. This diminutive snake is only known to occur in 3 small, elevated regions of southern California. These are in the Tehachapi, the San Bernardino, and the San Jacinto Mountains. Despite its threatened status, this snake can be reasonably common in suitable habitats.

9 Rocky Mountain Rubber Boa

Charina bottae utahensis 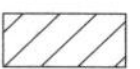

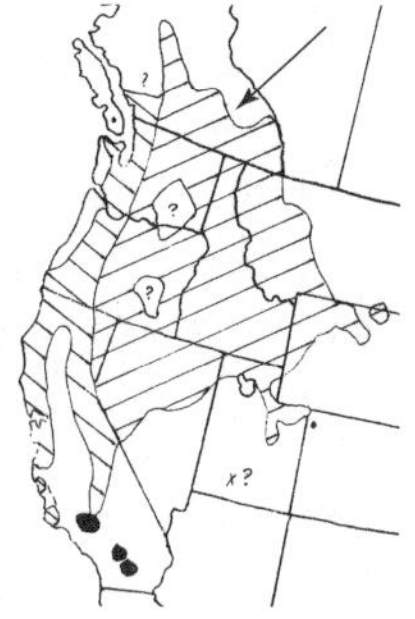

This is one of the two larger forms. It is very similar to the coastal rubber boa, but has 44 or fewer scale rows, a parietal scale that is mostly or fully divided, and 192 or more ventral scutes. This is the inland race of the rubber boa, which ranges southeastward from southcentral and southeastern British Columbia to northcentral Wyoming, then southwestward to central western Nevada.

10 Desert Rosy Boa

Lichanura trivirgata gracia 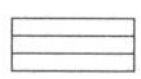

Nonvenomous Like all members of this family, the desert rosy boa is entirely nonvenomous.

Abundance Despite being a true mainstay of the pet industry for more than three decades, rosy boas remain a relatively common snake over much of their range. They persist even in suburban settings and can be common in ranchland settings where rodents abound due to ample year-round supplies of grains.

intergrade

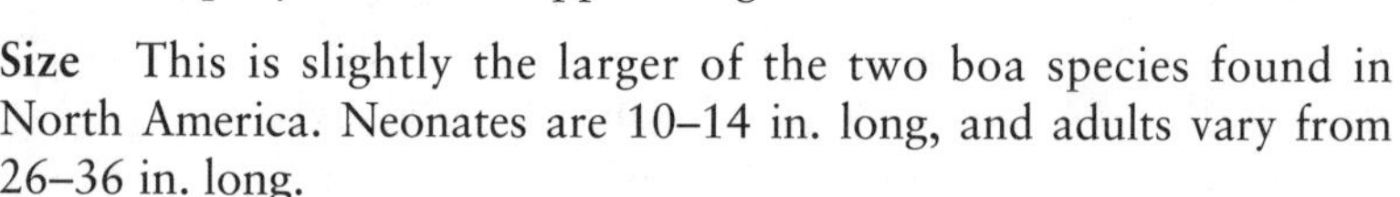

Size This is slightly the larger of the two boa species found in North America. Neonates are 10–14 in. long, and adults vary from 26–36 in. long.

Range The desert rosy boa occurs in inland regions of southern and southwestern California, and southwestern Arizona.

Habitat This is a snake that is associated with arid and semiarid scrublands, rocky deserts, desert oases, canyons, talus, and other such rockstrewn regions. Although rosy boas often seem most common near canyon and desertland streams, they are by no means restricted to such locales.

Prey Besides the typical fare of rodents, rosy boas accept such prey as small ground-dwelling birds, lizards, smaller snakes, and amphibians. These snakes are powerful constrictors, but large rosy boas do not always kill very small prey before beginning to swallow it.

Reproduction A live-bearing species, female rosy boas produce 1–14 (normally 2–7) babies annually. Females of larger size and ample body weight produce more and larger babies. The neonates are 10–14 in. long.

Coloring/scale form The desert race of the rosy boa is defined by having three well-defined tan to reddish-brown to brick-red stripes against a ground color of tan to grayish-beige. While some spotting of the stripe color may be present in the ground color, this is usually sparse at best. The stripes are usually very prominent and quite straight-edged. Males usually have prominent anal spurs. The tail is short, but tapers to a point. The crown of the head is covered with small, fragmented scales. A row of supraocular scales separate the upper labial scales from the eye. The belly may vary from cream to grayish, and each ventral plate is usually noticeably darker anteriorly. The subcaudals are not divided. Neonates are colored and patterned similarly to the adults.

Similar snakes The combination of stockiness, suppleness, small head scales, no enlarged chin-shields, pattern (of most specimens) and rather short, but tapered, tail are diagnostic.

Behavior The rosy boa is far more surface-active than the related rubber boa. It is also active at much higher temperatures, but may aestivate, or at least be activity restricted during the hottest months of the year. Although this species is capable of burrowing, it seems to much prefer merely seeking cover beneath surface debris (including that generated by humans), or occasionally, in the already excavated middens of kangaroo rats or other burrowers. The rosy boa is primarily crepuscular and nocturnal in habits, but may begin to prowl early or remain active late in the morning in cool weather.

Comments The taxonomy of the rosy boa is very confused. David Spiteri has argued convincingly against the validity of the subspecies *gracia* and the use of the subspecies *roseofusca* for California snakes. He believes both to be of the subspecies *myriolepis,* a term used now by hobbyists to identify the brightly colored rosy boas of the central Baja Peninsula. His findings have been ignored more on a technicality than due to erroneous conclusions on Spiteri's part.

Additionally, it has been suggested that the subspecies *arizonense* be used for certain rosy boa populations in Arizona. As mentioned elsewhere, the continued use of the generic name "*Lichanura*" has also been challenged.

Because these snakes are so often kept captive, we feel that we should mention that if kept in humid situations, they often languish. In the humid southeast, or in high-rain or fog-belt areas, they should routinely be offered water only once or twice a week, and kept without water otherwise.

11 Coastal Rosy Boa

Lichanura trivirgata roseofusca 

This subspecies is often darker, and nearly invariably, less precisely patterned and contrastingly colored, than the desert rosy boa. The ground color of this snake varies between brownish, olive-gray, gray, or bluish-gray. Of the 3 stripes, which are irregularly edged and are brown, orange, or rust, the dorsal stripe is often the widest and most irregular. The stripe color also occurs as scattered spots between the stripes. The venter is predominantly dark, but the posterior edge of each scute is lighter. This race attains the largest size. Occasional examples may attain, or slightly exceed, 3.5 ft in length.

intergrade

A unicolored phase—the stripes are absent—occurs in southern San Diego County, California and adjacent Baja California.

The coastal rosy boa is found from southwestern California to northern Baja California. They can be common to abundant in suitable habitat.

12 Mexican Rosy Boa

Lichanura trivirgata trivirgata 

The smallest of the three races, this primarily Mexican race has a very limited range in the area covered by this guide, where it occurs only in *extreme* southern Arizona, from just east of Organ Pipe Cactus National Monument westward to the southwestern corner of the Cabeza Prieta National Wildlife Refuge. It is unusual to find specimens more than 30 in. long. This race of the rosy boa has a very light (cream to straw-yellow) ground color, and very precisely edged chocolate to black stripes. It is rarely seen in the United States, but is reasonably common in western Sonora, Mexico.

intergrade

Advanced Snakes
Family Colubridae

As currently defined, this is a vast and unwieldy assemblage to which most of the world's snakes are assigned. The contents of this family are rendered somewhat more workable by the erection of several subfamilies, and of tribes within the subfamilies.

Although generally referred to as harmless, several of these snakes have toxic saliva and some have enlarged teeth at the rear of the upper jaw. All should be handled carefully.

The colubrine snakes vary widely in appearance and lifestyles. Many are short, stocky, and terrestrial. Some are glossy-scaled burrowers. Others are slender speedsters that may as readily ascend trees as seek refuge on the ground, and yet others are persistently arboreal, seldom descending to ground level.

For this book, we are recognizing the subfamilies Colubrinae, Dipsadinae, Lampropeltinae, and Natricinae, and have relegated 3 genera, *Contia, Diadophis,* and *Heterodon,* to problematic status, affinities undetermined. Additionally, for the sake of clarity, we are recognizing the colubrine tribe Sonorini, a subgroup that contains numerous burrowing snakes, some of which are rear-fanged, and many of which were once in the subfamily Xenodontinae. This tribe has been elevated to subfamily status, the Sonorinae, by some researchers.

Racers, Whipsnakes, and Allies
Subfamily Colubrinae

This subfamily includes the most typical of the colubrines, the racers and whipsnakes, and their allies. Most of the species are nonvenomous, but the vine snakes and the lyre snakes have a rather mild venom and fangs near the rear of the upper jaw with which to administer the venom.

Racers
Genus Coluber

Although they are broadly subspeciated in eastern North America, only 2 forms of the racer occur in the west. These are the eastern and the western yellow-bellied racer. Because the ranges of the 2 are not extensively contiguous, there is a growing tendency by researchers to consider the western yellow-bellied racer a full species. We resist this concept. Racers are absent from vast areas in our southwest.

Generally thought of as terrestrial serpents, racers can and do climb readily.

Racers are noted for their alert demeanor, readiness to bite if molested, and considerable speed. Ontogenetic changes are marked.

Hardly could a scientific name be more erroneous than the specific designation "*constrictor*" that has been bestowed upon this species, for the racers are, most emphatically, *not* constrictors. They merely grasp their prey and swallow it alive, occasionally making a cursory attempt to immobilize a struggling prey item with a loop of their body. But they never constrict.

All members of this genus are oviparous, and produce eggs with a characteristic "pebbly" shell.

The scales are smooth, arranged in 17 rows at midbody (usually dropping to 15 rows anterior to the vent), and the anal plate is divided.

13 Eastern Yellow-bellied Racer

Coluber constrictor flaviventris 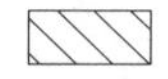

Nonvenomous However, like other racers, if cornered this fast and feisty snake will strike energetically; if carelessly held it will bite repeatedly. It can draw blood, but the wounds are rather insignificant. They should, however, be washed and cleaned with an antiseptic.

Abundance Although common, this alert snake may flee before it has been seen. As would be expected, it is most common where there is adequate ground cover, but it may also be seen in open situations well away from vegetation.

Size This racer is adult at 36–48 in. long. Rarely, a specimen may attain or exceed a length of 5.5 ft. The record size is 5 ft. 10 in. Hatchlings are from 8–11 in. long.

Range This quietly colored but pretty snake ranges widely from Iowa and Arkansas westward to central Montana and central New Mexico. An isolated population exists in central eastern Arizona.

Habitat This snake may be found in a broad cross-section of habitats. Look for it in mesquite-prickly pear associations, in shrubby fields, in open woodlands and riveredge situations, and in grasslands. It is common in the vicinity of debris-strewn deserted homesteads, farms, and ranches.

Prey Although lizards and frogs seem the principal prey items of the adults, small rodents, nestling birds, and insects are also accepted. Juveniles accept locusts, crickets, cicadas, and non-noxious caterpillars, but will also eat lizards and frogs, and newly-born mice or hatchling birds, when they are encountered.

Reproduction Egg laying occurs in early summer. Females may produce from as few as 4 to as many as 28 pebbly-shelled eggs. Incubation lasts 45–65 days. Larger females seem to produce larger clutches. Hatchlings are about 11 in. long.

Coloring/scale form Like the other races of this far-flung species, the eastern yellow-bellied racer has smooth scales and a divided anal plate. The dorsal ground coloration is bluish, blue-gray, greenish, greenish-gray, or brownish-green. The sides may be lighter than the dorsum. The interstitial skin and leading edges of the dorsal and lateral scales may be quite dark. Upper and lower labial scales are white to yellowish, and the venter is creamy to a rather bright yellow. This race usually has 7 upper labial scales. Its pupils are round.

The hatchlings have a ground color of tan to buff or gray with dark-edged, dark gray to brown dorsal saddles and dark spots on the side. These are best defined anteriorly and either fade noticeably or are absent posteriorly. The venter is light. There is no postorbital stripe.

Similar snakes The green snake is smaller, bright green dorsally and butter-yellow to white ventrally. Gopher snakes have heavily keeled scales. Great Plains rat snakes have weakly keeled scales and a dark spearpoint atop their head. Glossy snakes are patterned dorsally and, at all stages of their life, have a postorbital stripe. Night snakes and lyre snakes have vertically elliptical pupils.

Behavior Although it is primarily terrestrial, the eastern yellow-bellied racer may readily ascend shrubs and bushes. They are alert to all nearby movement and may either freeze or flee if approached. When alerted or hunting, this snake may raise its head well above body level in an attempt to better see and assess a given situation. If unable to flee, this snake may stand its ground and strike savagely.

The alacrity with which a startled yellow-bellied racer disappears into even sparse cover can be nearly as disconcerting as their occasional aggressive stance.

Comments Allopatry, the separation of range, does not in itself equate with speciation. For this reason, we continue to consider the western yellow-bellied racer (discussed next) a subspecies of C. *constrictor* rather than a full species.

14 Western Yellow-bellied Racer

Coluber constrictor mormon 

This subspecies ranges from southcentral British Columbia in the north to southern California in the south and extends as far east as western Montana and western Colorado.

This race of the black snake is very similar to he eastern yellow-bellied racer in appearance and habits. However, it has 8, rather than 7, upper labial scales.

In the North American west the western yellow-bellied racer inhabits riparian situations, pond edges, and other areas where water is usually or always available, and where its amphibian prey may be found. It also occurs in semi-aridlands where it preys on lizards. It does not prefer true desert, but is occasionally encountered in such habitats.

This westernmost representative of the species reportedly has smaller egg clutches than the eastern forms. Clutches seem most often to number 4–8 eggs.

Smooth Green Snake

Genus Liochlorophis

This is a monotypic genus. The smooth green snake, a tiny, secretive insectivore, is the sole representative. This is the brightest green snake in the North American west, and it has a yellow-tinged white belly.

Its vision seems acute.

An oviparous species, its eggs have been known to hatch in as few as 4 days.

The smooth green snake has only recently been removed from the genus *Opheodrys* and placed in the genus *Liochlorophis*. The scales are smooth and in 15 rows.

This snake is related to the racers.

15 SMOOTH GREEN SNAKE

Liochlorophis vernalis 

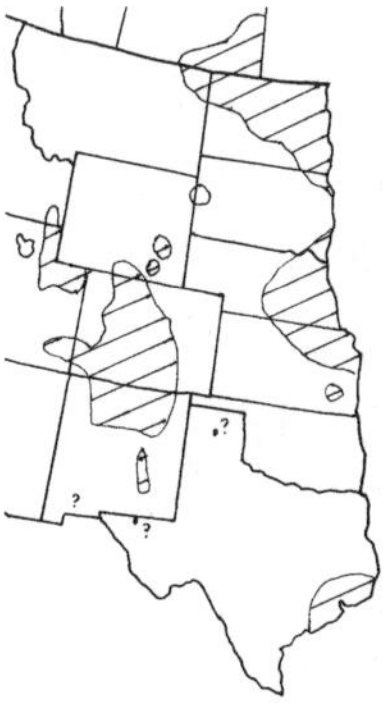

Nonvenomous This small snake seldom bites and is entirely nonvenomous.

Abundance This snake remains common in some areas, but has become uncommon, or disappeared entirely from others. Like those of other insectivorous snakes, populations of the smooth green snake have suffered in areas where insecticides are regularly or heavily applied.

Size Most smooth green snakes vary between a foot and a foot and a half in total length. Occasional specimens may near, or slightly exceed, 2 ft long. Hatchlings are about 5.5 in. long.

Range The smooth green snake is widespread in eastern North America, but of spotty distribution in the west. West of the 100th meridian, the smooth green snake occurs in eastern Montana, Wyoming, Colorado, Utah, New Mexico, and Chihuahua, Mexico.

Habitat This is a well camouflaged diurnal snake of fields and fencerows, orchards, and meadows. It is also found in open, damp woodlands, and may regularly be found in shrubby clearings or woodland edges. This snake prefers moist areas where it prowls slowly, usually in a terrestrial search, for its prey. It is often found, especially when preparing to shed, beneath boards, newspapers, or other human generated surface debris. Although the smooth green snake is fully capable of climbing, it is less prone to do so than the more southerly rough green snake. However, it often ascends into tufts of leaning grasses, low shrubs, and vines.

Prey Caterpillars, crickets, and spiders seem to make up the bulk of the diet of this pretty little snake. Other non-noxious insects are opportunistically accepted.

Reproduction Up to a dozen (usually 3–8) eggs are laid during the summer months by female smooth green snakes. The incubation duration is curiously variable but, in all cases, comparatively short. Reports of eggs hatching in as short a time as 4 days, or as long as 4 weeks, following deposition have been handed down. However, an incubation period of 10–20 days seems most common.

Coloring/scale form This is the only uniformly leaf-green (rarely, olive) snake in the western United States. Its belly varies from white to yellow. Upper labial scales are yellow. Prior to shedding and soon after death, the colors are muted, often being gray or bluish-gray. Until their postnatal shed, hatchlings are grayer or of a more olive than leaf-green color. The scales are smooth—nonkeeled—and in 15 rows. The anal plate is divided.

Similar snakes None within the scope of this book.

Behavior This is a nonobtrusive snake that relies on camouflage rather than flight as protection. If startled, it often ceases all movement in hopes of avoiding detection. This species seldom displays overt hostility. Rarely, if extremely frightened, this species may gape, displaying the dark interior of its mouth.

Comments The leaf-green color alone will readily identify this very non-obtrusive snake. Its insect-eating habits should endear it to gardeners throughout its range.

Subspecies Difficult-to-differentiate subspecies are occasionally assigned to this snake, but the current trend seems to be to just consider the smooth green snake a somewhat variable, nonsubspeciated, form.

Coachwhips and Whipsnakes

Genus Masticophis

These snakes are closely allied to the snakes of the racer genus *Coluber*. The coachwhips and whipsnakes are alert, slender serpents that often seek prey by periscoping their head above the surrounding grasses and ground plants. Their vision is apparently acute, and they seem to rely as much on visual as on chemical cues when pursuing prey. All manner of prey—frogs, lizards, smaller snakes (including those of their own kind), small mammals and birds—are opportunistically eaten. Because of their response to visual cues, coachwhips and whipsnakes readily locate and predate the nests of birds in shrubs and low trees. The food is not constricted.

The snakes of this genus are primarily diurnal and are often out and active on even the hottest of summer days.

Many of these snakes are of somewhat similar appearance. This is particularly true of the many races of coachwhip, *Masticophis flagellum* ssp., some of which occur in several color phases that may broadly overlap one another. Origin and scalerow count can be important in arriving at a positive identification. The scalerow count varies from 15–17. The scales are smooth, the anal plate is divided.

While rather narrow (bluntly lance-shaped), the head is deep and well defined from the slim neck. Whipsnakes are most often striped; coachwhips are plain or barred.

Although they would prefer a rapid and uneventful escape to a standoff, if cornered, coachwhips and whipsnakes vibrate their tail, assume a striking S and some (especially the coachwhips) will bite strongly. Some may even approach an offending object (such as a human) as they strike. All are nonvenomous. Bite wounds should be cleansed and treated if necessary.

Like the closely allied racers, the whipsnakes lay eggs with a characteristic granular shell.

16 SONORAN MOUNTAIN WHIPSNAKE

Masticophis bilineatus bilineatus

Nonvenomous

Abundance It is difficult to accurately assess populations of many of the wide-ranging whipsnakes—this one included. They are certainly not rare, but like a "Will-o'-the-wisp," Sonoran whipsnakes are everywhere, and nowhere. We seldom find them when looking specifically for them, but often see them crossing country roads or mountain trails, or along canyon streams when we are driving or hiking on nonspecific missions.

Size Although this snake can reach 5.5 ft in total length, its extreme slenderness causes it to look smaller. An average adult is 3.5–4.25 ft long.

Range This snake ranges westward from extreme southwestern New Mexico to central Arizona. The range extends far southward into Mexico.

Habitat The Sonoran whipsnake is pretty much a habitat generalist, being found in all but the most arid desert regions. Look for it by day as it basks or hunts in grasslands, thornscrub, open woodlands, rangelands, and in the proximity of mountain and desert streams.

Prey Lizards, amphibians, smaller snakes, newly born mice and rats, and hatchling birds are all prey items to this whipsnake. Adept at locating birds' nests, the snakes readily ascend shrubs and low trees in their search for nestlings.

Reproduction From 4–12 pebbly-shelled eggs are laid in early summer. Incubation last for about 2 months, and the hatchlings are about 13 in. long.

Coloring/scale form This is a beautiful, if rather quietly colored snake. Dorsally, the head and tail are often a warm-brown (they may be gray to nearly charcoal) while the neck and mid-body regions are grayer. The venter is yellowish, often brightest subcaudally. The chin is unspotted on snakes from the eastern portion of the range but may be spotted on specimens from more westerly areas. A light stripe, best defined anteriorly and narrowly bordered with darker pigment, is present on the upper half of scale row 3 and the lower half of scale-row 4. A broader light stripe involving most of scale row 1 and the lower half of scale row 2 is also present. A dark stripe, often broken, is present on the lowest one third of scale row 1. A dark stripe borders the top of the upper labial scales and a short light stripe is usually present on the side of the nose. The scales are smooth and usually number 17 rows at midbody.

Similar species The striped whipsnake has 15 scale rows at mid body. Garter snakes are proportionately stocky and have keeled scales.

Behavior This is an alert and difficult to approach snake. They may occasionally be surprised as they hunt frogs and lizards along canyon-bottom streams in the early morning, but even when cool, the snakes are remarkably agile and adept at evading a captor. If pursued, the snake may flee quickly, then stop and lift its head above the ground vegetation to assess the status of the situation.

Comments This pretty snake may be occasionally seen on the grounds of the Arizona-Sonora Desert Museum and along the roadways in Saguaro National Monument, Chiricahua National Monument, and other such places designed for general public access. Unless you are lucky enough to find a quietly resting specimen, however, you may see little more than a streak of gray as the snake crosses the roadway.

17 Ajo Mountain Whipsnake

Masticophis bilineatus lineolatus 

This race is no longer recognized as distinct by all researchers. It was distinguished from the Sonoran Mountain Whipsnake by a very narrow (only one half of one scale row) upper stripe and by a strongly spotted chin. Specimens having these characteristics are most common on Ajo Mountain in western Pima County, Arizona.

18 Sonoran Coachwhip

Masticophis flagellum cingulum

Nonvenomous

Abundance This and the several other subspecies of coachwhips are commonly seen snakes. In arid areas, they can be seen with frequency around stock-tanks, flooded playas, and smaller, even more temporary, waterholes.

Size Although a slender species, this snake, like other races of the coachwhip, is somewhat stouter proportionately than the whipsnakes of other species. A length of 6 ft is commonly attained.

Range This race of coachwhip ranges far southward into Mexico from western Santa Cruz County and immediately adjacent Pima County, Arizona.

Habitat This is a snake of mesquite-prickly pear, palo verde-creosote bush, and other thorn scrub associations, rangelands and gravelly deserts. Although it ranges far into the aridlands, it is also frequently encountered in riparian situations. Although predominantly terrestrial, it is able to climb well and regularly ascends trees and shrubs to bask and hunt.

Prey Small mammals, birds (especially nestlings) and their eggs, lizards, other snakes, and amphibians are the normal prey items of this snake. Hatchling and juvenile specimens readily accept insects such as locusts and cicadas.

Reproduction Gravid females lay their clutch in the early summer. From 4–18 (rarely a few more) eggs are placed in a protected moisture-retaining substrate. When conditions are ideal, incubation can take only 45 days. It more normally lasts 60–70 days. Hatchlings are about 13.5 in. long.

Coloring/scale form This race of coachwhip, like most others, is very variable in color. Several distinct ground colors, as well as pattern variables, are known. The origin of a given specimen must be carefully considered when a positive identification is attempted.

The Sonoran whipsnake is typically a pinkish snake with broad, darker red to brownish-red bands. The bands are usually wider than the lighter fields between them. Pattern and color is more intense anteriorly. A pale, narrow collar is usually present. The ground color may vary from pink, through tan or light reddish-brown, to black.

Specimens lacking the dark bands are well known, but seem more common in Mexico than in Arizona.

The large supraocular scales partially shade the eyes and give these snakes a scowling appearance.

The large, non-keeled (a dark longitudinal line in the center of each scale may give the appearance of keeling) scales are in 17 rows at midbody. They may also be tipped and/or edged dorsally with dark pigment. This gives them a "braided" look from which the common name is derived. The anal plate is divided.

Similar species See the accounts numbers 19–23 for comments on additional races of the coachwhip. Racers of the genus *Coluber* are not red; whipsnakes are usually striped.

Behavior It seems to most who see it that this snake has but a single speed—fast. However, it often basks quietly in the early morning sun, crawls slowly with its head and neck elevated well above the ground cover of its desert homeland, climbs agilely in shrubs and trees, or may seek seclusion in the burrow systems of small mammals or in the deep cracks formed by the quickly drying ground.

Comments This snake often becomes a road-casualty because of its propensity for stopping to eat road-killed small animals. It is a fast snake that may, if closely pursued, stop and turn to face its enemy (man included), then striking and biting savagely. Conversely, if actually captured, it may play dead, angling its head sharply downward, and allowing rather indiscriminate handling without retaliation.

Subspecies An additional 5 races of coachwhip are found in the western United States. All are variable and many can be difficult to identify with certainty. Again we state that knowing the exact origin of any given snake may do more to allow a subspecific identification than the appearance of the snake.

19 BAJA CALIFORNIA COACHWHIP

Masticophis flagellum fuliginosus 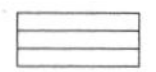

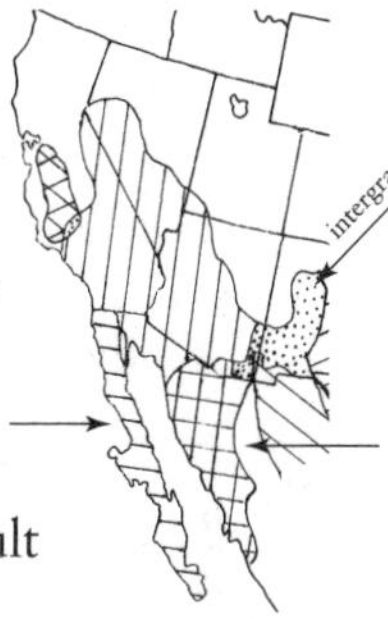

This subspecies enters the United States only in extreme southeastern San Diego County, California. Although this snake occurs in both a light (pinkish, through yellowish, to light-gray; most common on southern Baja) phase and a dark (dark grayish-brown; occurs throughout the range) phase, only the dark phase is known from its very tiny range in the United States. This race of coachwhip has narrow, light, longitudinal lines on its anterior sides. The normal adult size is 5–6 ft.

20 LINED COACHWHIP

Masticophis flagellum lineatulus 

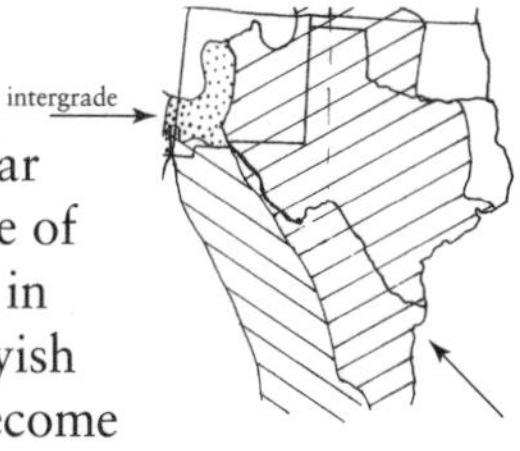

This subspecies is found in the extreme southeastern section of Arizona, along the international boundary in New Mexico, and far southward into Mexico. It attains an adult size of about 6 ft. This race is seemingly less variable in color than many of the others. It is a light grayish tan anteriorly and may retain that color, or become suffused with a light pink posteriorly. Dark dorsal neckbands are poorly defined or absent. The underside of the tail (subcaudal scales) may be a rather bright pink. Each anterior body scale bears a dark, longitudinal, central line. Together these produce a lineate pattern.

21 Red Coachwhip

Masticophis flagellum piceus 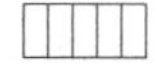

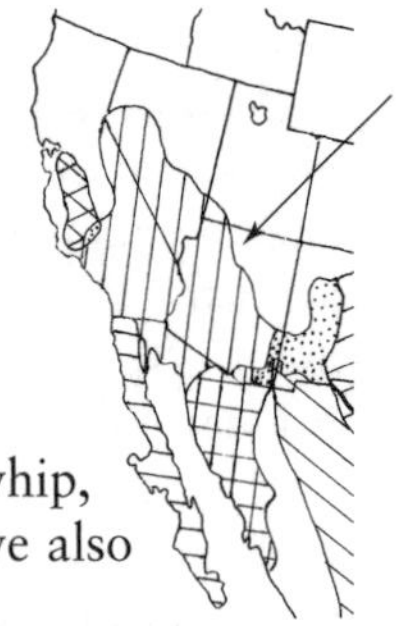

Also referred to as the red racer, this subspecies ranges widely over most of Arizona, southern Nevada, and southern California. It intergrades widely with the western coachwhip in western Texas where, as would be expected, coachwhips with a suite of confusing characteristics exist. Intergrades between the red coachwhip and the Baja California coachwhip, the San Joaquin coachwhip, the Sonoran coachwhip and the lined coachwhip have also been documented.

The red coachwhip exists in 3 well differentiated color phases, as well as in several intermediate colors and patterns. The principal phases are red and black, but a yellow phase also occurs. In the former the principal color is an unpatterned black, except for posteriorly and on the tail, where some red pigment (especially beneath the tail) is usually visible. The red phase is just that, primarily red dorsally and laterally, but with a variable amount of black present on the nape. The top of the head may be tan or red. Narrow light crossbars are usually present anteriorly. The red phase of this slender 6-ft-long snake is remarkably beautiful. The yellow phase is similar to the red in all contrasting markings, but rather than red, the ground color is an olive-yellow.

22 San Joaquin Coachwhip

Masticophis flagellum ruddocki 

Due to habitat degradation in California's San Joaquin Valley, this subspecies is now an uncommon snake. It is protected by the state of California. This is a rather dull-colored race of coachwhip, having a ground color of tan, grayish brown, or yellowish brown. It lacks a contrastingly colored head and, if neckbands are present, they are poorly defined, at best. The belly may be lighter than the dorsum in color, and the subcaudal scales are tan to pale pink.

23 Western Coachwhip

Masticophis flagellum testaceus 

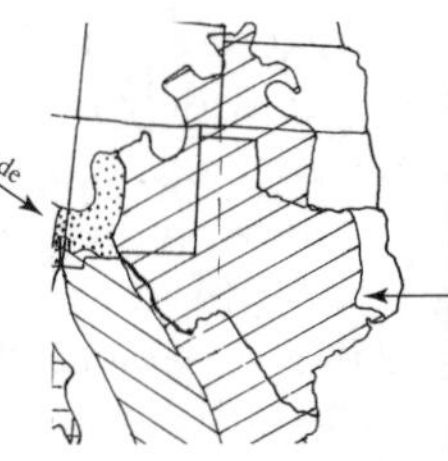

This subspecies is occasionally referred to as the "central coachwhip," a name that, because many far more westerly races exist, seems somehow more fitting. This race ranges westward from central Texas and southwestern Nebraska to western New Mexico. It is immensely variable in both pattern and ground color.

The pattern variations include "unicolored" (no contrasting dark bands), narrow-banded (common), and broad-banded (generally less common but predominant in some areas). The colors may be tan, olive-brown, yellow-brown, dark-brown, silvery-gray, or red of many shades. Although dark nape markings may be present, they are almost never in the form of strongly contrasting bars.

With a record size of 6 ft 8 in., this is one of the largest races of coachwhip.

24 Alameda Striped Racer

Masticophis lateralis euryxanthus 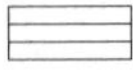

Nonvenomous

Abundance Because of continued human encroachment on open lands, the preferred habitat of this snake is being increasingly reduced. It is now extirpated from large portions of its range and uncommon in many others. It is listed as a threatened species and is protected by the state of California.

Size Although adult at 3–4 ft, occasional specimens may attain, or slightly exceed, 5 ft.

Range This threatened species is protected by the state of California. It occurs only in a relatively small area near San Francisco.

Habitat Moisture-holding canyons, riparian situations, escarpments, rocky hillsides and their associated scrublands, open woodlands, and pond edges are home to this beautiful, but increasingly rare, whipsnake. Of the two races (see account number 25, below), this one has the most limited distribution.

Prey Frogs, salamanders, lizards, smaller snakes, suitably sized rodents, and small birds (especially nestlings) all figure in the diet of this snake. Insects such as locusts, crickets, and cicadas are important dietary items to juvenile specimens.

Reproduction Up to a dozen eggs (but usually no more than half that number) are laid in late spring or early summer. Depending on temperature and humidity, incubation takes 55–90 days. The hatchlings are about 13 in. long.

Coloring/scale form Anteriorly, the lateral stripes and the ventral scales of this snake are orange. Both fade somewhat posteriorly, but the underside of the tail brightens to a pinkish orange or a clear pink. This subspecies has wide lateral stripes involving all of scale row four, the upper half of scale row three and the lower half of scale row five (counting up from the ventral plates). The dorsal color varies from warm- (juvenile) to dark-brown, or black (adult). The top of the head may be a shade lighter than the body color. This species has 17 rows of scales at midbody. The anal plate is divided.

Similar species The patterns of all other whipsnakes are "busier," less precise, if you will, than that of the Alameda whip snake. Each scale in the light lateral stripe of the striped whipsnake (**26**) has a dark, longitudinal, central stripe. Garter snakes have keeled scales.

Behavior Like other whipsnakes, this species relies primarily on its acute vision while hunting. They often move with their head periscoped above the top of ground cover as they search for their insect or lizard repast. The Alameda whipsnake is fast, agile, alert, and difficult to approach.

Comments The two races of this snake are often referred to collectively as California striped racers. They are among the most beautiful members of the genus.

25 California Striped Racer

Masticophis lateralis lateralis

This subspecies is quite like the Alameda race in appearance, but has a narrower lateral stripe (only 2 one half scales wide) that is paler (cream to yellow) in color, and a much larger range. This race ranges southward from northcentral California, along both slopes of the Sierra Nevadas, to central Baja Norte. In the San Francisco Bay region it is replaced by the more brightly colored Alameda whipsnake (**24**). The California whipsnake remains rather common in some areas.

26 Desert Striped Whipsnake

Masticophis taeniatus taeniatus 

Nonvenomous

Abundance This seems to be a fairly common snake that is often encountered in the vicinity of stock tanks and near long-persisting rivers and ponds. It is alert and may evade detection by stealthy retreat.

Size This slender speedster occasionally attains 6 ft in length. Most adults, however, are 3.5–4.5 ft long.

Range The desert striped whipsnake ranges from extreme western Texas and adjacent Mexico in the south, to southcentral Washington in the north.

Habitat In the southern part of its range this snake seems most frequently associated with open woodlands in mountainous terrain. Further north it also occurs in mountain ranges, but may also be found amidst desert thornscrub, in grasslands, and in juniper-studded rangelands at lower altitudes. It is often found along river- or pond-edges where amphibians are common and water is readily available.

Prey This snake accepts the typical whipsnake fare. Amphibians, lizards and smaller snakes, birds (especially nestlings and eggs), and small rodents are all important dietary items. Vision plays a larger part than scent-trailing in the procurement of food. This snake often elevates its head above the ground vegetation to better see the lizards and other small vertebrates on which its preys. Juvenile whipsnakes readily eat insects such as locusts, crickets, and cicadas.

Reproduction The clutch of 3–12 rough-shelled eggs is laid in late spring or early summer. Incubation lasts 2–3 months. Hatchlings are very slender and about 14 in. long.

Coloring/scale form The desert striped whipsnake is blackish to brown or gray dorsally. The gray specimens may have a bluish or greenish overcast. There is a busy pattern of (usually) 3 grayish white, white, or cream stripes on each side. The uppermost light stripe is the widest. It involves all of scale row 4, the upper half of scale row 3, and the lower half of scale row 5. Each scale in scale row 4 has a dark, longitudinal, central dash, making this uppermost stripe appear divided. The scales on the side of the head have white edges or spots. A narrow, black, vertical marking is visible behind the eye on lighter colored specimens. The belly is yellowish and the subcaudal scales are pink or coral. This whipsnake has 15 rows of scales at midbody. The anal plate is divided.

Similar species Coachwhips lack well-defined longitudinal striping. Both the Alameda and the California whipsnake have clear-cut stripes varying from cream to orange in color. The Sonoran whipsnake can be very similar in appearance but its uppermost light stripe is not divided by dark streaks in the center of the scales. Garter snakes have keeled scales.

Behavior Preferring to flee if frightened, some striped whip snakes will stand their ground and strike if cornered. Others will merely lie quietly and allow themselves to be handled with no evidence of temper.

Comments Like all whipsnakes, this is a fast and alert snake with excellent vision. It is difficult to approach.

Subspecies The single additional subspecies, the central Texas whipsnake, *Masticophis taeniatus girardi,* occurs east of the area covered by this book. Although older texts show the Schott's and Ruthven's whipsnakes as races of this species, they are now considered full species. Both of these latter also occur east of the region covered by this book (See *Snakes of North America: Eastern and Central Regions* by Tennant and Bartlett and *A Field Guide to Texas Snakes* by Tennant for coverage of these forms.)

Vine Snakes

Genus Oxybelis

This genus is of neotropical distribution. Only a single species, the brown vine snake, *Oxybelis aeneus,* reaches northward into the United States, and it is occurs only in the mountain canyons of extreme southeastern Arizona. There are several other neotropical species in this genus. All are clad in hues of brown, gray, green, or combinations of those colors. All are very well camouflaged, very slender, and primarily arboreal.

All of these snakes are dubbed "mildly venomous," with no real research having been done on the drop-for-drop toxicity. All of these snakes have well developed, grooved fangs in the rear of their upper jaw that effectively allow venom to enter a bite-wound. The toxin of all causes at least some localized to moderately generalized discomfort. Although most are reluctant to bite humans, we feel that these snakes should be treated with a great amount of care and respect.

27 Brown Vine Snake, *Oxybelis aeneus*

Mildly venomous This is a rear-fanged snake that has a toxin of unresearched composition and unknown potential. The few bites known have caused some localized swelling and localized numbness.

Abundance It is always difficult to hypothesize on the relative abundance of a snake as cryptic as this one. This is nowhere more true than when at the periphery of a range and in a relatively remote area. Certainly the brown vine snake is abundant just a short way south of the Arizona border in Mexico. Since the mid-1920s, just a few dozen specimens have been found in various canyons in southeastern Arizona. But because many of these canyons are remote, on private land, and not subject to frequent human visitation, it is virtually impossible to know what fragment of the actual population the found specimens constitute. Based upon what little is known about these snakes in their very limited range north of the Mexican border, we would venture a guess that *Oxybelis aeneus* is probably an uncommon species in Arizona.

Size Most specimens of this pencil-thin snake are between 30 and 50 in. in total length. Occasional adults (especially those from Latin America) are a full 60 in. long. The excessive slenderness causes all specimens to be judged smaller than they actually are. Hatchlings are somewhat more than a foot in length.

Range This species ranges northward from southeastern Brazil to southeastern Arizona. In Arizona, it is known only from the Pajarito, Patagonia, and Tumacacori mountains.

Habitat In the United States, the brown vine snake seems restricted to several semi-arid canyons and their environs situated at elevations of 2,500–4,500 feet. In this habitat, the snakes are persistently arboreal, but when arboreal highways, such as intertwining limbs or tree to tree vines are not present, do readily descend to the ground to move from copse to copse.

Prey We have found the brown vine snake to be a lizard specialist. They readily eat small swifts, tree, and side-blotched lizards, often grasping the lizard at midbody and quickly working it to the rear of the mouth where the fangs can be employed. The venom works quickly, soon rendering the lizard immobile. The prey is usually swallowed, headfirst, before death occurs. Other authors have mentioned that these snakes also consume insects, birds, frogs and small mammals. Although we have found the larger *Oxybelis fulgidus* readily eats all of these extraneous prey items, we have never had a brown vine snake take any food other than lizards.

Reproduction Little is known about the reproductive biology of this snake. One female, purchased from a dealer in Colima, Mexico, laid 4 elongate, cylindrical eggs in the snake bag where she was kept for nearly 2 weeks; 3 of the eggs desiccated, but 1 hatched after about 7 weeks of incubation. How long the eggs were in the bag before being discovered is unknown. The baby was about a foot long, but was weak and succumbed within a few hours of emerging.

Coloring/scale form Dorsally this snake is primarily a brownish-(dead-vine) gray, with the head and anterior neck being more richly colored than the body. There is a darker horizontal eyestripe that begins at the nostril and continues well onto the neck. The chin and the ventral half of the neck is a bright yellow. This fades to grayish brown on the posterior neck and continues to the tail tip. The outer edges of the ventral scutes may bear dark flecks. The head is long, the snout sharply pointed both when viewed from above or in profile.

The non-keeled scales are in 17 rows; the anal plate is divided; the tail is long (about 2/5th the total length) and very slender.

Similar snakes There are no other snakes similar to the brown vine snake in the United States.

Behavior The brown vine snake is persistently arboreal, but does occasionally cross open areas on the ground. When moving, either on the ground or through the shrubs, it holds its head and neck well above the body level. The head is always held almost level or with the nose tilted just slightly upward. This is an alert snake with keen vision. At times it moves swiftly, head periscoped well upwards, in what would seem to be an effort to scan its surroundings (for approaching enemies?). At other times this snake moves haltingly, head and neck waving slowly, looking for all the world like a broken twig swaying in the breezes. The tongue is often extended straight forward, forked tips tightly together, and held in that manner for some seconds. When threatened, this snake often gapes widely, exposing the dusky interior of its mouth, and faces the enemy, but even if lifted at this time it will seldom bite.

Comments It is hoped that additional field research in the mountains from which this snake is now known, or in others nearby, will prove this snake to be more elusive than rare. Its life history in Arizona is as badly in need of study as its population statistics.

Patch-nosed Snakes

Genus Salvadora

These are speedy, largely diurnal, racer relatives of moderate size and sandy to brown or buff ground colors. The enlarged, free-edged, wrap-around, rostral scale is distinctive of the genus. The middorsal area is the most richly hued and is separated from the lighter sides by prominent dark stripes. The belly is light and may be clouded with slightly darker pigment.

Lizards are the primary prey item, but amphibians, smaller snakes, and nestling rodents are opportunistically accepted. Patch-nosed snakes have acute vision upon which they rely when hunting. They also quickly take note of potential danger and are quick to flee. They are primarily terrestrial, but may pursue lizards upwards into shrubs. These snakes are oviparous.

Patch-nosed snakes may be active throughout the day, even in the hottest weather.

There are 3 species in this genus in western North America. All have smooth scales (occasionally weakly keeled near the vent) in 17 rows at mid-body and a divided anal plate. These snakes can be confusingly similar in appearance, and the origin of a given specimen should be carefully considered when a positive identification is attempted. Additionally, the presence or absense of a dark lateral stripe and the scale row on which it appears, as well as the number of small scales separating the posterior pair of chin-scales, are important criteria.

28 BIG BEND PATCH-NOSED SNAKE

Salvadora deserticola 

Nonvenomous This pretty striped snake may be either defensive, inflating its body, striking and biting, or mild mannered and not bite even when first caught. This and other patch-nosed snakes are devoid of venom.

Abundance As would be expected, this snake can be uncommon in marginal habitats and along the periphery of its range, but can be of common occurrence in ideal, interior habitats.

Size Most specimens seen are 20–30 in. long. Exceptionally, a length of 3.5 ft (record 45 in. [Tennant, 1998]) may be attained. These are slender snakes. Hatchlings are 8–9.5 in. long.

Range *Salvadora deserticola* ranges westward in the United States from Texas' Big Bend region to southeastern Arizona, and from there well southward into Mexico.

Habitat This snake is rather generally distributed in sandy or gravelly aridland habitats throughout its range. It frequents dry riverbeds and is associated with creosote bush and mesquite communities. It may be found in rocky open desert lands as well as in areas rather well vegetated with desert scrub.

Underchin: Texas and mountain patch-nosed snakes

Underchin: Big Bend patch-nosed snake

Prey The Big Bend patch-nosed snake prefers lizards and smaller snakes as its prey, both groups being abundant in its desert homeland. However, it also eats reptile eggs, nestlings of ground nesting birds, and nestling rodents. Prey can be caught while these fast-moving snakes are prowling, or lizards, small snakes, and their eggs may be rooted up from beneath the sand.

Reproduction This is an oviparous snake. It, like other patch-nosed snakes, breeds quite early in the year and may occasionally lay its eggs as early as late April. A clutch may number between 3 and 10 eggs, with from 4 to 8 being the usual number. Incubation takes from 78 to 90 days. Despite this early oviposition date, this species is not known to multi-clutch.

Coloring/scale form This pallid snake looks like it has been colored in pastels. There is a broad pale middorsal stripe (about 3 scale rows wide). This is edged ventrally by a two-scale-row wide dark stripe. The dark stripe is even edged dorsally, but sawtoothed ventrally. Below the dark stripe is another light line, this one about one and a half scale rows wide. The light line is bordered by a narrow dark line, which is 4 scales above the ventrals anteriorly. The venter is pinkish to pinkish orange. The chin is light. There are 2 or 3 small scales separating the posterior chin shields. There are 9 supralabial scales. Two supralabial scales (usually) touch the eye. The (patch-like) rostral scale is large, free-edged, curves up over the nose, and has a small groove on the ventral surface. The smooth dorsal scales are in 17 rows at mid body, the anal plate is divided.

Similar snakes Point of origin will help differentiate the various patch-nosed snakes. The patch-like rostral scales are distinctive of this genus, but the enlarged rostral scale of the leaf-nosed snake is somewhat similar. However, both species of leaf-nosed snake have dark dorsal saddles—not stripes. The mountain patch-nosed snake lacks a dark lateral stripe. The Texas patch-nosed snake has a very wide dorso-lateral dark stripe, and the dark lateral stripe is on scale row 3. The various races of the western patch-nosed snake have either one or no labials touching the eye (use range maps to help distinguish this very similar species. The various striped whipsnakes have normal-shaped rostral scales. Garter snakes have keeled dorsal scales.

Behavior This is a fast, alert, and agile snake that is diurnally active during cool weather, but which may be seen crossing paved arid land roadways at dusk, or more rarely, after dark during the hot days of a desert summer. It is often seen in or near brush patches, and it is very capable of putting on rather amazing bursts of speed when startled. When pursued, it careens for brushy or rock-strewn areas, and seeks seclusion in fissures or crevices, or occasionally, in rodent burrows or beneath rocks. This patch-nosed snake can climb, but usually does not.

Comments This pretty desert snake is a racer/whipsnake relative. Prior to being elevated to species-status, this snake was long considered a subspecies of the desert patch-nosed snake.

29 MOUNTAIN PATCH-NOSED SNAKE

Salvadora grahamiae grahamiae 

Non-venomous

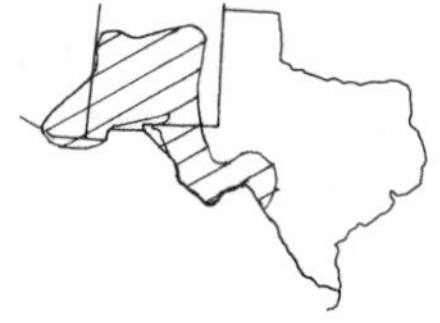

Abundance This is a common, but seldom abundant, snake that is widely spread but which, unless in hand where identifying characteristics can be carefully checked, may be easily confused with Big Bend or western patch-nosed snakes.

Size Although this desert speedster may occasionally attain a length of 3.5 ft (record 37.5 in.), specimens over 3 ft long are rather uncommon. Most found are 18–28 in. long. Hatchlings are 8.5–10.5 in. long.

Range The mountain patch-nosed snake ranges eastward from central Arizona to western Texas. It barely enters Mexico in the states of Sonora and Chihuahua.

Habitat This snake is usually associated with expanses of rocky, open deserts with arid mountainsides and suitable areas of mesas and buttes, and in similar, usually remote and often unpopulated, situations.

Prey The primary prey items of this snake are lizards. Small snakes and reptile eggs also figure prominently in its diet. Although they may be opportunistically eaten, the eggs and nestlings of ground-nesting birds and nestling rodents are far less important dietary items.

Reproduction This is an oviparous snake. It becomes active very early in the year and apparently breeds in March and April. Eggs are laid in mid-spring. A clutch may number 3–10 eggs, with 4–8 being the usual number. Incubation takes 78–90 days. Despite this early oviposition date, this species is not known to multi-clutch.

Coloring/scale form This is a precisely marked snake that often has only the dark dorsolateral stripes (the thin lateral lines are lacking or imprecisely delineated at best). The buff to yellowish middorsal stripe is two scale rows wide. It is bordered on either side by a dark stripe of about similar width. All stripes are even edged along both edges. The eyes are large; the rostral scale is "typically" wrap-around and triangular in shape. The base is broad and bears a small groove. There are 8 upper labial scales. At most, this species has only a single small scale between the rear chin scales. The smooth scales are in 17 rows at midbody, and the anal plate is divided.

Similar snakes See the accounts for the other patch-nosed snakes, pages 62–68. To the east of the range of this book, the Texas patch-nosed snake occurs. It is much more contrastingly marked, with dark dorso-lateral stripes that are 3 scale rows wide. The western patch-nosed snake has 9 upper labial scales, with only one reaching the eye, and has broad dark dorsolateral stripes (which may appear hazy). Its light middorsal stripe is 3 scales wide, and the dark lateral stripe (if present) may be on either or both the 3rd and 4th scale row. Striped whipsnakes lack the modified rostral scale. Garter snakes have keeled body scales.

Behavior This fast, agile, and alert snake is diurnal during the cooler weather, but may be crepuscular, or even nocturnal, during the hot days of a desert midsummer. This patch-nosed snake will usually dash into brush or boulder-strewn cover when startled. Fast and agile though it may be, this snake often relies on ambush to catch its lizard prey.

Comments Because of the lack of the dark lateral stripe and the narrowness of the dark dorsolateral stripe, this race of patch-nosed snake usually appears the lightest in overall coloration.

Additional subspecies With a record size of 47 in., the larger and very precisely patterned Texas patch-nosed snake, *Salvadora grahamiae lineata,* occurs east of this book's coverage and is discussed in Tennant and Bartlett's "eastern-and-central-regions" counterpart.

30 Desert Patch-nosed Snake

Salvadora hexalepis hexalepis 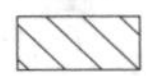

Nonvenomous

Abundance This is a common, but well-camouflaged, snake that is rather easy to overlook unless your paths directly cross.

Size While adult at 26–36 in. in length, occasional, very large desert patch-nosed snakes have attained 46 in.

Range This is the southeasternmost representative of the 3 races. It ranges westward from southeastern Arizona to southcentral California, and then south to eastern central Baja and central Sonora, Mexico.

Habitat Desert patch-nosed snakes are denizens of the arid and semi-arid southwest. They occur in brushlands, thornscrub, cactus-creosote bush associations, on rocky hillsides, in canyons, and other such varied areas. It is often found beneath human-generated debris and natural ground-surface cover.

Prey Lizards figure prominently in the diet of this desert and brushland snake. Suitably sized rodents (especially nestlings) and the nestlings of ground-nesting birds are also important dietary components.

Reproduction Patch-nosed snakes of all species are oviparous. They may mate relatively early in the year, and heavily gravid females are seen as early as mid-spring. The eggs number from 3 to 12 (usually 6–8) in each clutch, and it is possible that a healthy female may occasionally double-clutch. The eggs are smooth-shelled and incubation varies from 75–95 days. Hatchlings which are paler than, but otherwise replicas of, the adult measure about 10 in. in length.

Coloring/scale form The upper sides and the top of the head are pale gray. The three-scale row-wide middorsal stripe and lower sides are a distinct, but pale yellow. The belly is cream, often shading to the palest of oranges posteriorly, and especially beneath the tail. The eyes are large and the rostral scale is very large, has free edges, and wraps up over the tip of the snout. The internasal scales are not separated by the wraparound rostral. There are 9 upper labial scales, one of which reaches the eye. The loreal scale is often divided into 2 or 4 smaller segments. The scales are in 17 rows, and except near the vent where they are weakly (females) to moderately strongly (males) keeled, are smooth, and the anal plate is divided.

Similar snakes Leaf-nosed snakes are much smaller and are blotched or spotted, rather than striped. The Big Bend patch-nosed snake has 2 upper labials in contact with the eye and a single loreal scale. The ranges of these two patch-nosed snakes abut only eastern Arizona.

Behavior This common snake is diurnal and may be active even at midday in sweltering temperatures. It may react to the approach of a human by fleeing in a burst of speed, or if cornered, by coiling, inflating its body, and striking vigorously. When the body is inflated the interstitial skin is easily visible and patterns seem intensified. Patch-nosed snakes are often active early in the year when many sympatric species are still quiescent. They often crawl with the head lifted well away from the ground, but do not periscope their head above the ground cover as routinely as their racer relatives. Patch-nosed snake do, however, seem to rely on their acute vision when hunting. These snakes can also burrow rather adeptly in loose soils.

Comments The Big Bend patch-nosed snake (**28**) was long considered a subspecies of *S. hexalepis* but is now rather generally afforded specific status by taxonomists.

31 Mojave Patch-nosed Snake

Salvadora hexalepis mojavensis 

This is a pale version of the desert patch-nosed snake. The stripes, although dark-bordered and straw to pale yellow, are often not strongly in contrast with the ground color. The top of the head is brown(ish). This snake may have anterior crossbars that largely obscure the anterior striping. The loreal scale is usually not divided. The upper labials are usually separated from the eye by a few small subocular scales. It ranges from northwestern Nevada and southcentral Utah, southward to southern California and central Arizona.

32 COASTAL PATCH-NOSED SNAKE

Salvadora hexalepis virgultea

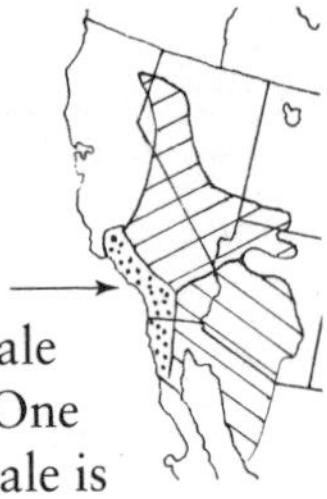

This subspecies ranges along the coastal strand of southern California and northern Baja Norte. It tends to have sides of light gray or sandy brown, a reduced area (one or two rows above the ventral scutes) of yellow on the lower sides, and the top of its head is usually brown. The vertebral stripe is usually only 2 scale rows (one full row and a half row on each side) wide. One upper labial scale usually reaches the eye. The loreal scale is fragmented into 2 or 4 small scales.

LYRE SNAKES

Genus Trimorphodon

The lyre snakes range widely through Middle America, but enter the United States only in west Texas and the southwestern states. Taxonomic instability plagues these snakes, but we have elected to follow older examples and recognize 3 forms in the American west. Only the Texas lyre snake occurs to the east of this work. They derive the common name from the dark, lyre-shaped, marking on the back of the head. The broad head is well differentiated from the slim neck. The body is slender and supple. The lyre snakes have a vertically elliptical pupil and a lorilabial scale—a scale between the loreal and the labial.

Lyre snakes are inhabitants of scrubby deserts, rocky hill- and mountainsides, and wooded canyons. They emerge from crevices and other areas of seclusion in the evening and remain active far into the night. Lizards are the preferred prey of the lyre snake, but nestling birds and rodents and smaller snakes may also be occasionally accepted.

The scales are smooth and in 21–27 rows; the anal plate may be either divided or undivided.

This rear-fanged snake produces a venom that effectively overcomes ectotherms. It seems less effective on endotherms. Humans, bitten, have developed mild swelling, redness and some sensitivity at the bite site, but no lingering or serious effects. Although lyre snakes are often reluctant to bite, large examples should be handled with caution.

33 Sonoran Lyre Snake

Trimorphodon biscutatus lambda 

Mildly venomous This is one of our larger rear-fanged snake species. Venom yield is unknown, and drop-for-drop toxicity is also an unknown factor. Although short, the grooved rear teeth are capable of affording a relatively effective delivery system. Despite this snake's reluctance to bite, and the current feeling by many that the lyre snake is harmless to man, we feel that this snake—especially large examples—should be handled with caution.

Abundance Lyre snakes are secretive, but are often fairly common in areas of suitable habitat.

Size Most of these snakes encountered in the field are 24–36 in. long. The largest examples in North America are about 4 ft long. (Tropical races attain a considerably larger size.)

Range The range of this race extends southward from southeastern Nevada and southwestern Utah to far south on the Mexican mainland.

Habitat Although it may occasionally be found well away from rocky situations, for the most part this is a snake of rocky deserts, escarpments, boulder-strewn aridlands, and fissured outcroppings. Typical plant communities in lyre snake habitat include mesquite, creosote bush, saguaro, and ocotillo.

Prey Lizards of many kinds are the principal prey of the various lyre snakes. Rock-crevice dwelling lizards, found while the snakes methodically search the escarpments and outcroppings that they frequent, are those that figure most prominently in the diet of the lyre snakes. Besides lizards, lyre snakes prey on rodents, bats, birds, and perhaps, snakes.

Reproduction The reproductive biology of this snake is poorly known. It would seem, however, that despite the temperate ranges inhabited by the northern races, the lyre snakes have retained an aseasonal breeding capability more suited to their tropical origins. Up to 20 eggs have been produced in a single clutch by captive females. More typically, the clutch size is 5–12 eggs.

Coloring/scale form The ground color of the Sonoran lyre snake often closely approaches that of the rocky substrates on which the snake usually dwells. The ground color can vary from a rather rich brown to the palest of sandy grays. The color is usually darkest mid-dorsally and lightest on the lower sides. There are usually about 28 light-centered, light-edged, darker dorsal blotches. Irregular small blotches are present on the lower sides. There is a well-defined lyre- or >-shaped figure present on the top of the head and the first blotch is usually noticeably elongate. The eyes have vertically elliptical pupils, and the head is much broader than the proportionately slender neck. The belly is off-white to pale yellow and is patterned with irregular dark spots. The spots are largest and most prominent at the outer edges (sides) of the ventral scutes. The smooth scales are in 20-24 rows at midbody, and the anal plate is usually divided.

Similar snakes The gray-banded kingsnake has round pupils and lacks an intricate pattern on the top of the head. Gopher snakes have heavily keeled body scales. Glossy snakes have round pupils and a thick neck. Night snakes have elongate black spots on the sides of their neck.

Behavior These nocturnal snakes are often surface active even in the driest conditions, but also prowl extensively following heavy rains. They remain out well into the wee hours of the morning and are often seen crossing paved trans-desert roadways. Although these snakes spend much time on the ground, they are fully capable of climbing rock faces and shrubs as they search crevices and branches for their prey. Although they seldom bite, lyre snakes will, if confronted, raise their anterior and swing into an intimidating striking pose.

Comments Taxonomic status in this group has not yet been fully agreed upon. We have elected to follow the suggestions of Scott and McDiarmid (1984) in subspecies recognition.

34 California Lyre Snake

Trimorphodon biscutatus vandenburghi 

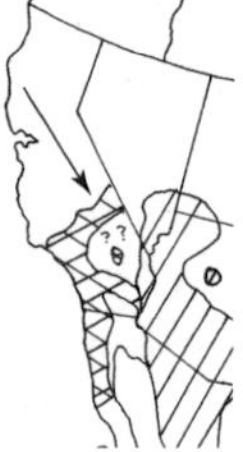

This is the more westerly race of the lyre snake. It is rather poorly differentiated subspecies, has a higher average number of dorsal blotches (35) than the Sonoran race, and the anal plate is usually undivided. Individuals from the white-sand deserts of southern California can be so pallid that the dorsal blotches are difficult to define. It ranges southward and southwestward from the vicinity of Inyo County, California, to central Baja California.

35 Texas Lyre Snake

Trimorphodon biscutatus vilkinsonii 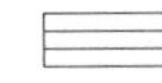

Quite different in appearance from any of the other races, this subspecies lacks a well-defined head pattern, has fewer than 24 (some specimens have as few as 17) comparatively narrow, widely separated, primary dorsal blotches, and may have a slight greenish cast to its limestone gray or earthen brown ground color. A clutch of 7 eggs monitored by August Rentfro (pers. comm. 1998) was laid the last week of June. The 8-in.-long babies hatched after 77 days of incubation. This beautiful snake is rather generally distributed from Texas' Big Bend to central New Mexico, but is nowhere common. It is seen most often in boulder-strewn areas and rocky hillsides along the Rio Grande.

Subfamily Colubrinae

Tribe Sonorini

As currently defined, there are 6 genera of burrowing snakes of the American West in this group. Herndon Dowling considers this assemblage a subfamily, the Sonorinae.

The genus *Phyllorhynchus,* the leaf-nosed snakes, is tentatively included here (John Cadel, pers. comm), but Dowling considers this genus a member of the Old World subfamily Oligodontinae.

Sand Snakes

Genus Chilomeniscus

This genus is represented in the southwestern United States by only a single species. It is brightly colored, but a persistent burrower that is seldom seen. It is a sand-swimming species with a narrow head, smooth scales, and a concave venter. It occurs primarily in loose sand habitats, but may be occasionally found in gravelly areas. It seems particularly abundant in areas that support the growth of both mesquite and creosote bush.

36 Banded Sand Snake

Chilomeniscus cinctus 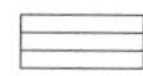

Nonvenomous

Abundance Banded sand snakes are fairly common, but because of their fossorial proclivities, are not often seen. When they do surface it is usually after nightfall or during heavy rains.

Size This is one of the smallest snakes of the southwestern United States. It is adult at 6.5–9.5 in. in total length, but is of fair girth.

Range This species ranges southward from central and western Arizona, well into Mexico.

Habitat A desert snake, the banded sand snake utilizes a specialized burrowing method termed sand-swimming. It is a creature that should be looked for in areas of fine to coarse yielding sand, often in the vicinity of plant communities of mesquite, creosote bush, saguaro, and ocotillo.

Prey The sand snake eats roaches and other insects and their pupae that it encounters while burrowing. They seem especially fond of tenebrionid beetle larvae and pupae. Sand snakes are, apparently, able to overcome and eat centipedes.

Reproduction Two females (each about 8.5 in. long) caught in early June while gravid laid 2 and 4 eggs, respectively.

Coloring/scale form This is a beautiful little candy-cane snake. The ground color is cream to yellow, often brighter, or even shading to strawberry, dorsally, and the black saddles, which reach well down onto the sides of the body, actually encircle the short, stout tail. The dark saddles may be narrow and numerous or broad and few. The head is narrow, the snout is flattened, the lower jaw is prominently countersunk, the nostrils are valvular, the eyes are small but fully functional, and the nose is light in color and weakly convex. The concave belly is off-white to pale yellow. The unkeeled scales are in 13 rows and the rather large rostral scales curve back over the snout, separating the internasal scales. The anal plate is divided.

Similar snakes The internasal scales of both species of shovel-nosed snakes are not separated by the rostral scale. Banded examples of the ground snake lack the prominently countersunk lower jaw, and the scales are usually in 15 rows, at least anteriorly. The Arizona coral snake has 15 rows of scales and is distinctively patterned in broad rings of black, red, and yellow.

Behavior The banded sand snake is a persistent burrower that is seldom seen by day but may wander extensively on the surface at night. It often forages just under the surface of the sand. Meandering, indented tracks are left behind the snakes when the dry sand filters into their burrows behind them. It is probable that nearly all of their food is encountered beneath the ground surface, but one small sand snake was found in the early evening west of Tucson, Arizona, on the surface of the ground as it swallowed a very small centipede.

Comments It is not uncommon to see from one to several of these little snakes crossing isolated desert roadways after nightfall on hot summer nights. Although the light dorsal areas of many may be decidedly reddish, it is not uncommon to find sand snakes hued dorsally in yellow. The very short (but pointed) ringed tail, countersunk lower jaw, and separated internasal scales are quite diagnostic.

SHOVEL-NOSED SNAKES

Genus Chionactis

This is a genus of 2 (possibly 3) species of burrowing, sand-swimming, desert snakes that, like the banded sand snake, have a narrow head, a concave belly, and non-keeled scales. The rostral scale (the scale on the tip of the snout) is large, cornified, and spade-like. These snakes are slender and supple, often strike animatedly when frightened, and are usually seen above ground only after nightfall. They can be abundant in prime, loose sand habitats. They are occasionally found by day near or amid the root systems of cacti, mesquite, creosote bush, or other desert shrubs.

37 COLORADO DESERT SHOVEL-NOSED SNAKE, *Chionactis occipitalis annulata* 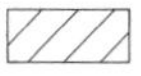

Nonvenomous

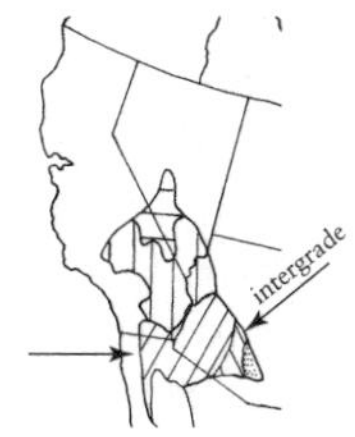

Abundance Because of its fossorial habits, even where it is an abundant species, the Colorado Desert shovel-nosed snake is seldom seen in natural habitat. It does often crawl on the surface in the early evening or during and following rain storms.

Size This is a slender-bodied burrowing snake that is adult at 11–14 in. Occasional specimens of 16–17 in. have been authenticated.

Range This shovel-nosed snake ranges from central and western Arizona to southeastern California and southward to northern Mexico.

Habitat This is a fossorial desert snake that swims rapidly through loose-sand habitats. It is most frequently seen in areas of fine sand, but may also be encountered in regions typified by coarser sand. It has been found both where vegetation is sparse, and where vegetation is relatively thick. The mounds of yielding sands associated with the root systems of desert shrubs and kangaroo rat middens are also excellent microhabitats.

Prey This is just one of many small desert snakes that feed exclusively on invertebrate prey. Insects, spiders, centipedes and small scorpions are all eaten. The larvae and pupae of tenebrionid beetles are relished. Much of the food is found during the snakes' burrowing activities.

Reproduction Comparatively little is known about the reproductive biology of the shovel-nosed snake. It is oviparous and lays 2–5 eggs (occasionally more) in each clutch. Egg deposition occurs in the late spring to early summer. Multi-clutches have not been documented.

Coloring/scale form The ground color of the Colorado Desert shovel-nosed snake is of some shade of pale yellow to cream. There are usually 25 or fewer, well-separated, rather narrow, dark (usually black) bands, many of which completely encircle the body (including the belly). In each wide yellow band there is *usually* a narrow, partial band of pale red. A broad, dark marking, in the form of an open U, curves backwards over the top of the head from each eye. The first neck band is broad and does not encircle the body. The nose is light in color. The rostral scale is broad and shovel-like, and the forehead is rather flat. The tail is not noticeably shortened. The scales lack a keel, are usually in 15 rows, and are shiny. The anal plate is divided. The two internasals are in contact on the top of the snout. The sloping snout is flat in profile. The belly is concave, an adaptation to help the snake swim through the loose sand. The lower jaw is noticeably countersunk.

Similar snakes The Arizona coral snake is brightly ringed in red, black, and yellow and has a black nose. The banded sand snake is shorter, stouter, has a very short tail, has scales in 13 rows, and the internasals are separated by the rostral scale. The nose of the ground snake is not specialized for burrowing, and there is usually some dark shading on each light scale. The Organ Pipe shovel-nosed snake is more strongly crossbanded, has brighter colors, and usually 20 or fewer black crossbands.

Behavior Shovel-nosed snakes generally move quickly (if disturbed, frenziedly) with an S-shaped, side-to-side movement. If on a smooth roadway they may slide about in their efforts to move quickly. If threatened they will draw the anterior of their body into an S and strike repeatedly. This persistent burrower is seldom seen above ground except following rains or after darkness has fallen.

Comments These are interesting little desert snakes that are often present in numbers much greater than thought. Should you choose to see one, slowly drive a paved desert road after dark and watch for the little snakes in the glow of the headlights. Unless you are absolutely certain what species it is you are seeing, it is best to just look and don't touch.

In 1967, *Chionactis saxatilis* (the mountain shovel-nosed snake) was described from the Gila Mountains of southwestern Arizona. Taxonomists have long questioned the validity of this taxon, and it has been virtually unmentioned in the ensuing years.

38 Tucson Shovel-nosed Snake

Chionactis occipitalis klauberi 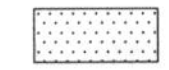

This, the easternmost race, is one of the most colorful. It is found primarily in Pinal and Pima counties, Arizona. The black primary bands of this shovel-nosed snake are quite wide dorsally, narrow dramatically on the sides, but often continue across the belly. More poorly defined secondary bands of black are usually present. The red, although fairly bright, is often reduced to small dorsal blotches.

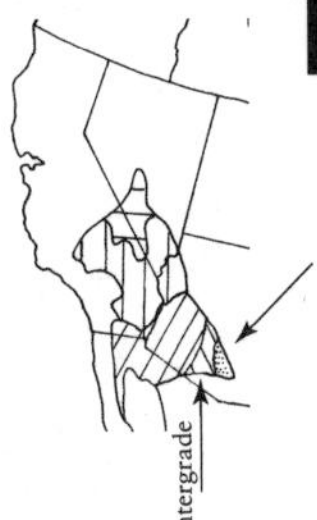

39 Mojave Desert Shovel-nosed Snake

Chionactis occipitalis occipitalis 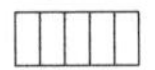

Ranging westward from central Arizona and southern Nevada to central southern California, this race often lacks red, being merely busily patterned with dark brown (occasionally black) and yellow. If red is present, it is pale. The Mojave shovel-nosed usually has 40 or more dark crossbands. Most do not span the belly.

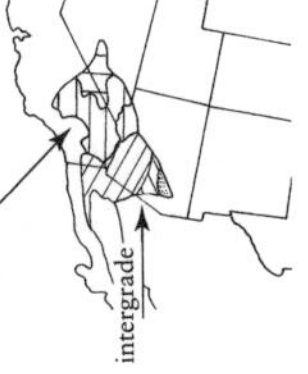

40 NEVADA SHOVEL-NOSED SNAKE

Chionactis occipitalis talpina 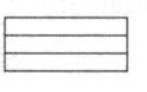

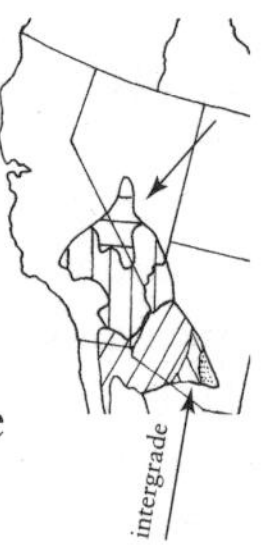

This is the northernmost representative of this species. It ranges westward to eastern central California from southwestern Nevada. It is the palest race, having brown rather than black primary crossbands, a hint of brownish secondary bands in the light fields, and a creamy ground color. Many bands do not continue across the belly. Some red *may* be present in the light areas. There is a high number (152 or more) of ventral scales.

41 ORGAN PIPE SHOVEL-NOSED SNAKE

Chionactis palarostris organica 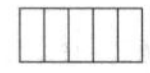

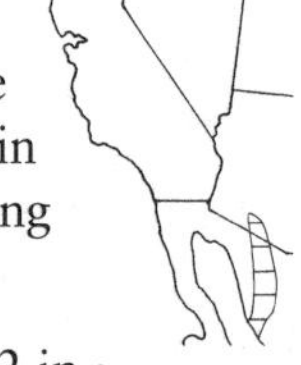

Nonvenomous

Abundance Actual population statistics are lacking. This is an uncommonly encountered snake species in the United States. It is seen with somewhat more frequency in Mexico. Confirm its identification by carefully eliminating all other look-alike species.

Size This is a tiny burrowing snake. It is adult at 10–12 in.; 15.5 in. is the largest documented size.

Range In the United States, this species is known only from Organ Pipe Cactus National Monument, Pima County, Arizona. The range extends southward into Sonora, Mexico.

Habitat This snake is associated with gravelly and rocky flats in areas vegetated by saguaro, ocotillo, creosote bush and associated shrubs.

Prey Insects and their pupae, spiders, small centipedes, and perhaps other arthropods are eaten by this shovel-nosed snake.

Reproduction Virtually nothing is known about the reproductive biology of this species. A badly mangled female, found dead on the road in early June, contained either 3 or 4 eggs.

Coloring/scale form This is a smooth-scaled, shiny, diminutive, and beautiful snake. The red markings are saddles, not rings, and are rather narrowly edged with the yellowish ground color. There are about 20 black rings, which narrow ventrally. The snout, and most of the belly, is yellowish. The snout is weakly convex. The lower jaw is countersunk. The scales are in 15 rows, and the anal plate is divided.

Similar snakes Although it is often stated that when viewed from above the Organ Pipe shovel-nosed snake is remarkably similar to the Arizona coral snake, we see the similarity as superficial, at best. The coral snake has a *black* nose and clear, *wide rings* of red and yellow. *C. palarostris,* on the other hand, has a light colored nose, *narrow* yellow rings, and saddles (not rings) of red. Other species of shovel-nosed snakes in the Organ Pipe Cactus National Monument region have a snout that is *flat* (not convex) in profile, usually more than 20 black rings, and poorly defined pink to strawberry red saddles.

Banded specimens of the ground snake do not have prominently countersunk lower jaws and usually lack most yellow dorsally. The long-nosed snake is much larger when adult and has black flecks in the red and yellow fields and yellow flecks in the black.

Behavior This is a secretive snake, but seems to be a somewhat less proficient burrower than its congenerics. It is at home beneath rocks and vegetable debris. It remains hidden by day, but may prowl above ground after dark, or occasionally, following afternoon rains. It is actively defensive, drawing its neck back into an S and striking animatedly if threatened.

Western Hook-nosed Snakes

Genus Gyalopion

The genus *Gyalopion* is represented in the western North America by 2 species. Of these, *G. canum,* the western hook-nosed snake, occurs from central Texas to eastern Arizona, and *G. quadrangulare,* the desert hook-nosed snake, pushes northward from its Mexican stronghold only into extreme south central Arizona. Both are accomplished burrowers that feed on invertebrate prey items.

Because of their strongly upturned rostral scale, these snakes look superficially like diminutive hog-nosed snakes. They are proportionately stout, with short, stout tails that taper quickly to a point. Both species have smooth scales in 17 rows. *G. canum* has a divided anal plate while that of *G. quadrangulare* is single.

42 WESTERN HOOK-NOSED SNAKE

Gyalopion canum 

Nonvenomous This small snake has grooved, slightly enlarged teeth at the rear of its upper jaw and a proteinaceous saliva that seems designed to benumb the snake's invertebrate prey. The western hook-nosed snake is harmless to humans.

Abundance Western hook-nosed snakes are fairly common, but because of their fossorial proclivities and nocturnal habits, are not often seen. Heavy summer rains may induce them to the surface in fair numbers.

Size This is another of the tiny burrowing snakes of the southwestern United States. It is adult at 6.5–9.5 in. The largest recorded adult was just over 15 in. long.

Range The range of this species in the United States extends westward to southeastern Arizona from central Texas. It also occurs in northern interior Mexico.

Habitat This little desert snake is associated with thornscrub and creosote bush at lower elevations, but also occurs in mountainous regions at more than a mile in elevation. Although a secretive burrower, it often prowls the desert surface after nightfall, and may be found crossing paved roadways well into the wee hours of the morning.

Prey Spiders are the primary prey items of most of the hook-nosed snakes, but other invertebrates such as insects, their larvae and pupae, scorpions, and centipedes are also eaten.

Reproduction Little is known about the reproductive biology of this snake. A single egg was attributed to one female; a road-killed female found in early June in Texas' Big Bend region contained two eggs.

Coloring/scale form The ground color of the western hook-nosed snake is tan, cinnamon, or gray(ish). There are from 25 to more than 40 dark brown dorsal bands. All bands may be similar in intensity or there may be primary bands and secondary bands. The bands are usually best defined dorsally where they are bordered both anteriorly and posteriorly by a narrow dark edging. They are narrow, well-defined, and well-separated. If present as a series of alternating primary and secondary bands, the latter may be present on only one side, be present on both sides but broken dorsally, or be virtually entire. The lowermost two rows of lateral scales are white except where patterned by the dark dorsal bands. The head is only slightly wider than the neck. The eyes are small but fully functional and have round pupils. A dark subocular blotch and a wide, dark, interorbital bar are both present. A second dark marking is present on the back of the head as either a complete bar or as a dark spot on each side. The smooth scales are in 17 rows. The rostral scale is large, pointed, sharp-edged, upturned anteriorly, and entirely separates the internasal scales posteriorly. The venter is white to off-white. The anal plate is divided.

Similar snakes Rather than being free-edged and sharpened anteriorly, the rostral of both species of leaf-nosed snakes curves back up over the snout. The rostral scale of the western hog-nosed snake is strongly keeled above. The top of the Mexican hook-nosed snake's (*Ficimia streckeri*) head lacks dark bars. The desert hook-nosed snake has far more extensive dark areas on the top of its head and very wide dorsal blotches.

Behavior As mentioned, the western hook-nosed snake is a persistent burrower that is seldom seen by day but which may wander extensively on the surface at night. It seems particularly surface-active on evenings following summer rains. As a defense mechanism, when prodded, this species writhes animatedly and pops its cloacal lining in and out, producing a snapping sound.

Comments Look for these little snakes crossing isolated desert roadways after nightfall on hot summer nights. Although a mildly venomous snake, western hook-noses are of absolutely no danger to humans.

43 Desert Hook-nosed Snake

Gyalopion quadangulare 

Nonvenomous This small snake has grooved, slightly enlarged teeth at the rear of its upper jaw. Its saliva contains enzymes and proteins that are thought to act both as predigestants and in benumbing the snake's invertebrate prey. The desert hook-nosed snake is harmless to humans.

Abundance Little is known about the actual population statistics of this snake in Arizona, but it is the least frequently seen of the three species of hook-nosed snakes in the United States. Since in Arizona it is at the periphery of its range, this is not entirely unexpected. It is much more frequently seen (but, perhaps, no better understood) in Mexico.

Size This seldom-seen species is adult at 6.5–9.5 in. Large adults may be a foot in length.

Range This is another of the tiny Mexican burrowing snakes that range northward as far as southeastern Arizona. There it is best known from Santa Cruz County, but may also occur in Pima and Cochise counties. Its exact range in the United States remains badly in need of defining. In Mexico this species ranges southward along the Pacific Coast to the state of Nyarit.

Habitat This desert snake is associated with thornscrub and creosote bush desert at lower elevations, but also occurs at altitudes of more than 4,000 ft in the Patagonia and Pajarito mountains. It is known to be a burrower in habitats that vary from canyon bottoms to open grasslands. It is induced to the surface by summer rains and has been found on rare occasions crossing paved roadways after nightfall.

Prey Spiders are, apparently, the prey of choice of this hook-nosed snake, but it also consumes other invertebrates such as scorpions, centipedes and, perhaps, insects and their larvae and pupae.

Reproduction Other than the fact that it is oviparous, virtually nothing is known about the reproductive biology of this snake.

Coloring/scale form This is the brightest colored and most spectacularly marked of the hook-nosed snakes of North America. The 30-36 black saddles are broadest and best defined dorsally and tend to be wider anteriorly than posteriorly. The downward projecting lateral extensions are infiltrated interstitially by light gray. The dorsal ground color between the dark saddles is a pale grayish-white. A 2.5–5-scale wide, rust-red to terra-cotta lateral stripe is present on the upper sides. This is broken by the black of the lateral projections of the dorsal markings. Below the red stripe the lateral color is again grayish-white. The belly is a uniform white, often with a greenish overlay. A dark interorbital extends rearward and is contiguous with a broad nuchal blotch. The cheeks are rust-red. The eyes are small, have round pupils, and are fully functional. The projecting rostral scale is sharp-edged and upturned but is not keeled dorsally, and posteriorly, separates the internasal scales. The scales are smooth, in 17 rows, and the anal plate is not usually divided.

Similar snakes Rather than being free-edged and sharpened anteriorly, the rostral of both species of leaf-nosed snakes curves back up over the snout. The rostral scale of the western hog-nosed snake is strongly keeled above, and the body scales are also keeled. The top of the Mexican hook-nosed snake's (*Ficimia streckeri*) head lacks dark bars. The western hook-nosed snake lacks the distinctive rust-colored flanks and has narrow dorsal blotches.

Behavior As previously mentioned, the desert hook-nosed snake is a persistent burrower that is seldom seen by day but which may wander extensively on the surface at night. It seems particularly surface-active on evenings following summer rains. The defense mechanism of writhing and animatedly popping its cloacal lining in and out (this produces a snapping sound) used by the Mexican and western hook-noseds has not been documented in the desert hook-nosed.

Comments Look for these little snakes crossing isolated desert roadways after nightfall on hot summer nights. Although a mildly venomous snake, desert hook-noseds are of absolutely no danger to humans.

Leaf-nosed Snakes

Genus Phyllorhynchus

This genus of small burrowing snakes is represented in the American southwest by 2 species, each with 2 subspecies. They often emerge from their burrows after nightfall or following rains. They may then be seen crawling on the desert sands or crossing desert roadways.

Both species have a huge, free-edged, wrap-around rostral scale that may help them burrow more efficiently or root out their secluded lizard prey.

These are feisty little snakes that, if threatened, will not hesitate to draw their neck into an S and strike repeatedly. Their tiny size precludes them being considered a serious threat.

The dorsal scales of both species are in 19 rows. The dorsal scales of the males of some subspecies are weakly keeled, while those of the females of all races are smooth. The internasal scales are separated by the wrap-around rostral. The anal plate is undivided. The pupils are vertically elliptical.

44 Pima Leaf-nosed Snake

Phyllorhynchus browni browni

Nonvenomous

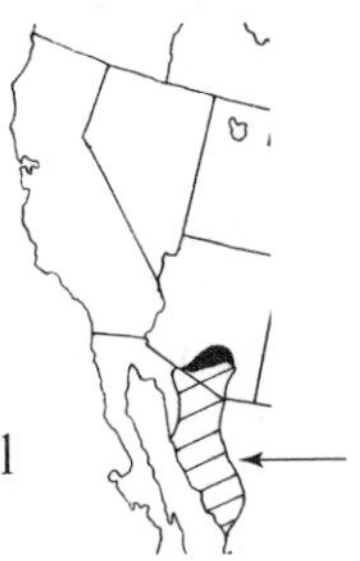

Abundance This is probably a common to abundant species, but as with many persistent burrowers, actual population statistics are difficult to ascertain. Certainly, the Pima leaf-nosed snake is a commonly seen species when it crosses paved desert roads on late spring and summer nights. At that time it is not unusual to see several specimens each evening.

Size Although a record size of 20 in. is mentioned, most specimens are much smaller. Typically, Pima leaf-nosed snakes are 10–16 in. long.

Range In the United States the range of this species is restricted to central and southcentral Arizona. However, south of the border, this snake ranges far southward into Mexico.

Habitat This is a species of sandy and gravelly desert flats. It seems most common where plant associations of saguaro-creosote bush-mesquite occur or in areas of thornscrub.

Prey It has been reported that lizards and their eggs, and in particular, the banded gecko and its eggs, are the primary diet of this small snake. However, at the moment, this seems speculation rather than fact. Captives have refused most items offered (including banded geckos), but supposedly have occasionally eaten side-blotched lizards, their eggs, and the eggs of house geckos.

Reproduction Little is known with certainty about the reproductive biology of the Pima leaf-nosed snake. It is thought that only a single clutch, numbering 2–6 eggs, is laid in the late spring or early summer. A single hatchling (still with egg-tooth) found crossing a roadway in late August measured a fraction over 6 in.

Coloring/scale form This is one of the prettiest and most distinctively colored and patterned of our western snakes. The ground color may be white (with just the faintest blush of pink) to cream. The 17 or fewer brown dorsal blotches are darkest near their outer perimeter and fade to a lighter brown centrally. The dark blotches are much wider than the bands of light ground color that separate them. The belly is immaculate white. The nose is white on the sides but may be smudged with dark pigment dorsally. Pupils are vertically elliptical; the scales are smooth (occasional males have weakly keeled scales) and in 19 rows; the anal plate is undivided.

Similar snakes Most other snakes that occur within the range of the Pima leaf-nosed snake (including the clouded leaf-nosed snake) have a much busier, less precise dorsal pattern. The anterior edge of the rostral scale of the western hog-nosed snake is free and sharply pointed. The various rattlesnakes have tail tip rattles (unless the tail tip has been amputated), facial pits, and fragmented scales on top of their head.

Behavior If given the opportunity, these little snakes will crawl quickly to safety if frightened. However, if closely confronted, they will unhesitatingly strike at a threatening object and will vibrate their tail. These snakes are accomplished and persistent burrowers that are often surface-active during and after the summer rains ("monsoons").

Comments Unless Lady Luck is truly with you, searching for leaf-nosed snakes in their desert homelands can be an exercise in futility. They may occasionally be found beneath surface debris, but are most easily found as they cross paved desert roadways on humid summer nights.

Together, the 2 races of *Phyllorhynchus browni* are referred to as saddled leaf-nosed snakes.

45 MARICOPA LEAF-NOSED SNAKE

Phyllorhynchus browni lucidus 

This subspecies is not currently recognized as valid by all researchers. It occurs in the northwestern and most westerly portions of the range of this species. It has 17 or fewer precisely delineated dark dorsal blotches that are narrower than the separating bands of light color.

46 CLOUDED LEAF-NOSED SNAKE

Phyllorhynchus decurtatus nubilis

Nonvenomous

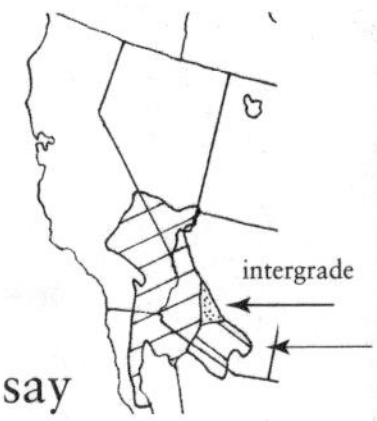

intergrade

Abundance The clouded leaf-nosed snake is often seen crossing paved roadways on summer evenings and may emerge from its burrow to prowl the surface of the sand following afternoon rains. Although no definitive population studies have been completed, it seems safe to say that this is a common to abundant species.

Size Most specimens found are 11–15 in. in length. The record length is 20 in.

Range This race occurs only in southcentral Arizona and immediately adjacent northern Mexico.

Habitat This is another of the persistent burrowers in the snake fauna of the Sonoran Desert. It occurs both in sandy areas and on gravelly flats. It seems quite common near desert plant community associations of saguaro-creosote bush-mesquite. It is occasionally found beneath surface debris, such as fallen cacti or human-generated litter.

Prey The clouded leaf-nosed snake apparently is a lizard- and lizard egg-eating species that has been said to specialize on banded geckos and their eggs. Little is actually known about the diet of this desert snake.

Reproduction It is thought that an adult female produces only a single clutch of a small number of eggs (2–6) annually. Deposition occurs from late spring to mid-summer. Hatchlings, which are 6–7.5 in. long, seem to make their first appearance in early to mid September.

Coloring/scale form This is a variable but strongly patterned race of leaf-nosed snake. The ground color may be tan, buff, pinkish, or gray. There are usually 35 or more narrow, dark-edged, brown, dorsal saddles. Smaller brown spots alternate between the dorsal blotches on the sides. A narrow, brown, chevron-shaped band (directed anteriorly) crosses the head, encompasses the eyes, and continues to the lip. The belly is an immaculate white. The scales are in 17 rows at midbody. Females have smooth dorsal scales; those of the male are keeled. The anal plate is undivided; the pupils are vertically elliptical.

Similar snakes The anterior edge of the rostral scale of the hog-nosed snake is free and strongly upturned. Gopher snakes are much larger and have strongly keeled scales. Night snakes have large dark blotches on the posterior of their head and nape. Patch-nosed snakes are striped. Rattlesnakes have the tail tip rattle (unless the tail tip has been amputated), a sensory pit on each side of the face, and fragmented scales on the top of their head.

Behavior This is a nocturnal snake that is most often encountered on quiet transdesert roadways at night. The free-edged, wrap-around rostral scale is characteristic of the genus.

Comments A third race of this snake occurs on the Baja Peninsula and a fourth on the western Mexican mainland. Together, these 4 races are referred to as spotted leaf-nosed snakes.

47 Western Leaf-nosed Snake

Phyllorhynchus decurtatus perkinsi 

This is a very pale subspecies of the spotted leaf-nosed snake. The ground color is white or silvery to the palest pinky-buff, and the small dorsal saddles are infiltrated centrally with light pigment. The small lateral spots are often not clearly defined. The belly is immaculate white. The top of the head may be largely devoid of dark markings. A teardrop-shaped dark marking runs from the bottom rear of the eye to the angle of the jaw. This race ranges southward from southern Nevada to central south Arizona, eastern south California and on into Mexico.

intergrade

Ground Snakes

Genus Sonora

There are few snakes in America as variably colored as the members of this genus. Depending on the simplicity or complexity of the pattern and colors, it may be easy or difficult to mistake a ground snake for other small snake species. In general, it might be said that ground snakes lack any distinctly overt identifying characteristics. They are a very typical small snake species. The head is only moderately distinct from the neck. The scales are in 13–15 rows and are smooth. The anal plate is divided. *A loreal scale (usually distinct, sometimes partially fused to another scale) broadly separates the second upper labial from the prefrontal scale on each side.* This is an important identifying characteristic.

Ground snakes are usually associated with well drained plains, prairies, semideserts, and desertedge habitats. These secretive little snakes may be found in numbers in areas where flat surface rocks are abundant. *Sonora* feed upon small arthropods and occasionally on tiny geckos and their eggs. These snakes are oviparous. They have a weakly toxic saliva but can in no way be considered of danger to humans.

48 VARIABLE GROUND SNAKE

Sonora semiannulata 

Nonvenomous The ground snake has a very mildly toxic saliva. They are harmless to humans.

Abundance This is a common little snake, often the predominant species, although more seldom seen than many others. When the ground snake does surface it is usually after nightfall or during heavy rains.

Size This small snake is adult at 8–12 in. (very rarely to 18 in.) in total length and is rather stocky. Hatchlings are 4–5 in. long.

Range This species ranges southward from central and eastern Kansas to Zacatecas, Mexico, then westward to the Baja Peninsula and northwestern Nevada. Disjunct populations occur as far northward as southwestern Idaho, Utah, southeastern Colorado, and northcentral Kansas.

Habitat A desert, semi-desert, grassland, ranchland species, the ground snake is primarily associated with open, rocky areas. It is commonly found beneath both natural (rocks) and human-generated surface debris. It is often found beneath rocks near stock tanks, in the beds of periodic streams and rivers, and nearly any other habitat which offers ample cover and some amount of moisture.

Prey The ground snake feeds on arachnids, including some noxious types such as small scorpions and centipedes. Crickets and other such insects and their larvae and spiders are also accepted. It is not known

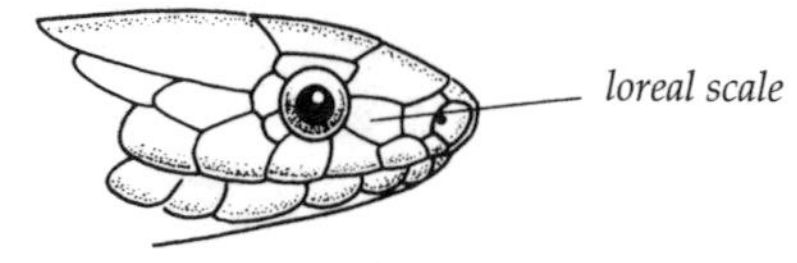

whether the toxic saliva aids in overpowering insects, as a predigestant, neither, or both. Degenhart (1996) reports finding a *Sonora* attempting to swallow a road-killed Texas banded gecko. It is not known whether these nocturnal lizards figure prominently in the diet of the ground snake.

Reproduction Two females (each about 8.5 in. in overall length) caught in early June while gravid laid 2 and 4 eggs, respectively. From 1 to 6 have been recorded. Incubation duration is about 60 days.

Coloring/scale form The ground snake is one of the most variable of American snakes, both in coloration and in pattern. Among other color and pattern schemes, these little terrestrial snakes may be unicolor russet, buff, or gray (sometimes with a vaguely darker head); may be distinctly banded in two tones of gray; may be greenish-buff or gray with a prominent terra-cotta vertebral stripe (which may or may not be broken by broad black saddles); banded russet and buff; banded gray and pink; be pinkish or russet dorsally, have black saddles, and yellowish sides; or be of a single ground color but have a dark spot on each light scale. The head is relatively narrow, but is slightly wider than the neck. A loreal scale is present. The lower jaw is not significantly inset. The unkeeled scales are usually in 15 rows, at least anteriorly; there may be only 14 rows posteriorly. The anal plate is divided.

Similar snakes Because of the myriad color combinations and patterns exhibited by the ground snake, it can be mistaken for many other species. None of the black-headed snakes have any banding or contrastingly colored middorsal stripe and all lack a loreal scale. Blind snakes have no functional eyes. Banded sand snakes and shovel-nosed snakes have a noticeably inset lower jaw and flattened snouts.

Behavior The ground snake is so persistently secretive that it may be present in vast numbers, but never seen. It is occasionally surface-active on warm rainy nights or warm humid nights, especially in the spring of the year. Males are more frequently found wandering than females. Look for this variable but pretty snake beneath surface debris (especially rocks) in open grassy, or sandy areas. It is probable that nearly all of this snake's food is encountered beneath ground surface rocks.

Comments The ground snake is unusual in that, individually, it varies from drab to gaudy. There may be a tendency for a given color to predominate in a given geographic area, but more often than not, several colors and patterns may be found sympatrically. Throughout much of their range, despite the use of herbicides, insecticides, and habitat degradation, these secretive little snakes remain one of the more common reptiles.

Black-headed Snakes

Genus Tantilla

In our southwest, the members of this genus are small, slender burrowers. Most are characterized by a black crown and, sometimes, a black nape. The head color may or may not be separated from the neck color by a light band.

The unicolored dorsum is often the color of the substrate on which these snakes are found. There is no loreal scale, an important fact when trying to separate these snakes from certain colorations of the ground snake. They are even more difficult to separate from each other. Hemipenial structure is often used by taxonomist to help identify a snake in hand. If it is necessary to resort to this latter, it is only the males that can be identified with any certainty. Rely strongly on range to facilitate identification.

The black-headed snakes are creatures of sandy, well-drained areas. They may occasionally be found beneath flat stones and building debris, and even more occasionally, they may be surface active. Despite their persistent secrecy, these snakes vary by species from common and fairly well-known, to rare and poorly understood.

The scales of these oviparous snakes are in 15 rows; the anal plate is divided.

Although possessing a toxic saliva and grooved rear teeth, the crowned snakes are reluctant to bite and are considered harmless to humans.

Additional morphological studies of many species in this genus are necessary before taxonomic stability will be achieved.

49 Southwestern Black-headed Snake

Tantilla hobartsmithi 

Mildly venomous Harmless to humans.

Abundance Although very seldom seen, this little snake is not thought to be rare. On the very rare occasions when they do surface it is usually after nightfall or when they are driven to the surface by flooding or heavy rains.

Size This is among the smallest snakes of the southwestern United States. It is adult at a slender 6.5–9.5 in. in total length and has a record size of 15 in. It is conjectured from data gathered from other *Tantilla* species with an adult size similar to *T. hobartsmithi* that hatchlings will be about 4.5 in. long.

Range The southwestern black-headed snake has a discontinuous range, occurring in several disjunct colonies in southern, central, and western Arizona, southern Utah, extreme central-western Colorado, southern California, and extreme northern Sonora, Mexico.

Habitat A desert and grassland snake, the southwestern black-headed snake occurs in areas as diverse as those that host growths of yucca, mesquite, creosote bush, as well as in juniper scrublands and open coniferous woodlands. However, it seems most common at low elevations in limestone habitats. This snake is persistently fossorial, and burrows readily through yielding soils, as well as seeking cover beneath fallen desert plants, rocks, and human-generated surface debris.

Prey Although insects and other arthropods are on its list of acceptable dietary items, it is probable that like others of this genus, the southwestern black-headed snake preys primarily on centipedes which are immobilized by the toxins in the saliva.

Reproduction Other than the fact that this snake is oviparous, we know little about its reproductive biology. From 1 to 3 (usually one) eggs are laid per clutch. It is thought that some females may double clutch. Deposition occurs during the months of June and July. Based on what little is known about the breeding habits of some eastern species, it is conjectured that the incubation for the southwestern black-headed snake is about 60+ days.

Coloring/scale form The brightest color on this pretty little smooth-scaled snake occurs on the belly. This is bright orange centrally. The dorsal coloration is brownish to gray. The outer edges of the ventral scutes are whitish, sometimes with an opalescent cast. The dark cap is largely restricted to the top of the head and seldom goes lower on the sides of the head than the bottom of the eye. It extends rearward approximately 2 or 3 scale rows past the parietal shields. There may be (but often is not) a vaguely defined, narrow, light collar separating the dark head color from the gray body color. There is no loreal scale (see diagram, page 82). The scales are in 15 rows and the anal plate is divided.

Similar snakes Rely primarily on range to identify this snake. Except in southeastern Arizona where it and three other species occur, the range of this species is not known to overlap with the range of any other black-headed snake. Also see accounts for the Huachuca, Plains, and Yaqui black-headed snakes.

Behavior Little is known about this snake except that it is persistently fossorial, and remarkably adept at burrowing from sight when it is brought to light. Most specimens are found beneath surface debris, but rarely, it is scratched out of loose earth or it may be surface-active at night, even at relatively cool temperatures. Additional study of the life history of this and of other black-headed snakes is much needed.

Comments This species used to be called the Utah black-headed snake and designated scientifically as *Tantilla planiceps utahensis*. Taxonomic stability is not yet assured.

50 Plains Black-headed Snake

Tantilla nigriceps

Slightly venomous This small snake has a mildly toxic saliva and grooved teeth at the rear of its upper jaw. However, it is reluctant to bite and is considered harmless to man.

Abundance This is a seldom seen, but not uncommon, snake species.

Size This is another relatively small black-headed snake. It is adult at 7–10 in. long, and the largest recorded specimen was only 14.75 in. This is a slender species.

Range This little snake ranges eastward and southward from northcentral Colorado to western Kansas and northern Mexico.

Habitat Grassy plains, desert grasslands, moist, rocky hillsides, and similar habitats are colonized by this snake. It is seldom seen above ground, but is often found beneath natural (rocks and fallen plants) and human-generated surface debris. It seems most common in sandy, yielding soils.

Prey Although insects and their larvae, spiders and millipedes are included in the diet of this snake, like others in this genus, the Plains black-headed snake seems very partial to centipedes. The toxin produced by this snake rather quickly quiets and paralyzes these potentially formidable, multisegmented arthropods.

Reproduction This small snake produces 1–3 (usually just 1) eggs per clutch. It is thought that some females may double clutch. Deposition occurs sometime during the late spring or the summer months. The incubation period is 60+ days.

Coloring/scale form This little snake has an olive-gray to yellowish-gray dorsum, and a pinkish to orange mid-ventral area. To either side of this strip of color the venter is white. The dark cap extends from 2 to 5 scales posterior to the parietal shields and tends to be pointed rather than smoothly rounded. The dark cap-color usually extends downward only to the top of the upper labial scales. A light collar is usually absent.

Similar snakes Rely heavily on range to aid in identifying this species. If it is found in southeastern Arizona, also check the accounts for the Huachuca, the southwestern, and the Yaqui black-headed snakes.

Behavior As are all of the black-headed snakes, this species is very secretive. It hides beneath both natural and human-generated surface debris and has also been found in the fissures caused by rapidly drying earth. It is frequently surface-active on relatively warm nights, especially during damp or rainy weather. It is an accomplished burrower that seems most common in areas of sandy, yielding soils.

Comments As mentioned, the many species in this genus can be perplexingly difficult to identify with certainty. Rely on range and all differentiating characteristics.

BLACK-HEADED SNAKES

51 WESTERN BLACK-HEADED SNAKE

Tantilla planiceps

Mildly venomous Harmless to humans.

Abundance Like other members of this genus, the western black-headed snake is seldom seen, but is quite common in suitable habitat.

Size Although this slender snake has a recorded maximum length of 15.5 in., seldom is an example of more than 12 in. seen. Most specimens found are 6–10 in. long. Extrapolating from known egg size, it is probable that hatchlings are 3.5–4.5 in. long.

Range This snake occurs in coastal California from the vicinity of San Francisco Bay southward to mid-Baja California.

Habitat This secretive snake is a persistent burrower that occurs in habitats as diverse as grasslands, open hardwood areas, and semi-deserts. It is most often found beneath rocks, logs, and human-generated debris.

Prey Insects and their larvae and other arthropods—but especially centipedes—comprise the diet of this snake. The centipedes, which are themselves highly predaceous, are usually grasped behind the head, envenomated, but not swallowed for a matter of minutes until benumbed by the venom.

Reproduction Very little is known with certainty about the reproductive biology of this species. From 1 to 4 eggs are produced in each clutch, and it is surmised that double clutching is a possibility. The elongate, cylindrical eggs are laid in the late spring to summer and take 60–80 days to hatch.

Coloring/scale form The dorsum is colored in earthen hues of from olive- to yellowish-brown. The venter is white, except for a pinkish to orangish central strip. The black cap extends from two to three scale rows posterior to the parietal scales, is vaguely rounded or straight on its posterior edge, and usually drops well below the mouthline posterior to the corner of the jaw. There is usually a moderately defined to well-defined narrow, light collar posterior to the black of the head. The collar may be edged posteriorly by half-dark scales.

Similar snakes While the range of no other black-headed snake overlaps that of this species, the range of the southwestern black-headed snake (**#49**) does near it. The silvery legless lizard lacks a black cap and has eyelids.

Behavior This is a poorly known, secretive snake. It is occasionally disclosed when surface debris (both natural and human-generated) is turned. It has been found to be occasionally surface-active on warm nights and may be especially so following late afternoon or evening rains in the spring.

Comments The California black-headed snake has a more extensive dark cap than any of the other 5 western species. Black-headed snakes almost never attempt to bite anything other than their arthropod prey species.

52 Huachuca Black-headed Snake

Tantilla wilcoxi wilcoxi

Mildly venomous Like all other species in this genus, the venom of this black-headed snake is of no danger to humans.

Abundance The Huachuca black-headed snake is thought to be very rare in its limited Arizona range. It is not particularly uncommon south of our border.

Size The record size for this species is 14 in. Specimens 7–10 in. are more commonly found. It is hypothesized that hatchlings measure 3.5–4.5 in.

Range This Mexican snake enters the United States only in the vicinity of the Huachuca Mountains in southeastern Arizona.

Habitat A secretive and fossorial species, the Huachuca black-headed snake may occasionally be found beneath plant debris, surface-rocks, and human-generated debris. It occasionally actively crawls on the surface of the ground at night in warm, preferably damp, weather.

Prey There is no reason to suppose that the diet of this black-headed snake is different from that of any other. Centipedes are probably the primary prey.

Reproduction Other than the fact that this is an oviparous snake, virtually nothing is known with certainty about its reproductive biology. We hypothesize that egg count, deposition sites and dates, and incubation durations are much like those of our other southwestern species of black-headed snakes.

Coloring/scale form The dorsal color is brown to olive-brown. Some lateral scales contain a dark spot. The venter is white anteriorly and shades to orange posteriorly. The black cap is of reduced length on this species, not including the rear tips of the parietal scales. The white collar is relatively well-defined, includes the rear tips of the parietals, and at least one subsequent scale row. It is bordered posteriorly with dark scales. Most upper labials are light, but the black cap tips downward at the rear of the mouth, includes the rear half of the last supralabial scale, and touches (or may extend below) the jawline.

Similar snakes This is the only black-headed snake in southeastern Arizona with the posterior tips of the parietal scales included in the white collar.

Behavior This snake seeks cover beneath toppled plants, flat rocks, other natural cover, and human-generated debris. It is an accomplished burrower that may go well below the surface of the ground. It may be surface-active at night in warm weather, especially following rains or when conditions are humid.

Comments This is one of the most infrequently seen snakes in our area. Most of our comments regarding the Huachuca black-headed snake are hypotheses derived from knowledge of other species. This race is occasionally referred to as the Chihuahuan black-headed snake.

53 Yaqui Black-headed Snake

Tantilla yaquia 

Mildly venomous The weakly toxic saliva of this species is harmless to humans.

Abundance This species is apparently uncommon in its limited United States range. It is not particularly so in Mexico.

Size This is the smallest of the 5 species of black-headed snakes in the North American west. The Yaqui black-headed snake attains an adult size of only 13 in., and those most frequently seen are 6–9 in. long. Hatchlings are about 3.5 in. long.

Range This is another Mexican species that barely enters the United States where it is known to occur only in southeastern Arizona and immediately adjacent New Mexico.

Habitat In the United States, this uncommon snake occurs in loose soils in evergreen and deciduous woodlands. Many specimens have been found in riparian situations. In Mexico it also occurs on the coastal plain. As secretive as any other member of this genus, the Yaqui black-headed snake has been found beneath rocks, fallen vegetation, and human-generated debris.

Prey With centipedes being a prime prey item, the Yaqui black-headed snake also accepts insects and their larvae.

Reproduction From 1 to 4 eggs (often 1) are laid in each clutch. It is not known whether this species multiple clutches.

Coloring/scale form The Yaqui black-headed snake has a dorsum of light brown to olive-brown or tan. The black cap extends for up to 4 scale rows posterior to the interparietal suture. The cap is widest anteriorly, extending under the eye and including all but the upper labial scales. The cap narrows posterior to the eye, producing a prominent light cheek-patch, then widens again, tipping downward to or past the corner of the mouth. The collar is variably distinct, but is usually broad and at least partially edged by dark scales posteriorly. The belly is orangish posteriorly and cream-colored anteriorly. The smooth scales are in 15 rows, and the anal plate is divided.

Similar snakes No other black-headed snake in the North American west has a white cheek-patch.

Behavior This snake is secretive and nocturnal. Numerous specimens have been found crossing paved roadways in southeastern Arizona, particularly following afternoon rains. It is an efficient burrower, but is often found beneath surface debris.

Comments Very little is known about the life history of this peripheral species in the United States. Although this snake was once divided into two subspecies, it is now considered monotypic.

Night Snakes

Subfamily Dipsadinae, Genus Hypsiglena

There are no members of this subfamily in western America except the night snakes of the genus *Hypsiglena.* East of our range, in Texas and eastward, 3 other dipsadines are the cat-eyed snake, *Leptodeira,* the black-striped snake, *Coniophanes,* and the pinewoods snake, *Rhadinea.*

The vast majority of the dipsadines are of Central American distribution. Most are small, many are terrestrial leaf-litter dwellers, but some are extensive arboreal, and a few have tails that are very easily broken off.

Dowling (pers. comm., 1999) feels this genus belongs in the subfamily Leptodeirinae.

Depending on the authority quoted, the wide-ranging night snake is either represented in the western North America by a single randomly variable species or by up to 6 subspecies. A current trend is to recognize 4 races, but since to us, these 4 seem no better defined than the 2 that are not recognized, we have mentioned all 6 geographic races. The single best-developed identifying characteristic is the presence of 2 or 3 large neck blotches (which may rarely be entirely absent). The number of these, their comparative size, and their general size and shape may help differentiate the subspecies. However, all characteristics are variable, so we urge you to also consider range when attempting an identification. The dorsal ground color (between the dorsal spots) is often considerably lighter than the lateral ground color. Night snakes are profusely spotted both dorsally and laterally. The venter is usually immaculate.

Night snakes are small, preferentially nocturnal, and have vertically elliptical pupils. The body scale rows are either 19 or 21. The scales are smooth; the anal plate is divided. This snake seldom attempts to bite. While lizards are the preferred prey, some night snakes will also accept small frogs. The toxic saliva not only benumbs and kills the prey rather quickly, but may act as a predigestant as well. The dorsal color of the night snakes usually closely matches the substrate on which they are found.

These secretive snakes emerge from hiding as the daylight wanes and may be active far into the night. They are primarily terrestrial and may be quite common in areas where flat rocks, cactus skeletons, or other surface debris provide ample surface cover. This is an oviparous species.

Depending on the subspecies and the terrain in which it occurs, night snakes may be found from sea level to altitudes of more than 7,000 ft.

54 Desert Night Snake

Hypsiglena torquata deserticola

Slightly venomous The night snake has a toxic saliva that rather quickly paralyzes and kills lizards. However, having either non-grooved or only weakly-grooved teeth, this snake lacks the means to effectively administer the toxin. These snakes are considered harmless to humans.

Abundance This is a common snake, but due to its nocturnal habits, can be easily overlooked. It can even persist in suburban lots and gardens.

Size This is a small and slender snake. Those seen are most often 8–12 in. long. Although this snake may occasionally exceed 24 in., seldom is a specimen of more than 16 in. found.

Range This night snake ranges northward from Baja California to southcentral Washington in drier inland habitats. It is absent from most of the humid and rainy coastal strand.

Habitat The night snakes, in general, are serpents of arid- and semi-aridlands and are most common where surface cover, in the form of flat rocks, vegetable debris, and human-generated trash, are abundantly scattered. The unused burrows of small mammals, other reptiles, and spiders are also utilized as retreats by this snake. They may traverse considerable stretches of relatively open desert and are one of the most frequently seen snakes on trans-desert roads at night.

Prey Lizards are the preferred prey of the night snake, but small frogs and their larvae, smaller snakes, and some invertebrates, are also eaten. While captives have accepted newly born mice, it is not known whether specimens in the wild do so.

Reproduction Although a single-egg clutch annually seems the norm, at least some reproductively active females of this oviparous snake may lay 2 clutches of 2–9 (usually 3–6) eggs. Incubation lasts 50–65 days. Hatchlings are about 7 in. long.

Coloring/scale form The ground color, and to a lesser degree, the color of the darker dorsal and lateral blotches and spots, usually blends well with the substrate on which these little snakes are found. With a background color of very light brown, grayish, tan or cream, this desert dweller is one of the more pallid races. Both the dorsal blotches and lateral spots are deeper brown. The nuchal and nape blotches are very large and usually contact each other so widely that they appear as one enlarged blotch. However, when discernible as a separate entity, the nape blotch is narrow anteriorly and greatly broadened posteriorly. The head is not much wider than the neck and bears no pattern on the top. The pupils are vertically elliptical. The scales are smooth and in 21 rows. The belly scales are white and non-patterned; the anal plate is divided.

Similar snakes Glossy snakes and juvenile racers have round pupils; gopher snakes have strongly keeled scales and round pupils; lyre snakes have an intricate pattern on the top of their head.

Behavior This is a secretive little snake that blends well with its background even when out and active. They seldom strike or bite when handled and, when disturbed, may either wriggle frantically in an effort to escape or may coil and insert their head in the center. Because they are so persistently nocturnal and secretive, rather large populations may be present but unsuspected. They may be found beneath surface debris, under rocks, or even in the deep cracks formed when the ground dries quickly.

Comments This is a problematic subspecies, the validity of which is questioned by many researchers.

55 Texas Night Snake

Hypsiglena torquata jani 

One of the larger and prettier members of the genus, this subspecies is also the easternmost form. Its range extends westward from central Texas and extreme southern Kansas to southeastern Colorado and New Mexico. It also occurs far southward into Mexico. The record size for this form is 20 in., but most seen are 15 in. long or less. Hatchlings are 4.75-6.5 in. This can be a stout little snake (especially when a female is carrying eggs). The three black neck (nuchal) blotches are usually well-developed and extensive, and rounded posteriorly. The ground color— gray, olive-gray, or tan— often matches the rock substrate on which this snake is usually found. The 50 or more well-defined dorsal blotches are olive-green to drab. A snake of semi-arid to arid-land habitat, this little snake is often most common near some water source and where natural or human-generated surface debris offer ample hiding spots.

56 San Diego Night Snake

Hypsiglena torquata klauberi 

This snake has two fairly large nuchal blotches and a narrow nape blotch that is not widened posteriorly. All are usually discrete. Like all other races except the California night snake (which has 19 rows of scales), the San Diego race has 21 rows of smooth scales. This race ranges southward on the Pacific slopes and in coastal areas from the vicinity of Santa Barbara County, California, well into Baja California.

57 MESA VERDE NIGHT SNAKE

Hypsiglena torquata loreala 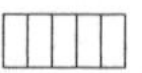

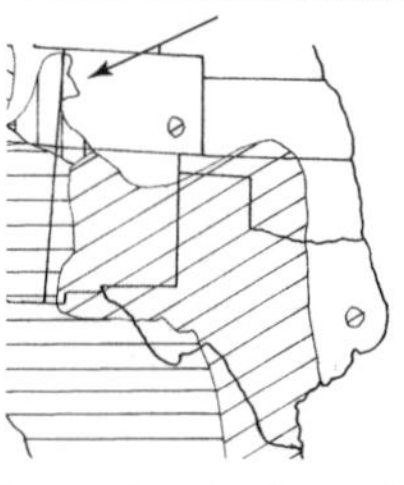

This is the only one of the four races to have two loreal scales on each side of the face. The other subspecies have only a single loreal on each side. The ground color of the back is usually noticeably lighter than that of the sides. The body scales are in 21 rows. The nuchal blotches are prominent, but the nape blotch is often lacking or represented by one or more small spots. This subspecies is found throughout eastern Utah and in immediately adjacent southwestern Colorado.

58 CALIFORNIA NIGHT SNAKE

Hypsiglena torquata nuchalata 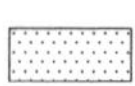

Look for this race on the slopes of the Sierra Nevada and the coastal ranges near the Sacramento and San Joaquin valleys, southward from Shasta County to San Luis Obispo County, California. This subspecies has only 19 scale rows. The nuchal blotches may converge to form a dark band behind the head, but are more often separated.

59 SPOTTED NIGHT SNAKE

Hypsiglena torquata ochrorhyncha 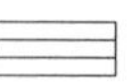

Ranging southward from northern Arizona, throughout most of that state, to northwestern mainland Mexico, this is a busily patterned race with the light dorsal ground color extending lateral to the dorsal blotches. The lateral nape blotches are well-defined and often contiguous with the narrow, forward projecting, median nape blotch. The scales are in 121 rows.

GLOSSY, RAT, KING-, GOPHER, AND LONG-NOSED SNAKES

Subfamily Lampropeltinae

In recognizing this subfamily, we have followed Ernst (1989). Some taxonomists consider this a tribe in the subfamily Colubrinae.

The Lampropeltinae contains many of the world's herpetocultural favorites. This includes the many rat, king-, milk, and gopher snakes that are bred by herpetoculturists by the thousands each year. There is, however, often considerably less known about their habits in the wild.

The snakes in this subfamily are powerful constrictors. Several species in differing genera have been known to interbreed when natural habitat partitions are removed or altered, or by bringing the snakes into contact in captivity. In most cases, the resulting offspring are viable, and breed readily. All are oviparous.

GLOSSY SNAKE

Genus Arizona

For the last several decades, this has been treated as a monotypic genus.

Currently, however, based as much on allopatry (a break in the range) and a few comparative morphological differences, there is a suggestion that at least 2 species may be involved. *A. elegans* (with 3 subspecies [*arenicola, elegans,* and *philipi*]) in North America has been called the eastern glossy snake, and *A. occidentalis* (with 4 North American subspecies [*candida, eburnata, noctivaga,* and *occidentalis*]) is referred to as the western glossy snake. The eastern races have been referred to as the long-tailed forms, the western races as the short-tailed forms.

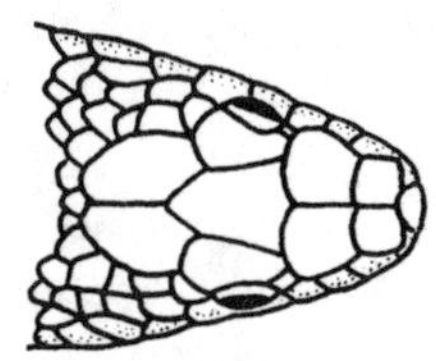

Prefrontal scales: glossy snakes

Although in the future we may actually recognize 2 full species, for the moment we will discuss the glossy snake as a single species and consider the 7 races of North America, variable subspecies. One, the **Texas glossy snake,** *Arizona elegans arenicola,* occurs to the east of the scope of this book, and is discussed in the counterpart to this guide, the *Field Guide to Snakes of North America—Eastern and Central Regions* (Tennant & Bartlett), also by Gulf Publishing. Additional races may be found in Mexico.

Glossy snakes are entirely nonvenomous, but may bite if provoked. The glossy snakes are considered relatives of the pine, gopher, and bullsnakes of the genus *Pituophis,* and like them, are oviparous. The glossy snake has nonkeeled body scales in as few as 25, or as many as 35, rows, occasionally one but usually two prefrontal scales, and an undivided anal plate. The head is narrow but distinct. The glossy snake is an efficient burrower, and very secretive, indulging in surface activity, primarily after darkness has fallen, to seek its prey of lizards, and, more rarely, small rodents. This snake is capable of constricting, but often does not constrict small prey items.

60 MOJAVE GLOSSY SNAKE

Arizona elegans candida 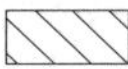

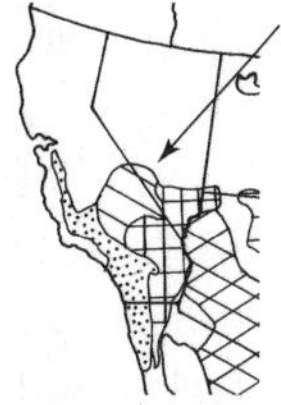

Nonvenomous As are all members of this subfamily, the Mojave glossy snake is entirely nonvenomous.

Abundance These are among the most frequently encountered of nocturnal serpents. They are surface-active even during prolonged droughts, and may prowl from dusk to the wee hours.

Size Although Stebbins relates a maximum length of 70 in. for a glossy snake, most are very much smaller. An average sized female is 30–42 in. long (males are noticeably the smaller sex in this snake species), and a specimen of more than 48 in. is large indeed. Hatchlings are 9.5 in.–12.5 in.

Range This race has a fairly small range. It occurs from Inyo County, California, eastward to the Death Valley area of western Nevada and westward and southward throughout much of the western Mojave Desert in California.

Habitat The Mojave glossy snake occurs in a variety of habitats. It may be found in open deserts, desert scrub, along rocky washes and river floodplains, chaparral and grasslands. It may be found along the edges of wooded areas, but tends to shun densely treed areas. It prefers areas with a soil of loose enough consistency to be easily burrowed in. Besides burrows of its own making, the glossy snake may utilize the burrows of rodents or other desert creatures, and may also be found beneath natural and human-generated surface debris.

Prey Although lizards figure very prominently in the diet of these snakes, they will also prey on suitably sized rodents, ground-dwelling birds, and smaller snakes. Sleeping diurnal lizards are the principal prey item of many glossy snakes. These snakes are fully capable of strong and sustained constriction, but may not always do so.

Reproduction Studies have disclosed that not all female glossy snakes in wild populations reproduce every year. Conversely, an occasional captive female will double clutch in a given year. This seems to have been undocumented in wild populations. Normal clutches contain 5–12 eggs. Clutches of 3–23 eggs have been recorded. Incubation lasts 68–80 days.

Coloring/scale form This is one of the light-colored desert races of glossy snake. The ground color is a light sandy tan to grayish tan. The dark blotches, which are buff, olive-buff, or olive-tan, and which are edged anteriorly and posteriorly with a darker olive, are noticeably narrower than the light spaces that separate them. The average body blotch count is 63 (53–73). There is a series of small lateral blotches that alternate in their placement with the dorsal blotches. The smooth scales are in 27 or fewer scale rows. The venter is a pale sandy-olive to light buff with an olive blush. Because of its proportionate narrowness, the head looks elongate. This race has 2 preocular scales and a proportionately short tail.

Similar snakes The gopher and bullsnakes have very strongly keeled body scales. The various rat snakes have weakly keeled mid-dorsal scales, a spearpoint pattern on top of its head, and a divided anal plate. Night snakes and lyre snakes have vertically elliptical pupils. Juvenile racers have a divided anal plate.

Behavior This is a nocturnal snake that is active at, and shortly after, dusk on cool evenings, but which may be active throughout the hours of darkness on hot summer nights. Glossy snakes are excellent and persistent burrowers, remaining hidden by day, and emerging at night. They may hiss and bluster when approached, but seldom actually bite.

Comments As a species, the glossy snake is easily identified. However, the various subspecies are more difficult to distinguish from one another. We suggest that you rely strongly on the range maps as an initial tool when attempting subspecific identifications. Scale row counts are also important.

61 DESERT GLOSSY SNAKE

Arizona elegans eburnata 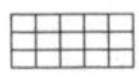

This is a pale race, often with poorly contrasting body markings. The ground color is a sandy cream, the dorsal blotches, which are weakly edged with slightly darker pigment anteriorly and posteriorly, are a pale olive-brown. The body scales are smooth and in 27 or fewer rows. This race usually has only one preocular scale. The average count of the narrow dorsal blotches is 68 (53–85). The blotches are narrower than the width of the ground color that separates them. This race has a short tail. This subspecies ranges southward from southern Nevada and adjacent southwestern Utah and northeastern Arizona, through eastern California, and into northeastern Baja California.

62 KANSAS GLOSSY SNAKE

Arizona elegans elegans 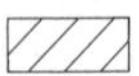

A wide-blotched, long-tailed race, whose ground color is tan to pale-brown and the dark-edged blotches are deeper brown. The average dorsal blotch count is 53 (39–69). The scales are smooth and in 29 or 31 rows. The blotches are wider than the lighter areas of ground color that separate them. There are usually two preocular scales on each side. This race is quite dark in color and has a proportionately long tail. It ranges southward from northeastern Colorado and southwestern Nebraska, through eastern New Mexico, northern and western Texas, well into northeastern Mexico.

63 ARIZONA GLOSSY SNAKE

Arizona elegans noctivaga 

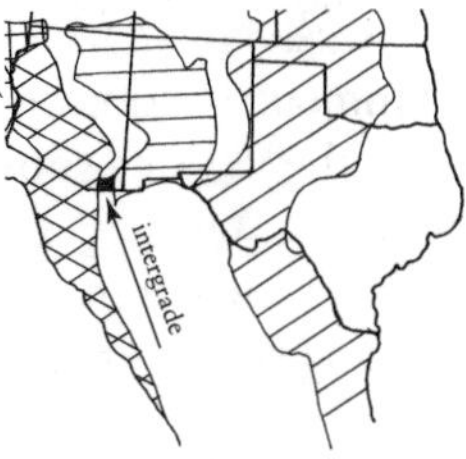

The ground color of this desert and brushland race is tan to light reddish brown. The dorsal blotches are deeper brown and are narrowly edged anteriorly and posteriorly with darker pigment. The midbody scale rows of this race may vary from 25–29, but are often 27.

It may have one or two preocular scales. The dorsal blotches are about the same width as, but may be slightly wider than, the light areas of ground color that separate them. There is an average of 66 dorsal (53–77) blotches. The venter is pale and unmarked. The lower labial scales usually lack dark markings. The tail is comparatively short. This race occurs over much of western and southern Arizona, to Sinaloa, Mexico. This race is quite similar to the (usually) darker California glossy snake, but its range is separated from that of the latter by the intervention of the very light colored desert glossy snake.

64 California Glossy Snake

Arizona elegans occidentalis

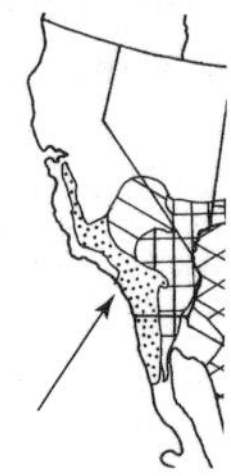

This is a variable, but usually relatively dark snake dorsally. It has a ground color of olive-tan to olive-brown and dark-edged blotches of deep-brown. This race also has dark markings on the lower labial scales and on the outer edges (sides) of the ventral scutes. There are 27 scale rows, 2 preoculars, and a short tail. The dorsal blotches are about equal in width to the light areas of ground color between them and average 63 (51–75) in number. This race (which looks very much like the Arizona glossy snake, but is separated from this more easterly form by the intervening range of the very pale desert glossy snake) ranges southward from the San Francisco Bay area through much of western California to northwestern Baja California.

65 Painted Desert Glossy Snake

Arizona elegans philipi

The ground color is a pretty buff. The saddles are a dark edged, darker brown. On this long-tailed race, the body scales are smooth and rarely in 29, but usually in 27 or fewer, rows. There is an average of 64 (53–80) dorsal blotches. Expect this race from southeastern Utah, through much of central and western New Mexico, to extreme northeastern Sonora and northern Chihuahua, Mexico.

intergrade

Trans-Pecos and Baja Rat Snakes

Genus Bogertophis

This is a bitypic genus of big-eyed, desert and rocky savanna, and riparian scrubland snakes. They are capable of prey constriction, but may not always do so. Both species are egg-layers. Some researchers consider the 2 snakes in this genus more closely allied to the bull- and gopher snakes than to the rat snake genus *Elaphe,* from which *Bogertophis* was only recently separated. These snakes seldom bite, and are entirely nonvenomous. The head is broad, somewhat flattened, and distinct from the slender neck. There is a row of scales—the suboculars—separating the eyes from the upper labials (lip scales). The body scales are weakly keeled, arranged in 31–35 rows, and the anal plate is divided. Both are primarily of Mexican distribution. However, one, the Trans-Pecos rat snake, is of regular occurrence in North America, being very well known in west Texas and in southcentral New Mexico. The main range of the more westerly Baja rat snake is on the southern Baja Peninsula. A very few specimens have been found in northern Baja and adjacent California.

66 Baja California Rat Snake

Bogertophis rosaliae

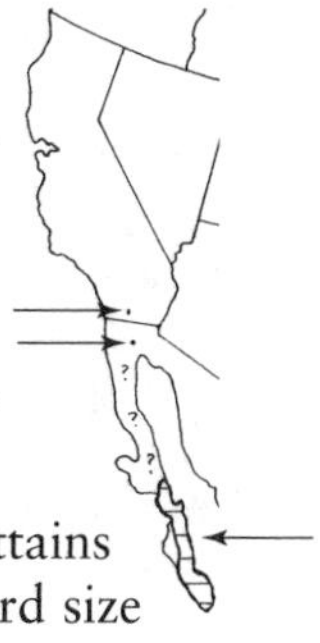

Nonvenomous This snake is entirely without venom. However, it is a nervous snake that may pull its neck into a defensive "S" and strike viciously when frightened or carelessly handled.

Abundance Perhaps as much because it is peripheral in the United States as for any other reason, this is a very rare, or at least, rarely seen, snake.

Size Although rather slender, this interesting rat snake attains a fair size. Adults of 3–4 ft are not uncommon, and a record size of 58 in. has been reported. Hatchlings are 11.5–13 in. long.

Range As currently known, the principal range of this pallid rat snake is in Baja California Sur, southward from the vicinity of Bahia de Los Angeles to the southernmost tip of the peninsula. It occurs also on some of Baja's offshore islands. A very few specimens have been found well north of the main range, in northern Baja California and in Imperial County, California. Could it be that this snake is actually more generally distributed than now known, or were the specimens found in northern Baja California and near Mountain Spring, California, refound releases? It is likely to take much dedicated observation to piece together the distributional puzzle now posed by the findings of this secretive snake.

Habitat In Baja this snake is associated with canyons, arroyos, and riparian scrub habitats. It seems most abundant near desert streams and springs. Even on Baja this snake does not seem overly common, but this may be due to a paucity of herpetologically oriented field activity on the peninsula.

Prey Hatchlings and juveniles held in captivity eat both rodent and lizard prey. Adults, also captive, eat many species of wild mice and laboratory mice. Whether juvenile or adult, the captive snakes have shown a preference for prey items of comparatively small size. Wild specimens have regurgitated bats, unidentified rodents, and iguanian lizards.

Reproduction *B. rosaliae* is an oviparous species. Most clutches contain from 2–6 eggs. Up to 10 eggs have been recorded. Hatching occurs after 73–87 days (up to 107 days has been reported) of incubation.

Coloring/scale form In general appearance this snake looks much like a (nearly) patternless Trans-Pecos rat snake, its much better known relative. The eyes are protuberant (but not overly large), and are separated from the upper labials by a row of subocular scales. The head is broad, the neck is slender. The body scales are usually in 31, 33, or 35 rows at midbody. The lateral scales are smooth, the dorsolateral scales are usually smooth, but the middorsal scales are usually very weakly keeled. The keels may be difficult to see. The anal plate is divided.

Adults vary from a (apparently very rare) silver-gray to olive-yellow, olive-gray, or reddish brown dorsally and are paler below. Hatchlings look delicately translucent, especially ventrally. Juveniles usually have a ground color of olive-yellow, olive-orange, to olive-gray. A vague, paler vertebral stripe with well separated, pale, partial bands extending downward is present. The markings are best defined anteriorly. They usually fade quickly with growth.

Similar snakes None within this snake's range. The Trans-Pecos rat snake is very similar in build and habits, but occurs far to the east of the Baja California range of *B. rosaliae.*

Behavior This is a nervous snake that is so uncommon in the United States that its behavior here is entirely unknown. It has been found to be primarily crepuscular and nocturnal on the southern Baja Peninsula, and captives have also shown a predilection for this activity pattern. Two juveniles that we once kept were occasionally active on overcast days, but even then, they seemed uncomfortable. These two snakes preferred to feed after darkness had fallen, but would occasionally eat by day if the food animal was placed in their darkened hide box.

Comments Virtually everything known about the breeding behavior and certain other aspects of this snake's natural history has been learned from captive breeding projects. When captive, this snake does not fare well in humid areas, but seems relatively hardy when maintained in arid regions of the country in dry terraria.

67 Trans-Pecos Rat Snake

Bogertophis subocularis subocularis

Nonvenomous This snake usually does not attempt to bite when encountered in the wild. However, it is fully capable of doing so, and a frightened specimen may strike repeatedly.

Abundance This snake is so secretive that it is difficult to make population assessments. In suitable habitats, it is certainly not rare, and it may even be relatively common. In West Texas, we have seen up to a half dozen post-hatchling sized "subocs" crossing roadways on a single warm autumn night. Likewise, during one late-summer night of looking, we saw five adult subocs on the road, all but one a male.

Size Occasional specimens of the Trans-Pecos rat snake may measure 5.5 ft in length. Most, however, are considerably smaller, measuring 3–4.5 ft long when adult. Except when in their largest sizes, when they "chunk up," the Trans-Pecos rat snake is a slender serpent. Hatchlings measure 11.5–14 in., are proportionately slender, have huge eyes, and appear translucent when viewed ventrally.

Range This pretty snake is a resident of the Chihuahuan Desert. It may be found southward from southeastern New Mexico, through western Texas, to central Durango, Mexico.

Habitat This desert snake is firmly associated with rock- and boulder-strewn mountainsides, escarpments, creviced cliff-faces, and other similar habitats. It is particularly common in rocky riparian areas that support tangled growths of desert scrub such as ocotillo, agave, creosote bush, shin oak, and cholla.

Prey The adults of this attractive snake prefer a diet of rodents, but also prey on lizards and bats. Hatchlings eat a proportionately higher number of lizards than the adults. Subocs seem to prefer comparatively small prey items. These snake are fully capable of constricting prey, but may not do so.

Reproduction The Trans-Pecos rat snake breeds much later in the year than many other snakes. Adult males are commonly found crossing trans-desert roadways in May, June, and July. It is thought that many of these are following the pheromone trails of receptive females. In captivity, reproductively active males are known to fight savagely, causing rather severe, bloody, wounds to one another. Egg deposition occurs in June, July and August. Following an incubation period of 62–75 (rarely to more than 100) days, the hatchlings emerge in late August, September, October, November, or rarely, early December.

Coloring/scale form This big-eyed (it has even been referred to as "bug-eyed") constrictor is restricted in distribution to the Chihuahuan Desert of the American Southwest and northern Mexico. In its most characteristic color and pattern, it is one of the most distinctive snakes of the Chihuahuan Desert. However, two lesser known colors also occur. These can be confusing.

In the Franklin Mountains of west Texas, just to the south of that covered by this book, the Trans-Pecos rat snake bears what we will refer to as the typical, black, H pattern on a silvery-gray to a steel-gray ground color. The unmarked venter is also a pale silvery-gray.

Elsewhere, and more typically, the pattern of 21 to 30 black H-shaped markings are on a straw-yellow, olive-yellow, to tan, ground color. The venter is unmarked and of an opalescent off-white to pale tannish yellow in coloration. This is the color phase seen most commonly over most of the range, including in New Mexico.

In both of the above phases, the neck is marked by two wide, parallel, black stripes. At a point, variable by individual snake, the crossbars of the H begin. Weak, perhaps only represented by a dark vertebral spot at first, by the time they are a third of the way toward the tail, the paralleling dorsolateral lines have become broken, and are usually fully joined by the crossbars, producing the H-shaped pattern for which this species is famous. White markings may show interstitially, especially where the crossbars of the H join the dorsolateral stripes. A series of lateral blotches, often poorly defined, is usually visible on each side.

Again, south of the area covered by this book, in Texas' Big Bend region, a very small percentage of the Trans-Pecos rat snakes are of a brighter yellow, atypically marked, phase (referred to by hobbyists as the "blonde phase"). On these, rather than dorsolateral stripes and Hs, the pattern consists of simple, light-centered, darker dorsal saddles and a single vertebral neck stripe. If lateral blotches are present on this phase, they are vague at best, and often are entirely lacking.

In all phases, the dorsal surface of the head is unpatterned, and a row of subocular scales separator the eye from the upper labial scales. The dorsal scale rows are in 31–35 rows. The lateral rows are not keeled, the dorsolateral rows *may* be very weakly keeled, the dorsal scale rows *are* weakly keeled; the anal plate is divided.

Similar snakes Within the scope of this book, the H shaped pattern (atypical patterns are not known from New Mexico) will distinguish the Trans-Pecos rat snake from any other species. If the snake is in hand, the row of subocular scales are also definitive.

Behavior Although they are quite apt to allow gentle handling without aggression being shown, occasionally Trans-Pecos rat snakes will draw back into a striking "S" and defend itself animatedly if approached.

This is primarily a nocturnal snake that may become active at dusk, but is more often seen well after darkness has encompassed its desert homeland. It may be found still actively prowling long after midnight.

Comments Until rather recently, this beautiful snake was included in the rat snake genus *Elaphe.* We discuss it, and the Baja California rat snake under the generic name of *Bogertophis* (established by Dowling and Price in 1988), but caution that additional work needs doing on the exact relationships of many of the rat snakes currently contained in *Elaphe.*

Additional subspecies None in the United States. The only other race, *Bogertophis subocularis amplinota,* occurs in southern Coahuila and Durango, Mexico. Intergrades between the 2 races are well documented.

RAT SNAKES
Genus Elaphe

Although this genus is abundantly represented in eastern North America, only a single species, the Great Plains rat snake, the westerly representative of the corn snake clan, occurs in the western portion.When adult, the snakes of this genus have weakly keeled dorsal and dorsolateral scales and unkeeled lateral scales. The juveniles of all lack scale keels. The number of scale rows varies by species and individually. The Great Plains rat snake has the scales arranged in 27–29 rows. The anal plate is divided.

If looked at in cross section, the rat snakes would be seen to be rounded on top, to have weakly convex sides, and to have a flattened venter. Rat snakes are agile climbers that can ascend virtually straight up a tree with only moderately rough bark and can even ascend smooth barked trees (though with more difficulty) if they choose.

Rat snakes are often drawn to barnyard and ranch settings by the proliferation of rodents.

Juveniles of the rat snakes usually feed on small lizards and treefrogs, while the adults consume rodents, rabbits, and some birds.

Most rat snakes kill or immobilize their prey animals by constriction.

If carelessly handled, many wild rat snakes will bite. Some strike savagely and repeatedly. Most quickly become accustomed to handling and become very tractable.

68 GREAT PLAINS RAT SNAKE

Elaphe guttata emoryi 

Nonvenomous Like other rat snakes, this snake is completely devoid of venom. It may attempt to bite if approached, but even wild specimens often allow themselves to be gently handled with no show of hostility.

Abundance This widespread and interesting serpent is a common sight in the more easterly part of its range, but in New Mexico, Colorado, and Utah, it appears to be more local in distribution. It can, however, be locally abundant where resources such as water availability, ample food, and adequate ground cover allow.

Size Great Plains rat snakes seldom exceed 4.5 ft in length and the record length is only 5.1 ft. Hatchlings are 10–12.5 in. long.

Range This is a wide-ranging rat snake of our central and western states and northeastern Mexico. In the American West, the Great Plains rat snake occurs in eastern New Mexico, southeastern Colorado, and in a disjunct population in central western Colorado and adjacent Utah. A single record exists from the extreme northeastern corner of Utah.

Habitat The Great Plains rat snake inhabits a variety of habitats. It is more dependent on a source of water than true desert rat snakes (such as the Trans-Pecos rat snake) are. Although it wanders widely, somewhere within its range there is usually a spring, stock tank, stream, pond, or lake, to which it can (and does) return when thirsty. It is often drawn to the vicinity of human habitations, not only for the water they provide, and because rodents are often drawn to like locations, but because human-generated surface debris provides ample areas for seclusion. Rock- or boulder-strewn areas in the vicinity of watercourses also provide excellent natural habitat. Fissures in canyonsides, escarpments, talus, the entrance and twilight zones of caves and mines, are all habitats utilized. Water availability due to irrigation practices has allowed the Great Plains rat snake to expand its range in some areas.

Prey Although the adults seem to prefer endothermic prey, such as bats, pocket mice and nestlings of larger rodents, birds and, occasionally, their eggs, they also may opportunistically eat ectotherms such as lizards. Lizards form a large percentage of the diet of hatchling rat snakes.

Reproduction This oviparous snake has relatively large clutches of rather large eggs. Much of the data available regarding the reproductive potential of this snake have accrued from captive specimens. Normally, clutches seem to contain 5–12 eggs, with larger females producing the larger clutches, and marginally larger eggs. Clutches of up to 16 eggs are not uncommon, and one of 25 has been mentioned. A second clutch, usually containing fewer eggs, may also be produced in years when food is plentiful. Hatchlings emerge after 55–70 days of incubation.

Coloring/scale form Although dull when compared to its eastern relative, the Great Plains rat snake is often a pleasing combination of brown on gray. However, this snake is variable, both inter- and intrapopulationally. The ground color can vary from a mid-gray to an olive-brown, and both the dorsal saddles and the lateral blotches may be a light olive-gray, olive-brown, medium-brown, or a rich chocolate brown. The saddles are often narrowly edged with darker pigment.

There is a dark spearpoint atop the head, a dark bar runs diagonally upward through each eye from the jawline, and converges on the top of the snout. The head markings may fade with advancing age.

The belly may be prominently checkered, diffusely checkered, or immaculate. The underside of the tail may or may not have dark stripes. There may be pockets of specimens with unpatterned bellies interspersed among those with prominently checkerboarded bellies. This appears to be an individual, rather than a populational, trait.

The lateral scales lack keels, but dorsolaterally and dorsally the scales are weakly keeled. The scales are in 25–31 rows and the anal plate is divided.

Similar snakes The blotched young of racers have smooth scales and lack the spearpoint design on the top of the head. Glossy snakes have smooth scales and a single anal plate. Bull and gopher snakes have a vertically oriented, wraparound rostral scale and heavily keeled dorsal and lateral scales.

Behavior We have most frequently encountered these serpents, from dusk to late at night, at times in fair numbers, on roadways. They were actively crawling when all other snake species seem to be quiescent. We have found them active, even when the landscape has been illuminated by a full moon, a time when many other snakes supposedly remain in hiding or at least, are said to limit their sphere of surface activity. They have also been found by day beneath debris, in tree hollows, or occasionally, actively crawling.

This snake is a powerful constrictor that seldom consumes prey before killing it.

Comments This is the least colorful member of the corn snake complex. Although we have included it as a race of the corn snake, some taxonomists consider this snake a full species, *E. emoryi,* and divide it into a northern race (*emoryi*) and a southern race (*meahllmorum*). If valid, the same subspecific designations may be made (as they once were) while retaining the Great Plains rat snake in the species *guttata.* Such nomenclature will then continue to show the Great Plains rat snake's obvious relationship with the corn snake.

Kingsnakes and Milk Snakes

Genus Lampropeltis

As currently understood, there are only 4 species of milk snakes and kingsnakes in the western United States. Of these, only one, the gray-banded kingsnake, is not subspeciated.

The scales of all members of this genus are smooth and appear shiny and polished. All species and subspecies have undivided anal plates.

The snakes of this genus are noted for their occasional ophiophagous (even cannibalistic) tendencies. Kingsnakes and milk snakes seem immune, or at least very resistant, to the venoms of the various venomous snakes with which they share their habitats.

The various races of the common kingsnakes have dark ground colors, while the gray-banded kingsnake and the various Arizona milk snakes can be clad in very brilliant colors.

Some of the milk snakes are remarkable mimics of the venomous coral snakes but have the ring sequence arranged differently. The coral snakes of North America have the two warning colors of a traffic signal—the yellow for caution and the red for stop—touching. The harmless milk snakes have the two caution colors separated by black.

69 Gray-banded Kingsnake

Lampropeltis alterna

Nonvenomous Most specimens are even reluctant to bite.

Abundance Once thought to be rare in Texas, it is now known that the gray-banded kingsnake is actually a common snake that is a master at evading detection. This may not be the case in New Mexico, where they are very much a peripheral species. In New Mexico these kingsnakes occur, as far as is known, only in and along canyons in the southernmost regions of two counties to a point just a few miles north of the Texas state line.

Size This is a moderate sized kingsnake. Adults are typically 26–40 in. long. The record size is 57.75 in.—just 2.25 in. shy of 5 ft! Hatchlings are 9.5–12.5 in. long. Hatchlings are quite slender, but gray bands bulk up some with growth. However, they never appear stout.

Range Although secretive—it is now known that fissured canyons and creviced roadcuts in western Texas and northern Mexico are the strongholds of this attractive snake—it is not a rare species. Within our region, the gray-banded kingsnake is known only from southern Eddy and Otero counties, New Mexico.

Habitat This is a species of rocky desert flats, fissured escarpments and canyonsides, road-cuts, and other such Chihuahuan Desert habitats. Most specimens seen by casual observers are in the process of crossing paved trans-desert roads, rather late at night. Hobbyists hunt roadcuts and canyons with powerful lights for this coveted species.

Prey Although adults opportunistically feed on both lizards and rodents (especially nestlings), in most cases it is the lizards that predominate in the diet. These snakes seem particularly adept at finding sleeping diurnal lizards that have sought nighttime refuge beneath the rocks and in the fissures and crevices through which the snakes prowl by night.

Some hatchlings and juveniles will accept only lizards as prey.

Reproduction Gray-banded kingsnakes routinely lay rather small clutches of fairly large eggs. From 4–9 are typically laid, and the record seems to be 15. As with many other snakes, we actually know far more about this species as a captive, than in the wild. The incubation duration in captivity varies between 60–70 days.

Coloring/scale form Although only the black banded, gray, alterna phase has been found in New Mexico, it is possible that the blairi phase may eventually also be found.

As indicated by both the specific name and the hobbyist vernacular, the alterna phase has broken black bands alternating with complete black bands on a gray ground color. If any orange pigment is present on this phase, it is usually restricted to the neck and the tail.

The blairi phase of the gray-banded kingsnake is more variable. The ground color may vary from dark gray to light gray. The dark crossbands may be narrow or wide, mostly black, with red or orange centers dorsally, and with white edging, or mostly red (or orange) with narrow black edging, and with each band bordered anteriorly and posteriorly with a narrow pale-ash or white edging.

The ventral coloration is gray with black blotches and spots. The dark coloration may occasionally predominate.

The body scales are smooth, in 25 rows and the anal plate is undivided.

Similar snakes The black-banded alterna phase is quite similar in color to the banded rock rattlesnake. However, the kingsnake lacks the telltale rattle and is of more slender build than the rattler. Lyre snakes are equally slender, tend toward a browner coloration, but have a vertically elliptical pupil (that of the kingsnake is round). There are no other snakes similar in appearance to the red saddled blairi phase.

Behavior The gray-banded kingsnake is primarily nocturnal in its surface-activity pattern. Unless a concerted effort is made to find it in its rock crevice habitat, it is seldom seen in the field. Most specimens are encountered on paved road, long after darkness has fallen. This snake seldom bites when handled, but can be nervous and erratic in its movements and efforts to escape. It may void and smear feces and musk on the hand and arm of the person holding it.

Comments This kingsnake has captured the interest of herpetoculturists and hundreds (perhaps thousands) of locality-specific hatchlings are produced by dozens (perhaps hundreds) of hobbyists each year. For many years the saddled blairi phase gray-banded kingsnakes were assigned a different subspecific name than the banded alterna phase examples. For pattern-phase identification purposes, hobbyists still continue to refer to these animals simply as blairi and alterna.

Additional subspecies Although it is still considered a component of the *Lampropeltis mexicana* complex, as currently understood, there are no subspecies.

70 California Kingsnake

Lampropeltis getula californiae

Nonvenomous This, like all members of this subfamily, is entirely nontoxic.

Abundance This is a common, even abundant, snake in suitable habitats. It is remarkably adaptable, and persists in some numbers not only in wilderness areas, but in farmlands, ranches, and even some brushy suburban areas.

Size Although some of the eastern races of this kingsnake (collectively the numerous races are referred to as the common kingsnake) may exceed 6.5 ft in total length, no western race nears this size. The California kingsnake, for example, seldom exceeds a total length of 4 ft, and lengths of 2.5–3.5 ft are far more common. Hatchlings are about a foot in length.

Range The range of the California kingsnake is extensive. This pretty constrictor can be found southward from southwestern Oregon and southcentral Utah, throughout California and the western half of Arizona, to the southernmost tip of the Baja Peninsula and northern Sonora.

Habitat The California kingsnake may be encountered in myriad habitats. It may be found in desert, semi-desert, areas of brush, grasslands, pastures and meadows, canyons, marshes, swamps, and other such habitat. It seems most common where there is access to either natural or artificial waterholes, or in riparian situations, but it may also be encountered far from standing water.

Prey There may be no snakes with a more catholic diet than the California (and related) kingsnakes. Turtle eggs and hatchling turtles, other snake (including venomous ones), lizards, frogs, salamanders, bird's egg and nestlings, small mammals, even large insects, are opportunistically eaten.

Reproduction The California (and all other) kingsnake(s) is oviparous, laying one or more clutches of from 2–24 eggs annually. The more normal clutch size is 5–12 eggs. Hatching occurs after 45–60 days of incubation.

Coloring/scale form The most common color phase has a deep brown to black ground color prominently marked with narrow-to-wide, cream-to-pure-white, crossbands that widen ventrolaterally. In some areas a striped phase occurs. This beautiful morph has a two or three-scale-wide vertebral stripe, usually entire but sometimes broken, on a chocolate brown ground color. The lateral scales often have some degree of white-tipping. Intermediates between the two phases are known. A "desert phase" has jet black ground color and narrow, stark-white bands. The banded phase has a dark and white belly; the striped phase has a chocolate belly. The California kingsnake has a great amount of white on its nose and white labial scales. It also has 23 rows of non-keeled body scales and the anal plate is not divided, but the scales beneath the tail (the subcaudals) are divided. Hatchlings and juveniles are very much like adults in coloration.

Similar snakes There are few snake that can be mistaken for the California kingsnake. Occasional specimens of the California Mountain kingsnake may lack red bands, but their white rings do not broaden ventrolaterally. Some long-nosed snakes also lack red. However, they have many undivided subcaudal scales.

Behavior California kingsnakes are usually nonaggressive when encountered in the field. Some may coil and strike, but many merely hide their head among their coils and allow themselves to be lifted unceremoniously. However, after being lifted, kingsnakes have a disconcerting habit of pressing their nose against a finger, thumb, or fingerweb, slowly opening their mouth, and biting and chewing. Although not dangerous, the episode is decidedly unpleasant.

During cool weather, California kingsnakes may prowl by day, but become crepuscular and nocturnal during the hottest weather.

Kingsnakes are powerful constrictors that coil tightly around their prey, be it a rodent or a venomous snake, to immobilize and kill it. After prey-death has occurred the item is swallowed. Kingsnakes seem largely immune to the toxins produced by the venomous snakes with which they evolved.

Comments Two quite different color phases occur on the Baja Peninsula. These phases were once thought to be subspecies, but are now considered variants of the California kingsnake. The names, *conjuncta* and *nitida,* are kept alive by hobbyists. The *conjuncta* phase has a brownish black ground color and poorly defined, silver-gray crossbands. The *nitida* phase has a similar ground color and a narrow and very poorly defined silvery-gray vertebral stripe that may be entire or fragmented. Neither phase is known from the United States, although an occasional "melanistic" California kingsnake, having reduced band contrast, is found.

Albino California kingsnakes are also well documented in the wild.

California kingsnakes in all of their natural patterns and colors, as well as many very unnatural ones, are now bred annually in captivity for the pet trade.

Kingsnakes from the disjunct population in southwestern Colorado look much like a banded phase California kingsnake, but are considered intergrades between it and the desert kingsnake. Those from the grasslands in Otero County, Colorado, look much like the desert kingsnake but are considered intergrades between that and the speckled kingsnake, *Lampropeltis getula holbrooki.*

Additional subspecies This kingsnake group is represented to the east of our range by numerous subspecies. In the west 2 additional subspecies occur, and they are discussed in the following sections.

71 Desert Black Kingsnake

Lampropeltis getula nigrita 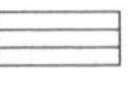

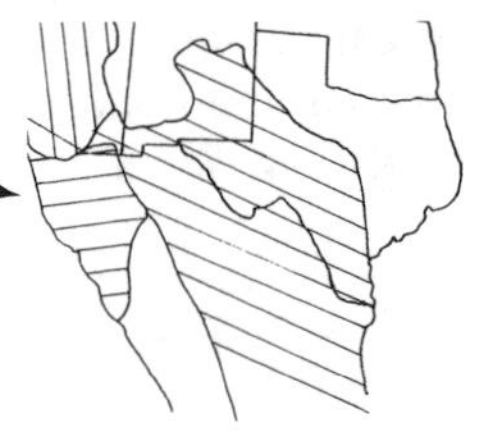

Mainly a northern Mexico inhabitant, this snake enters the United States from its Mexican stronghold only in extreme southeastern Arizona. It is also an arid- and semi-aridland race. Where its range abuts that of the California or the desert kingsnakes, intergrades are well documented. At its best, this is a shiny dark brown to black kingsnake, with few, if any, yellow markings, and often no evidence of a dorsal chain, dorsal banding, or dorsal striping. However, those found in the United States often have a tiny light dot on each lateral scale. If a pattern *is* present, it is invariably most evident on the sides. Hatchlings tend to show more yellow and stronger evidence of a pattern than adults, but usually become darker with each successive shedding. There is also an eastern race of kingsnake designated as the black king, *Lampropeltis getula nigra*. While related, these two are very different and should not be confused.

72 Desert Kingsnake

Lampropeltis getula splendida 

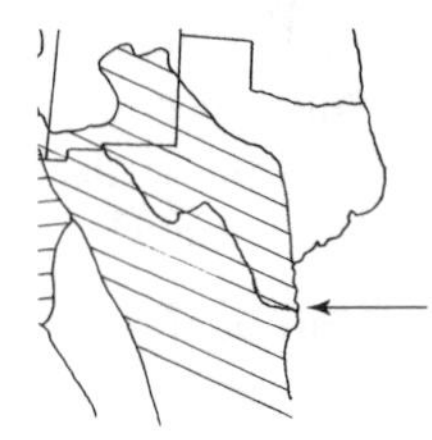

This is a pretty species with a variable and intricate patterning. The ground color varies from brown to black. The dark sides are usually prominently speckled with yellow, or yellowish cream. A series of narrow yellow(ish) crossbands divides the dark back into a variable number of saddles. There is much yellow on the labial scales and head of this snake. In the United States, the desert kingsnake ranges westward from central Texas, over much of southern New Mexico, to the southeastern corner of Arizona. Disjunct populations occur in northern New Mexico, and intergrade populations in southeastern Colorado and southwestern Colorado (see comments, above). Although well adapted to aridland and semi-aridland conditions, desert kingsnakes seem most common where surface water is always, or nearly always, available.

73 UTAH MOUNTAIN KINGSNAKE

Lampropeltis pyromelana infralabialis

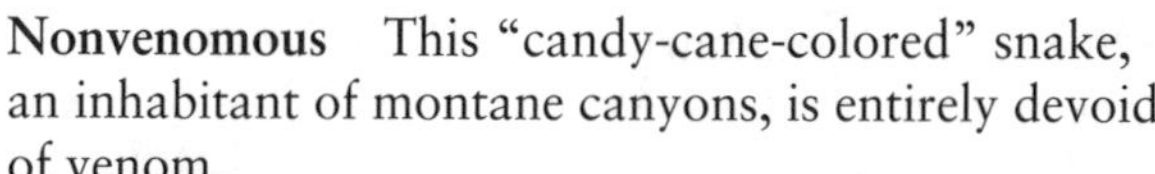

Nonvenomous This "candy-cane-colored" snake, an inhabitant of montane canyons, is entirely devoid of venom.

Abundance Because of the relative inaccessibility of their preferred habitats, these beautiful snakes are seldom seen. However, within suitable areas they are not uncommon.

Size This is one of the larger of the tricolored snakes of the United States. Although adult at 20–30 in., specimens of slightly more than 40 in. have been found. This is a slender snake species. Hatchlings are 7.5–10 in. long.

Range This subspecies ranges northward in various mountain ranges, from extreme northcentral Arizona, to central Utah and central-eastern Nevada.

Habitat Boulder-strewn, forested mountain canyons, especially those with permanent or persistent streams, are the favored habitats of the several races of this kingsnake. However, they have also been found at meadow-edge and at the foot of talus slides. Although they have been found as low as 3,000 ft in elevation, these snakes are most common at elevations of 4,500–9,000 ft.

Prey Lizards, snakes, frogs, and rodents (especially their nestlings) comprise most of the diet of this snake. It is probable that ground-dwelling birds, their nestlings, and occasionally their eggs, would also be eaten.

Reproduction Like all kingsnakes, this is an oviparous species. The eggs are relatively large, and the clutches relatively small. Egg deposition normally takes place in very late spring or early summer. An average clutch consists of 3–6 eggs. From 2–9 eggs have been recorded. Hatching (in captivity) occurs after 57–70 days of incubation.

Coloring/scale form A white nose easily identifies all races of this kingsnake. They have 23–25 scale rows and an undivided anal plate.

Differentiating the three subspecies that occur in our southwestern mountains can be difficult. Use range maps as well as white ring and lower-labial scale counts as identification tools.

This snake is vividly ringed in bands of red, black, and white (sometimes yellowish white or cream). The red is separated from the white by the black which is narrowest on the sides, but which widens dorsally, and which may actually divide the red bands vertebrally. The venter is paler than the dorsum, and red often predominates, followed in expanse by white, then black. The black markings are often interrupted or offset midventrally. There is usually a minimum of 42 white rings, but as many as 57 have been counted. Following the white nose, there is a broad, triangular, band of black (the anterior edge is basically a straight line across the snout), narrowest laterally, that begins on the the upper labials, covers the eyes, and widens posterio-dorsally to include the parietals. Hatchlings are diminutive replicas of the adults.

It is a decreased number of infralabial (lower lip) scales (9 rather than 10) and an increased number of complete (not ventrally broken) white rings (more than half) that differentiates this race.

The scales are arranged in 21–23 (often 21) rows at midbody; the anal plate is not divided.

Similar snakes The banded sand snake and the shovel-nosed snake are very small and have saddles of color, not rings, and do not occur within the range of the Utah mountain kingsnake. The long-nosed snake has many rows of subcaudal scales in a single row.

Behavior At high elevations, where nighttime temperatures tend to be unsuitable for nocturnal activity, the various Sonoran mountain kingsnakes are primarily diurnal. They can be found thermoregulating beneath flat sun-warmed stones, or coiled in open sunny patches. They may be found actively crawling in mid morning throughout the warmer months of the year. Remarkably visible in a cage, when this (and other tricolored) snake(s) is/are moving, the rings of brilliance blend so well with the background that the snake may be easily overlooked. It is not uncommon to find this snake along hiking trails in wooded, stream-drained, montane canyons. This is a nervous snake that seldom bites, but which will whip to and fro and smear musk and cloacal contents on its captor if carelessly restrained.

Comments Is this a variable but non-subspeciated snake, or should 2, 3 or even 4 races be recognized? It seems as if even the authorities are unable to agree. At some points in time, 2 races, *Lampropeltis pyromelana pyromelana* (the Arizona mountain kingsnake) and *Lampropeltis pyromelana woodini* (the Huachuca Mountain kingsnake) have been deemed valid in North America. At other times, the nominate race remained as a recognized entity, but it was *Lampropeltis pyromelana infralabialis*, (the Utah Mountain kingsnake) not *L. p. woodini* that was considered valid. At other times all 3 subspecies have been recognized. We have elected to recognize all 3.

74 Arizona Mountain Kingsnake

Lampropeltis pyromelana pyromelana 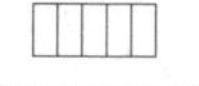

Like the other subspecies, this one has a beautiful and precisely delineated combination of red, black, and white rings. However, with age, it may tend to darken a little, and black pigment may suffuse and replace the red vertebrally. The belly is paler than the dorsum, and the red predominates. The black markings may be broken or offset midventrally. This race is similar in white ring count (42–61) as the Utah race. However, it has 10 lower labials, and at midbody the scales are often in 23 rows. This race occurs in some mountains of southwestern New Mexico, in southeastern and central Arizona, and in northcentral Mexico.

75 Huachuca Mountain Kingsnake

Lampropeltis pyromelana woodini 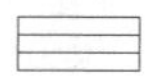

The validity of this subspecies is questioned by some researchers. The race, which takes its name from the mountain chain in southeastern Arizona (Cochise and Santa Cruz counties; also immediately adjacent Sonora, Mexico) where it dwells, has a comparatively low number of white body rings (37–42). It is a very brightly colored and precisely patterned subspecies. At midbody the scales are usually in 23 rows. The ventral color is paler than the dorsal color, and the red usually predominates in expanse. Like the Arizona mountain kingsnake, this race usually has 10 infralabials. With a record size of 44 in., this is marginally the largest race.

An additional race, *Lampropeltis pyromelana knoblochi*, bearing a more pastel red and a reduced amount of black pigment, occurs in northern Chihuahua, Mexico.

76 NEW MEXICO MILK SNAKE

Lampropeltis triangulum celaenops

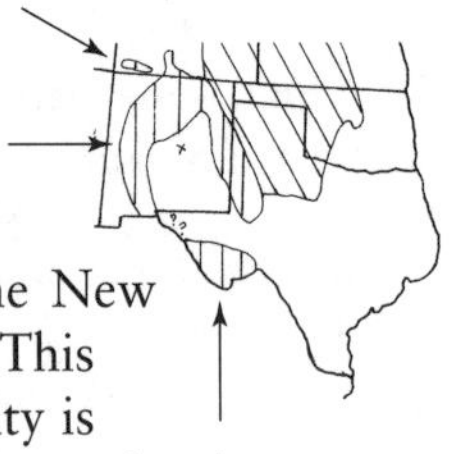

Nonvenomous Some specimens may assume a striking "S" and defend themselves furiously; others show no evidence of bad temper.

Abundance Because of its secretive habits, the New Mexico milk snake is often thought to be rare. This does not seem to be at all the case. Surface activity is triggered by rains, and (apparently) to a lesser degree by the passage of dry fronts that causes a falling barometric pressure. At such times the snakes may be seen prowling, perhaps as much in search of new territory as prey.

Size This is one of the smaller races of the milk snake. Most specimens found are 14–18 in. long, while the largest specimens are in the 22–30-inch range. Hatchlings are a slender 6.25–7.75 in. long.

Range Besides two small satellite populations in Arizona, the New Mexican milk snake occurs in a large but difficult-to-delineate area that begins in western Val Verde County, Texas, and extends northward in a narrow swath along the Rio Grande, through much of New Mexico, and culminates in two points in southcentral and southwestern Colorado. It may be found from sea level to elevations of more than 7,000 ft.

Habitat The New Mexico milk snake occurs in several habitats. It is most often found in rock- and boulder-strewn, riparian areas, but wanders far out into semi-desert and desert scrublands as well. It is also found in grasslands, forested areas, and sandhills, and from sea level to elevations of more than 7,000 feet. Like other subspecies of this wide-ranging snake, the New Mexico milk snake is often found beneath natural (rock and fallen tree trunks) and human-generated (boards, newspapers, etc.) surface debris. This snake is fully capable of burrowing, but also uses the ready-made burrows of lizards and small mammals.

Prey Lizards (especially skinks), and smaller snakes are eaten by this milk snake. Occasionally frogs are also accepted. Larger specimens also accept nestling mice and the nestlings of small ground nesting birds (such as sparrows).

Reproduction This oviparous snake lays 2–8 eggs. Eggs are laid in decomposing logs, sawdust piles, beneath moisture-retaining surface debris such as rocks and logs, or in fissures. Hatching occurs after 50–70 days of incubation.

Coloring/scale form The smooth scales of the New Mexico milk snake are arranged in 21 rows and the anal plate is not divided. The brilliant bands of (bright but not scarlet) red, black, and white (or yellowish) are conspicuous. The red bands are widest (and number 17–30—very wide to moderately wide), the white next so, and the black are the narrowest. The black and the white bands completely encircle the body (extending across the belly) but the red bands are often discontinuous on the belly. The black bands usually expand middorsally and may (rarely) interrupt the red banding vertebrally. The red and the white bands are separated by black bands. There is seldom any black tipping on the red scales, but some dark tipping may appear laterally on the white scales. The nose is primarily black, but usually bears some white spotting. Hatchlings are very similar to the adults but may be a little paler and have white (not yellow) bands.

Similar snakes The coral snake has the two caution colors, red and yellow, touching. Banded sand snakes and shovel-nosed snakes have saddles of color (not rings). Both have a white (yellowish) belly. The Sonoran mountain kingsnake has a white snout.

Behavior Except on cool days when it may be diurnally active, when this snake does indulge in surface activity, it is most usually only after darkness has fallen. It would appear to be most active during and following nighttime rains. Throughout its range (except in sandhill habitats), the New Mexico milk snake is associated with areas of surface debris such as rocks, logs, boards, or trash. It may secrete itself behind loosened bark on dead but still standing trees and stumps or, when possible, burrow into decomposing logs and stumps. In coniferous woodlands it may travel beneath the layer of needles that is usually present in such habitats.

This fossorial snake is well adapted both for burrowing and for following the burrows of other small snakes and small rodents.

Comments This is one of the prettier and more precisely colored of the milk snakes. It is in great demand by hobbyist/breeders. More research is needed to more precisely delineate its range.

77 Central Plains Milk Snake

Lampropeltis triangulum gentilis

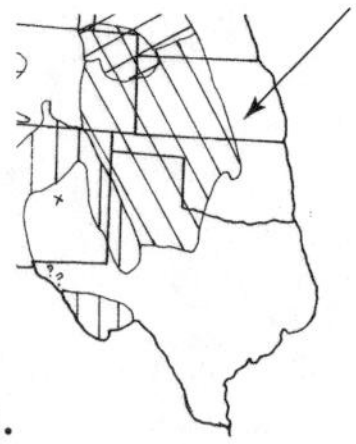

This subspecies is another small and beautiful tricolored snake. Adults are usually 18–24 in. long; the record size is 36 in. Hatchlings are a slender 6.25–7.75 in. long.

On this form, the red bands tend to be somewhat faded (red, orange-red to orange) and of almost the same (variable) width as the white (or pale gray) bands. The 20–40 red bands are separated from the white by narrower bands of black. The black bands and the white bands encircle the body, but the red bands are usually interrupted middorsally by black pigment. The scales are in 21 (occasionally 19) rows. The snout is white but the scale sutures are often black. In our area, this snake occurs only in the eastern half of Colorado. From there it ranges eastward to central-southern Nebraska and northern Texas. Although seldom seen and apparently rare in some locales, in other areas, if properly looked for, this will be found to be a common race of the milk snake. The Central Plains milk snake is a secretive creature that may be found in many various habitats. Among others, it occurs on rocky mountains and hillsides, in riparian settings, on prairies, and in canyons. It is fully capable of burrowing, but often chooses to secrete itself beneath surface debris or in the burrows of lizards or small mammals. It occurs from near sea level to elevations of more than 8,000 ft.

A clutch typically consists of from 3–6 eggs, but from 1–9 have been recorded.

Similar snakes The only snake that the Central Plains milk snake might be mistaken for (other than other races of this species) is one of the subspecies of *Lampropeltis pyromelana,* collectively called the "Sonoran mountain kingsnake." Both have white noses. However, the Sonoran mountain kingsnake does not occur in the range of the Central Plains milk snake.

78 Pale Milk Snake

Lampropeltis triangulum multistriata 

The most northerly of the 4 western races of milk snake, this snake prefers open rocky woodlands, rocky prairies, and escarpments where it secludes itself beneath logs, in stumps, behind loosened bark, under rocks, and other ground-surface litter. It ranges northwestward from extreme northeastern Colorado and southern Nebraska to central Montana.

Although adults of this race measure 16–26 in., occasional examples can measure 30 in. or slightly longer. Hatchlings measure 6.25–8.0 in. Perhaps due as much to its secretive habits as to an actual scarcity, the pale milk snake is considered uncommon to rare throughout its range.

The pale milk snake preys on lizards and small snakes, and if the snakes are large enough, on nestling rodents and nestlings of small ground-nesting birds.

This snake produces small clutches of 2–8 (rarely to 10) eggs, and the incubation period, varying, of course, by temperature, is from 60–70 days.

Typically, this is the palest of the milk snakes. The light bars are gray(ish) rather than white or yellow, the black is reduced in quantity and the 22–38 red bands are muted to orange-red or dusty-red. The top of the head is dark and the snout is whitish with orangish overtones and scattered dark markings. The bands do not completely encircle the body, usually leaving the midventral area an unpatterned light gray.

The body scales are smooth and usually in 19 rows. The anal plate is undivided.

Although there are no similar appearing snakes over most of the range of the pale milk snake, we suggest that you check the account for the Central Plains milk snake, the race that abuts the pale milk snake to the south for differentiating features.

79 Utah Milk Snake

Lampropeltis triangulum taylori 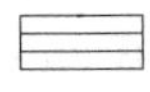

Very little is known about the natural history of this western subspecies. It has from 23–34 dull, but definite red saddles (not rings) that are often narrower than either the black or white (to pale gray) fields. The black bands may also be interrupted ventrally, leaving the belly predominantly grayish in color. The pattern of this little milk snake is well defined, but not clear cut. The scales in both the red and the white fields have some degree of dark-tipping. The nose is white with dark scale sutures and sometimes a pale orange blush.

This, the westernmost of the milk snake subspecies, is found in western central Colorado, and over much of Utah to the east and south of the Great Salt Lake. There is speculation that the easternmost and southernmost populations are of intergrade status. This form has been found at elevations to approximately 5,800 ft.

This is a secretive little snake that, over most of its range, is happened across mostly by accident. It is one of the more poorly understood of the milk snakes. It seldom bites, but if provoked sufficiently will assume a striking "S" and may even strike. Like other king- and milk snakes, this race will vibrate its tail when nervous.

Few snakes resemble this milk snake, and none do exactly. The Utah mountain kingsnake is larger and more precisely patterned.

80 Sierra Mountain Kingsnake

Lampropeltis zonata multicincta 

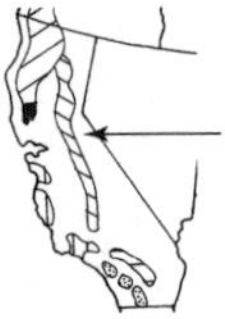

Nonvenomous The 5 races of this colorful snake, which together are referred to as California mountain kingsnakes, are entirely devoid of venom.

Abundance As with most of the tricolored kingsnakes, in areas of suitable habitat, the Sierra mountain kingsnake is more secretive than rare. At high altitudes, where low nighttime temperatures restrict movement during much of the year, this kingsnake may be surface-active by day. Where temperatures are more moderate, it may indulge in crepuscular and nocturnal, as well as some diurnal, activity.

Size Although these snakes may occasionally exceed 3.5 ft (the record is 48.25 in.!), most found are much smaller. A more normal length is 18–28 in., and any specimen measuring more than 30 in. must be considered large indeed. Hatchlings are 7.5–9 in. long.

Range The Sierra mountain kingsnake has been named for its range—the mountains of California's Sierra Nevada.

Habitat From sea level to elevated mountain fastnesses, from moist wooded canyons to chaparral—with the exception of desert, this snake is pretty much a habitat generalist. It seems most common and most generally distributed in moist coniferous woodlands, but may also be encountered with some regularity in more sharply drained areas. An ideal habitat would boast decomposing logs and a permanent, or semi-permanent, stream. This snake secretes itself in the gathered duff on forest floors, beneath surface rocks, and in rock and earthen fissures. It occurs also in talus slides (especially near the foot), near lumber-mills (favoring those with ample discarded slabs near a moist, wooded, periphery), and in other such habitats.

Prey The Sierra mountain kingsnake is an opportunistic feeder, preying upon lizards, snakes, amphibians, rodents and their nestlings, nestling birds, and possibly on bird's eggs. Larger snakes can, of course, eat a wider variety of prey.

Reproduction Small clutches of relatively large eggs are produced by this snake. An average clutch numbers from 3–5 eggs, but from 1–9 have been recorded. Hatching occurs following 50–65 days of incubation.

Coloring/scale form This subspecies is noted for its variable coloration. Most specimens are clad in scales of red, black and white. The red bands are usually precisely defined anteriorly, where they are at least twice as wide as either the black or the white bands. The red bands often narrow perceptibly posteriorly. The black bands may widen and break the red bands dorsally. The first white band is often comparatively narrow, and its rear edge is slightly posterior to the edge of the mouth. This race has an average of 35 (23–48) triads (black-red-black). Some, or all, triads may lack red; part, or all of the snake being patterned just in black and white bands. This reduction of red seems more an individual, than a populational, trend. The belly color is paler than the dorsum, with the white bands being particularly irregular. It is in the central high Sierra Nevadas that the snakes missing the red most often occur. This race normally has a black nose.

The body scales are smooth, in 21 or 23 rows at midbody, and the anal plate is entire.

Similar snakes Shovel-nosed snakes have saddles of color and an immaculate venter. Sonoran mountain kingsnakes have a large amount of white on their snouts, and their ranges do not overlap those of the various California mountain kingsnakes. Long-nosed snakes have numerous single scales beneath the tail.

Behavior All of the races of California mountain kingsnake are secretive and easily overlooked. During moderate temperatures, these kingsnakes tend toward a diurnal and crepuscular activity pattern. During very hot weather, they may be primarily nocturnal. This is especially so of snakes in low altitude populations.

Some California kingsnakes seem to react to handling rather with no display of nervousness or hostility. Others will wriggle nervously, and if held carelessly, will seek a soft patch of skin on their captor's arm or hand and will bite and chew.

There are no indigenous tricolored venomous snakes (coral snakes) in California.

Comments Because of their variability, the various races of the California mountain kingsnake can be very difficult to differentiate. We urge that you rely heavily on range when attempting identification. To make identification even more difficult, intergrades are also known. Even at best, the differences in the subspecies are subtle, often depending on the exact position of the first white band on the head and the number of black-red-black triads (three bands of color). But even these characteristics are overlapping. Additionally, the ranges of several subspecies are discontinuous, another factor that must be kept in mind.

81 Coast Mountain Kingsnake

Lampropeltis zonata multifasciata

This subspecies tends to be a narrow-banded, busily patterned form, on which the red bands are usually at least marginally the widest, with the white bands next so. The snout is black, but often has red patches or scales. With an average of 35, the triad count range is 26–45. The belly is paler and far more irregularly marked than the dorsum. The posterior edge of the first white band can be either behind or in front of the corner of the mouth. This band usually narrows (or may be interrupted by black pigment) dorsally. Rely primarily on range when attempting an identification of this snake. The Coast mountain kingsnake occurs in at least three disjunct areas in the coastal ranges, southward from the San Francisco Bay area southward to Orange County. Although it does occur in mountainous areas, it is not a rare snake in moist, shaded, rocky, sea level canyons. A particularly pretty phase (which may have the white replaced with yellow and which has a very low triad count, and which is quite likely of intergrade origin) occurs in the region of Mt. Hamilton, Santa Clara County, California.

82 San Bernardino Mountain Kingsnake, *Lampropeltis zonata parvirubra*

This subspecies has a higher average triad count than the previous two races. With a low of 35 and a high of 56, the average triad count is 41. The red bands are noticeably, but not excessively, the widest, followed next by white, then by the narrow black rings. Although all three colors are present, the belly markings are pale and irregular. The posterior edge of the first white band either bisects or is at the anterior edge of the last upper labial scale. The snout tends to be entirely black in this race. Usually only a few of the red rings are broken dorsally by black pigment. This race also occurs at low elevations. It ranges in the foothills and wooded, stream-drained canyons of Los Angeles, San Bernardino, and Riverside counties in southern California.

83 San Diego Mountain Kingsnake

Lampropeltis zonata pulchra

Of rather restricted distribution, this subspecies occurs in suitable rock and boulder-strewn habitats, from sea level to the foothills and isolated mountainsides, in Los Angeles, Orange, Riverside, and San Diego counties. With a black snout and similarly placed first white band (the posterior edge bisects the last upper labial, or may be slightly anterior to the anterior suture of that scale), except for a reduced triad count, this race is quite similar to the San Bernardino mountain kingsnake, discussed last. The triad count on the San Diego mountain kingsnake varies between 26 and 39, with an average of 33. The paler belly bears imprecisely delineated markings.

84 St. Helena Mountain Kingsnake

Lampropeltis zonata zonata

Despite being the nominotypical race, in a non-intergraded form, this race has a rather restricted distribution in wilderness areas just to the north, and slightly to the east, of California's San Francisco Bay area. This race has a low triad count—normally 24–30, with an average of 27. The snout is dark. The posterior edge of the first white band is posterior to the corner of the mouth. The black and the white bands are about equal in width, but both are narrower than the red bands. The belly is primarily a patchy blackish-gray and pale red, with the white bands often being broken ventrally.

Although the range of the California mountain kingsnake continues north into southeastern Oregon, and in a far removed (apparently) disjunct population in southern Washington, the specimens from northern California northward are considered of intergrade status. The parent races are the St. Helena mountain kingsnake and the Sierra mountain kingsnake. Although always of some combination of red, black, and white, these intergrades are quite variable in band width, dorsal suffusion of black. If unsubstantiated reports of California mountain kingsnakes in Yakima County, Washington, are eventually confirmed this will extend the known range well northward. Likewise, if reports of this species from Wasco County, Oregon, prove correct, it will do much to close the hypothetical gap between the southern Oregon and the southern Washington populations.

Two additional subspecies occur in Mexico. These are *Lampropeltis zonata agalma,* the San Pedro mountain kingsnake, and the curious little black and white *Lampropeltis zonata herrarae,* the Todos Santos Island kingsnake.

Gopher Snakes and Bullsnakes

Genus Pituophis

The members of this genus are moderately large to large snakes with heavily keeled scales; the ability to constrict; a rather belligerent nature; thanks to a glottal modification, the ability to hiss loudly; and a penchant for vibrating their tails. The heads of the bull and gopher snakes are narrow, but moderately wider than the neck. The rostral scale—the scale on the tip of the snout—is protruding, strong-

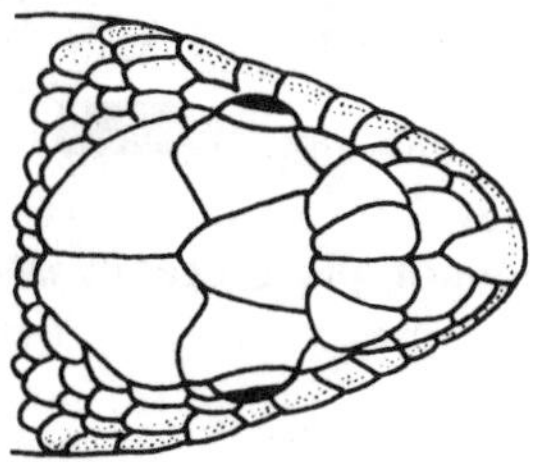

Prefrontal scales: bull-, pine, and gopher snakes

ly convex, and much higher than wide. There are usually four prefrontal scales. The body scales are in 27–35 (often 29) rows at midbody and the anal plate is undivided. A projecting supraocular scale makes the snakes of this genus appear as if they are scowling.

These snakes are accomplished burrowers, both pursuing their rodent prey (some seem to be pocket gopher specialists) in their underground burrows and choosing underground chambers in areas of moist soil for egg deposition. All members of the genus *Pituophis* are oviparous. Most clutches consist of relatively few, comparatively large, eggs. Occasionally, a very large clutch may be produced. Communal nesting is well documented in some species. As might be surmised, the hatchlings are also quite large, some exceeding 20″ in length.

Despite having a very different appearance, the snakes of this genus are rather closely allied to the rat and the kingsnakes. Captives of all three groups have been known to interbreed and produce fully viable young.

85 Sonoran Gopher Snake

Pituophis catenifer affinis

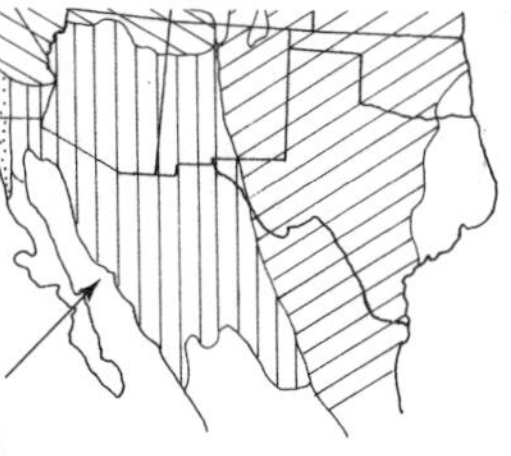

Nonvenomous Although some specimens may be defensive almost to the point of belligerence, this race, and all other gopher and bullsnakes are entirely devoid of venom.

Abundance Gopher snakes may actually be abundant in a given area, yet be so secretive (despite their large size, fossorial) that they are seldom seen by humans. Look for them in the spring of the year and during early summer when reproductively active males are trailing females. At such times they wander far afield. Hatchlings may be commonly seen in the early autumn, as they search for new and suitable habitat.

Size The normal size of this impressive snake is 5–6 ft, but specimens to slightly more than 7 ft long have been found. There is a tendency for females to be the larger sex. Hatchlings are relatively stout and 13.5–16 in. long.

Range The Sonoran gopher snake ranges southward from southern Colorado, through most of Arizona, New Mexico, and western Texas, to Sinaloa and northern Zacatecas, Mexico.

Habitat From suburban field to mountain fastnesses, from ranches and farmlands to remote canyons, from desert flats to irrigated fields and grasslands—these and more are the habitats of the Sonoran gopher snake. This, and related species, are among the most ubiquitous serpents of the American West. They may be found at elevations of from sea level to close to 9,000 ft.

Prey Although gopher snakes will accept many types of rodents and birds, they have an especial fondness for their namesake mammal, the pocket gopher. So ardently do the snakes pursue these and other burrowing rodents that the snakes remain below the ground in the mammal burrows much of the time. In the confines of a gopher or rat burrow, where space renders it impossible to throw a constricting coil around the prey, the snakes press the rodent prey against the sides of the rodent's own burrows, a particularly effective method of overpowering the toothy gophers. From one to several small mammals can be simultaneously overpowered by either this method or by typical constriction. Hatchlings are so large that most are capable of eating rodents up to the size of nearly grown mice.

Reproduction All gopher snakes are oviparous. Adult females actively seek secluded, moist depositories for their single, or very rarely, double, clutches of relatively few, large eggs. In the wild these are deposited in moisture-retaining burrows. The largest females lay both the largest and the most eggs. The eggs will hatch after an incubation duration of 60–75 days. The eggs are soft when laid, but soon become turgid. The permeable shells of fertile eggs will have a dry appearing, somewhat roughened surface. This becomes more accentuated as the eggs age and absorb moisture from the substrate. Clutch size is usually 3–12 eggs, but may rarely contain 20 or more.

Coloring/scale form Although clad in earthen-colored scales, this race is actually one of the prettiest of the gopher snakes. Against a dorsal and lateral ground color of light brown, tan, or straw-yellow, it has anterior blotches of medium-brown to almost russet. These do not contact the row of lateral spots. The dorsal blotches usually (but not always) darken to deep brown or black posteriorly and they may contact at least some of the lateral blotches that are in 3 alternating rows, the lowermost being the smallest. The supracaudal spots are almost black. The belly is yellowish and has a variable amount of bold, dark spots. The outer edges (sides) of the belly scutes are usually dusky.

This impressive snake has four prefrontal scales, an enlarged rostral scale, heavily keeled body scales (29–33 rows), a single anal plate, and a penchant for hissing loudly, striking savagely, vibrating its tail tip, and even approaching a person or other predator, when threatened. Hatchlings look very much like diminutive examples of the adults, but may be somewhat paler.

Similar snakes The glossy snake and the various racers have smooth scales.

Behavior During the spring of the year this is one of the most frequently seen snakes on both paved and dirt roadways. More often than not, those seen are males, probably following pheromone scent trails of receptive females. The Sonoran gopher snake seems to be primarily crepuscular, but may be active during the daylight hours in cool weather, and active long into the night during the hottest days of summer.

Comments No western American member of this genus is brightly colored, although some bullsnakes may be suffused with orange. In most cases, these snakes are clad in scales of variable brown, tan, and straw yellow. The dorsal ground color may be darker than the lateral color. Differentiating the several subspecies using only the subtle differences in pattern and coloration can be truly exasperating. Even scale row counts are variable, being as low as 27 or as high as 37. Intergrades occur frequently where the ranges of two races abut. Knowing the precise origin of the snake in question will do much to ease the confusion. An occasional albino specimen of several of the subspecies has been found.

86 San Diego Gopher Snake

Pituophis catenifer annectens

This race occurs south of the Pacific gopher snake. It also occasionally exceeds 6 ft in length but is far more commonly seen in 4–5-ft range. The anterior dorsal blotches are quite dark (nearing black on some specimens) and may fuse with each other and with the lateral blotches along each outer edge. This can produce a snake that is very dark in color. Many of the yellowish to tan ventral scutes have a dark spot (smudge) on their outermost extremes and may also have sparse spotting centrally. This race is found southward from Santa Barbara County, California, to central Baja California Norte. While this snake seems most common in coastal areas it is certainly not uncommon in either mountains or desert.

87 Pacific Gopher Snake

Pituophis catenifer catenifer

One of the more variable races in color and pattern, this snake occurs naturally in both blotched and striped morphs, and albino specimens of both are not particularly uncommon. The stripes can be variable in number and may not contrast sharply with the ground color. When present, the dorsal blotches are chocolate brown, usually discrete from each other and from the lateral spots, and well defined. The dorsal ground color is straw to straw-gray, and the lateral ground color is strongly gray. Although one of the larger races, having been measured up to 7 ft long, it is more typically seen at adult lengths of 4.5–5 ft. The scales are in 29 or more rows (often 31–35) and the anal plate is not divided. The range of this subspecies includes much of western Oregon and California.

88 GREAT BASIN GOPHER SNAKE

Pituophis catenifer deserticola 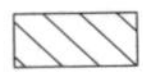

Recorded at a length of 6 ft, over much of its broad range it is typically well under 5 ft in length. This is often a dark subspecies of gopher snakes that may have an imprecise pattern of interconnected blotches. However, some specimens have a light ground color, and have small, precise and largely discrete, dorsal and lateral blotches. The center of each light colored dorsal scale bears a dark longitudinal line. The dorsal blotches of this inland race vary from almost black (or very deep brown) anteriorly to a pleasing dark to reddish brown posteriorly. The supracaudal markings are black and often interconnect with the lateral blotches. This creates the illusion of a light-blotched dark snake rather than the opposite. Scale rows vary between 27 and 35. The range of the Great Basin gopher snake includes southcentral British Columbia (Canada) southward to southeastern California, northern Arizona, and extreme northwestern New Mexico.

89 SANTA CRUZ GOPHER SNAKE

Pituophis catenifer pumilis 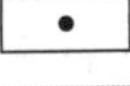

This is a rather small snake (to about 3 ft) with a grayish ground color and a blotching that is a dusty black. The dorsal blotches are small and usually discrete. The upper sides are lightest, forming a dorsolateral stripe about 3 scales wide. The small dorsolateral spots are arranged along the top of this stripe and the lateral spots along the ventral edge. The keeled scales are in 29 or fewer rows, the anal plate is not divided. This seldom seen race occurs only on Santa Cruz, San Miguel and Santa Rosa islands on the south side of California's Santa Barbara Channel.

BULLSNAKE, *Pituophis catenifer sayi*

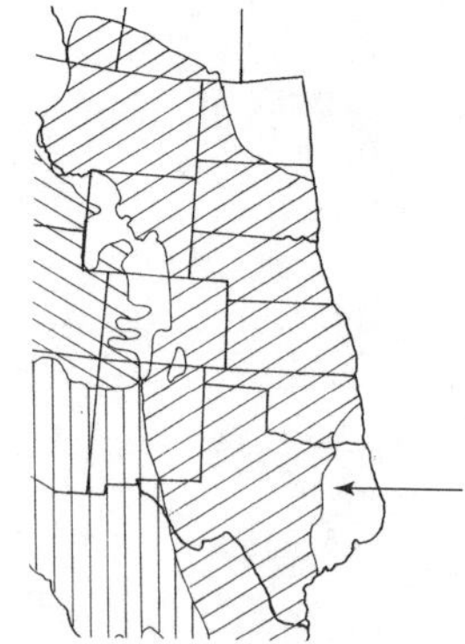

This is one of the most magnificent snakes of the American West. The strongly convex rostral scale of this snake is in the form of an acute triangle, being much higher than wide. Although most adult specimens seen are 3.5–5.5 ft long, the record length is 8 ft 4 in. Because this is a heavy-bodied snake, finding one of more than 6 ft in length is a memorable occurrence especially because the snakes are apt to be defensive and stand their ground. The ground color of the bullsnake varies from a pale straw-yellow to a rather brilliant medium-yellow (occasionally an evident, but pale, orange). The 40–66 dorsal blotches are dark brown anteriorly, lighter brown at midbody, and shade to nearly black posteriorly. The 3 rows of lateral spots are colored similarly to the dorsal blotches. The dorsolateral spots are irregular and often poorly defined and the ventrolateral row is equally so. There is a dark line from the eye to the corner of the mouth, and the upper and lower labial scales often have prominent, dark, sutures. The venter is yellow with scattered dark spots and smudges, and there are spots on the outer edge (side) of every second ventral scute. Some specimens are dark and have poorly defined markings, others are prettily and precisely marked. The bullsnake occurs over a vast expanse of range. It may be found as far north as southern Alberta and southwestern Saskatchewan, Canada, southern Tamaulipas, Mexico, in the south, and from central Illinois in the east, westward to western Montana. Disjunct populations occur to the east and west of the main range. In central New Mexico and western Texas the bullsnake intergrades extensively with the Sonoran gopher snake.

Besides the subspecies that occur in the American West, there are several Mexican forms of this variable snake species.

LONG-NOSED SNAKES

Genus Rhinocheilus

This is a genus of beautiful, but often busily patterned, tricolored snakes. Long-nosed snakes are associated with the arid- and semi-aridlands and are both secretive and capable burrowers. They may be found amid sheltering rocks, in crevices, rodent burrows, under debris, or otherwise hidden by day, but the snakes often prowl widely in the evening and by night, especially during or following rains.

Long-nosed snakes are considered kingsnake relatives. They may either hide their head in their body coils, or assume an S and strike animatedly if provoked. Juveniles are especially apt to bite if molested. If severely stressed, long-nosed snakes autohemorrhage from the cloaca while voiding musk and feces. Nasal hemorrhaging has also been noted. The precise mechanics of this hemorrhaging remain unknown, but it is thought to be restricted to females.

Long-nosed snakes are efficient constrictors, but often consume small prey items without constricting. While lizards seem the food of choice, small rodents and nestling birds are also eaten.

The head is slender, the nose is pointed. The smooth scales are in 23 rows and the anal plate is undivided.

91 Western Long-nosed Snake

Rhinocheilus lecontei lecontei 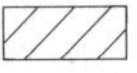

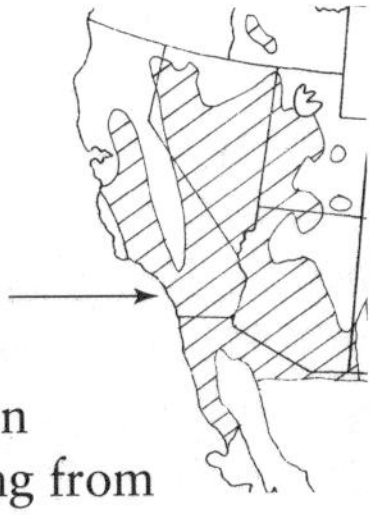

Nonvenomous These kingsnake relatives are devoid of toxic properties.

Abundance This is a common but very secretive snake.

Size Most of these slender snakes seen are 16–30 in. long. Specimens up to 42 in. long have been recorded. Hatchlings are of variable length, measuring from just over 6.5–11 in.

Range This race ranges westward from extreme southwestern New Mexico to northern California. It also occurs in northern Sonora, Mexico and far southward on the Baja Peninsula.

Habitat The long-nosed snake is a denizen of arid and semi-arid-lands. Look for it in rock- or boulder-strewn deserts, grasslands, and prairies. It is commonly seen crossing trans-desert roadways. It occurs primarily from sea level to elevations of about 3,500 ft, but may be rarely found as high as 5,400 ft in elevation.

Prey The long-nosed snake preys primarily on ectothermic creatures. Lizards and small snakes figure prominently in the diet of most specimens. Rodents and the nestlings (and reportedly the eggs) of ground-dwelling birds are also opportunistically taken.

Reproduction This is an oviparous species. One, or rarely 2 clutches of from 1–12 (usually between 3 and 6) eggs are laid annually.

Coloring/scale form The tricolored phase is the most common. The saddled (not ringed) pattern is pleasing, but busy. The red scales, which are often restricted largely to the vertebral area, are tipped or flecked with yellow and *narrowly* edged with white. Yellow tipping (flecking), especially prevalent laterally, is also present on the black scales, and many of the yellow scales are flecked with black. The narrow head is primarily yellow with black flecks and sutures. This race does not have a strongly upturned nose. The belly is yellow to cream and unpatterned except at the outer edges (sides) of some scutes. Some specimens lack all traces of red. On these, the whitish to yellowish ground color may not bear extensive flecking of black, but the black saddles are strongly flecked laterally with light pigment. The scales are smooth and in 23 rows, and the anal plate is nondivided. At least some of the subcaudal scales are not divided.

Similar snakes Other tricolored snakes have all subcaudal scales divided. All of the subcaudal scales of all kingsnakes are divided. The coral snake has *broad rings* of black, red, and yellow, with the two caution colors touching.

Behavior This is essentially a terrestrial, crepuscular and nocturnal snake that may be active throughout the hours of darkness. They are especially active following evening showers, and remain active even when conditions cool sufficiently to deter other snake species from ground-surface activity. Long-nosed snakes burrow well, but also use the ready-made burrows of lizards and small mammals.

Comments The black and white (or pale yellow) morph was long considered a subspecies in its own right. Dubbed *Rhinocheilus lecontei clarus,* the designation was dropped when it was learned that both bicolored and tricolored examples were present in a given population.

92 TEXAS LONG-NOSED SNAKE

Rhinocheilus lecontei tessellatus ☐☐☐☐

The easternmost representative of this species, this subspecies ranges southward from southwestern Kansas and adjacent Colorado, through much of Texas and New Mexico, and southward to San Luis Potosi, Mexico. With a subspecific designation of "tessellatus" one might expect a busier pattern than that of the nominotypical form. Such is not the

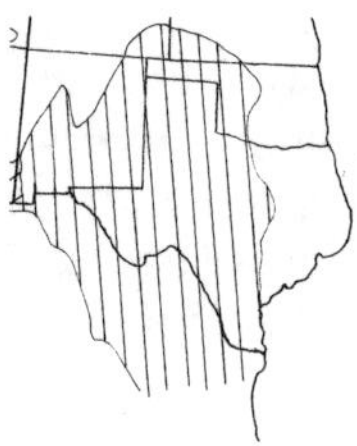

case. The principal difference is in snout conformation. The rostral scale of this race extends upward somewhat, giving a pert, slightly upward, tilt to the tip of the nose. Habits and habitats for this subspecies are the same as those of the western long-nosed snake.

There are additional Mexican subspecies.

GREEN RAT SNAKE

Genus Senticolis

Based on biochemical differences, as well as on differences in scale structure, osteology, and hemipenial morphology, this genus was erected 1987 by Dowling and Fries. The genus contains only the several races of *S. triaspis,* collectively termed the neotropical rat snake.

The genus is represented in the United States only in the mountains of extreme southeastern Arizona. Collectively, the ranges of the various subspecies run southward from Arizona where the subspecies *intermedia* is found, to northern Costa Rica, where the species is represented by the subspecies *mutabilis*.

93 GREEN RAT SNAKE

Senticolis triaspis intermedia

Nonvenomous This primarily Mexican subspecies is entirely nonvenomous. It is often short-tempered but bites are not of serious consequence.

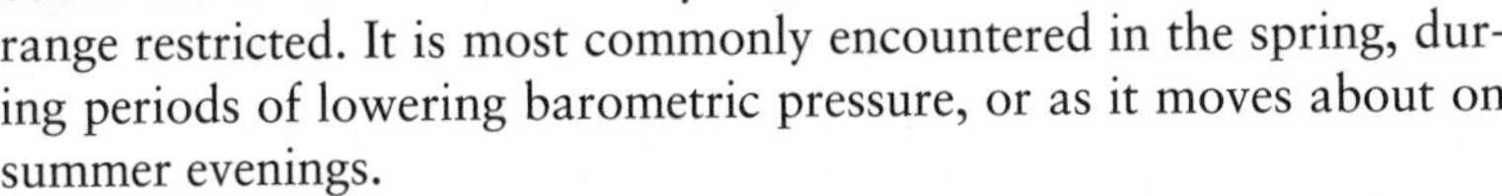

Abundance This is not an uncommon snake, but in the United States it is very habitat and range restricted. It is most commonly encountered in the spring, during periods of lowering barometric pressure, or as it moves about on summer evenings.

Size This is a slender species that often reaches 3–4.25 ft long, and occasionally attains, or barely exceeds, 5 ft. Females are noticeably the larger sex.

Range In the United States, this beautiful snake occurs only in a few mountain canyons in extreme southeastern Arizona and immediately adjacent New Mexico. It may be expected in many of the mountain ranges extending northward from Sonora into eastern

Pima County, Santa Cruz County, and Cochise County, Arizona, as well as in western Hidalgo County, New Mexico.

Habitat In North America, the green rat snake is most often associated with the scrub and forested vicinities of both intermittent and permanent montane canyon streams, generally at relatively high elevations (to more than 6,500 ft). They have been found resting by day in low brush, from 1–5 ft above the ground, but are also known to spend much time secluded in rock crevices and beneath boulders. They may remain inactive for periods of more than a week.

Prey Small green rat snakes readily accept suitably sized lizards, small frogs, and nestling rodents. Larger snakes expand their diet to include larger rodents, larger lizards, and ground- or brush-dwelling birds.

Reproduction This is an oviparous snake species. It seems to lay only a single small clutch (2–6) eggs annually. Incubation (in captivity) takes about 70 days. Hatchlings are 11.5–14 in. long.

Coloring/scale form Like many rat snakes, the green rat snake undergoes considerable ontogenetic change. The hatchlings have a ground color of olive-tan to tan or light olive-brown. About 70 darker dorsal blotches are present from the nape to the vent. These may be in the form of saddles, or offset into a checkerboard pattern vertebrally. The blotches fade rather quickly with growth, but may occasionally be faintly visible well into adulthood. Normally colored adult snakes are an unmarked olive to a rather bright green dorsally, and have an immaculate white to off-white or yellowish venter. The scales on the flanks are smooth, but dorsal scales are weakly keeled. The snout is rather long and when viewed from above, squared.

Similar snakes Adults of this snake are unlikely to be mistaken for any other snake species in their range. Range, and the weakly keeled dorsal scales differentiate this greenish snake from the smaller, more brightly colored, smooth-scaled green snake. The strongly blotched young might be mistaken for a lyre snake, a Great Plains rat snake, a racer, or a whipsnake. However, the lyre snake has a prominent intricate pattern on the top of its head and vertically elliptical pupils while the head pattern of the green rat snake is less well defined and its pupils are round. The Great Plains rat snake does not occur within the range of the green rat snake. Racers and whipsnakes have smooth dorsal scales. The scale rows of Arizona specimens number from 31–39 and the anal plate is divided.

Behavior Although it is unusual to do so, we found one green rat snake in a shrub shortly after noon. We have found all other Arizona specimens, save one, at, shortly before, or shortly after dusk. All were along canyon streams, most were near escarpments or in boulder-fields, one was in a campground, and one was on a woodland pathway. It is probable that this snake is primarily terrestrial, but it is fully capable of climbing agilely. These snakes seem most active during periods of lowering (or low) barometric pressure, such as that which accompanies the advent of storm systems. They are active at moderate temperatures throughout the warm months of the year.

Comments There is remarkably little known with certainty about the life history of this beautiful snake. Not only is it poorly known in the wild, but captive specimens often do not fare well.

Garter Snakes, Water Snakes, and Allies

Subfamily Natricinae

This subfamily has been removed from the Colubrinae by some researchers and elevated to a full family, the Natricidae. Although this is far from a new concept, it is one that has not been fully endorsed yet.

The garter snakes are particularly well represented in the North American West, but other genera, such as the water and red-bellied snakes are better represented in the eastern United States.

The snakes in this subfamily have keeled scales and most are aquatic to a greater or lesser degree. Despite often being referred to as harmless, all natricines are toxic to some degree, but are not of medical significance to humans.

American Water Snakes

Genus Nerodia

Although amply represented in eastern North America, there are only two species of American water snakes in our West. Both are rather large snakes which are often very short tempered and quite ready to bite. If lifted they are equally ready to smear an unpleasant combination of musk, feces, and urates on their captor.

As with many snakes possessing a Duvernoy's gland, the saliva of water snakes can contain complex proteins and enzymes which may prove mildly toxic to some persons. Occasional toxic reactions to the bites of closely allied genera are well documented.

All of the American water snakes are live-bearing. The two western species are quite aquatic. They are heavy-bodied serpents that fishermen and hikers regularly confuse with the venomous cottonmouth, a species that does not occur in the American West. Water snakes often bask by day, even in fairly cold but sunny weather. They often choose warmed concrete abutments, protruding rocks or snags, or limbs overhanging the water as basking sites. Basking water snakes are wary and will often drop into the water and dive at the first sign of disturbance. They may surface rather quickly and may either scull slowly in place or swim parallel with the shore to assess the severity of the disturbance. If again frightened they often submerge and remain so for long periods. Water snakes may be very active on warm, rainy or humid, spring and summer nights.

Females are usually the larger sex, and when nearing parturition can be of immense girth. Some species have more than 100 neonates in a single clutch.

Water snakes have heavily keeled, rather dull scales and, in nearly all instances, a divided anal plate. However, the several races of the plain-bellied water snake may have undivided anal plates.

94 Blotched Water Snake

Nerodia erythrogaster transversa

Nonvenomous Although the water snakes are considered nonvenomous, some persons have developed lividity (redness), swelling, and sensitivity at the bite site. We urge that care be used when handling the snakes of this genus. If you do get bitten, wash the site thoroughly with soap and water.

Abundance Throughout much of its range this is an abundant snake. This does not seem to be the case in New Mexico, where it occurs only in Eddy County.

Size The record size for this snake is 58 in., but most seen are somewhat smaller. The more usual length is 25–40 in. Females are the larger sex. Neonates are 8–12 in. long.

Range The blotched water snake enters the area covered by this book only in southeastern New Mexico. It occurs also in Texas, Oklahoma (and adjacent northeastern Arkansas), Kansas, and western Missouri. It is also found in northern Mexico.

Habitat In New Mexico, this interesting snake seems restricted to the Rio Grande, its tributaries, and some canals. It has not yet been found in stock tanks or other water-retention areas.

Prey Amphibians and their larvae and fish are the known foods of this snake.

Reproduction Virtually nothing is known about the reproductive biology of this snake in New Mexico. However, elsewhere in its United States range, the blotched water snake is known to produce up to 22 babies in the late summer. Clutch size varies from 5 to 15 neonates.

Coloring/scale form Considerable ontogenetic changes occur in this race of the plain-bellied water snake. Neonates are prominently blotched both dorsally and laterally. Anteriorly, the lateral blotches alternate with those on the dorsum. The ground color is gray, the blotch color varies from maroon to nearly black. As the snake matures, the contrasts fade and the blotches may all but disappear. On some specimens the only dorsal markings may be in the form of short transverse bars. Mud may adhere to the heavily keeled scales further obscuring the colors and pattern. The venter is primarily yellow but each scute may have a vague dark marking on each side. The keeled dorsal scales are usually in 25 (23–27) rows at midbody. A great majority of the specimens have divided anal plates.

Similar snakes Non-striped garter snakes have undivided anal plates. The Great Plains rat snake has weakly keeled scales. Glossy snakes have smooth scales. Gopher snakes have 4 prefrontal scales.

Behavior This is an interesting, but certainly not a pretty snake. They are usually unpleasant to handle, being quite feisty and not hesitating to bite as well as to writhe and void their cloacal contents on their captor if held carelessly. The blotched water snake is a strong swimmer, but prefers the sun-warmed shallows to the cold, or swiftly moving, depths. They are active by day, and during hot weather, at dusk and after dark as well. If surprised in a position where it feels escape is not a viable option, this snake will flatten its head and body and strike energetically.

Comments Studies of the life history of this snake in New Mexico should be undertaken. Their limited range renders them vulnerable to both natural disaster and human depredations.

Additional subspecies There are additional races in eastern America, as well as other Mexican subspecies.

95 NORTHERN WATER SNAKE

Nerodia sipedon sipedon

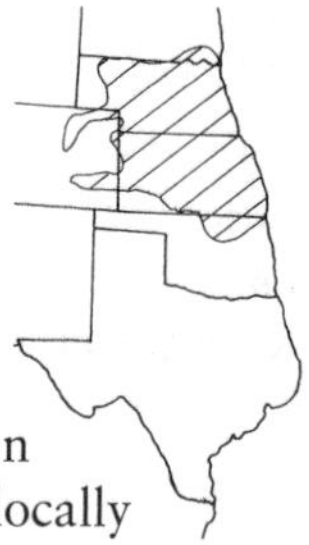

Nonvenomous Although juvenile northern water snakes will often allow themselves to be handled without biting, this is not usually the case with adults. We are considering these snakes nonvenomous but we urge that you read the cautions and comments in the genus discussion.

Abundance Although a common snake in eastern North America, it is, perhaps, more uncommon and locally distributed in its Colorado range.

Size Adults vary in size and may be 2–4.5 ft long, with females being the larger sex. Neonates measure 8.5–10.5 in. at birth.

Range The range of this eastern snake barely enters the American West. Within the scope of this book, it is found only in eastern Colorado. In the east it is found in suitable habitats from eastern Maine and southeastern Ontario, to the mountains of western North Carolina and eastern Tennessee, then westward.

Habitat This snake occupies pond and lake shores, river and stream edges (including areas with a fair current), marsh and swamp margins, oxbows, and may even occur in temporarily flooded areas. In Colorado, it occurs at elevations below 5,500 ft.

Prey Amphibians and fish are the primary prey items. Reports exist of adults eating crayfish and juveniles eating earthworms.

Reproduction This live-bearing snake normally produces litters numbering from a dozen to three dozen. Anecdotal accounts exist of more than 90 babies being born. Clutches are usually born in the late summer and the early autumn.

Coloring/scale form Although adults are often less brightly colored than juveniles, the northern water snake does not undergo particularly extensive ontogenetic changes. Mud may adhere to the keeled scales, making these snakes appear even less colorful than they actually are. To fully appreciate the brilliance and intricacy of the colors and patterns, look at the snake when it is either wet, or better yet, freshly shed.

The ground color of the northern water snake may be gray, buff, tan or brown. The markings are usually much darker than the ground color, but this is not invariably so. The markings of the juveniles are often blackish, as may be those of some adults. On other examples the markings may be reddish, with or without a black border. Typically the anterior markings are in the form of rather regular, broad bands. This pattern may continue posteriorly, or the banding may change to a combination of dorsal saddles and lateral blotches. Tail bands may be regular or irregular. The belly is usually strongly patterned, but may be sparsely so, or virtually unpatterned except for a sparse to liberal dusting of dark dots. If markings are present, they may be large and in the shape of dark bordered half moons or irregular triangles, apex directed posteriorly. They are usually arranged to each side of a complete or broken dark-edged light midline, and may be present only at the very edges of the ventral scutes. Any given specimen may combine any or all of these colors and patterns. Northern water snakes usually lack a horizontal dark ocular (eye) streak, have 21–25 scale rows, and a divided anal scute.

Similar snakes There are no other snakes in Colorado with which you can easily confuse the northern water snake. Glossy snakes have smooth scales. Hog-nosed snakes have a prominently upturned rostral scale. Bullsnakes have a sharp nose with an enlarged, wraparound rostral scale. The Great Plains rat snake has weakly keeled dorsal scales.

Behavior The northern water snake is usually bad dispositioned and quite prone to bite if grasped. It will also void cloacal contents on its captor. In the spring months, while nights are still cool, northern water snakes are sun-worshippers, basking throughout most of the daylight hours and foraging occasionally. As temperatures increase, the snakes are able to more easily maintain a suitable body temperature, even though they bask less and forage more. A snake seeking to bask will use almost any exposed, fairly dry, sunlit spot. Concrete or wooden bridge and dam abutments, rocks, beaver and muskrat lodges, exposed snags and limbs overhanging the water are but a few of the possibilities. Juvenile northern water snakes are less apt than adults to come ashore to bask. If frightened and unable to easily escape, these snakes flatten their head and body and strike energetically.

Comments These snakes may wander widely during the rainy season. They may then be encountered crossing roadways, and seen well away from immediate water sources.

Additional subspecies There are 3 additional subspecies in eastern North America.

Brown and Red-bellied Snakes

Genus Storeria

In North America there are only 2 species in this genus of diminutive, secretive, natricine snakes. Both species have a divided anal scute, keeled dorsal and lateral scales, and both species usually lack loreal scales, a scale usually present and situated between the preoculars and the posterior nasal scale on many other snake genera.

Brown snakes do not occur in western North America, and there is only a single subspecies of red-bellied snake.

While the members of this genus seldom (if ever) bite when grasped, none are loathe to void musk and smear feces and urates on their captor.

96 Black Hills Red-bellied Snake

Storeria occipitomaculata pahasapae 

Nonvenomous Normally, this snake cannot be induced to bite. Despite its affiliations with the garter and water snakes, it is entirely harmless to humans.

Abundance This snake is so secretive that exact population statistics are unknown.

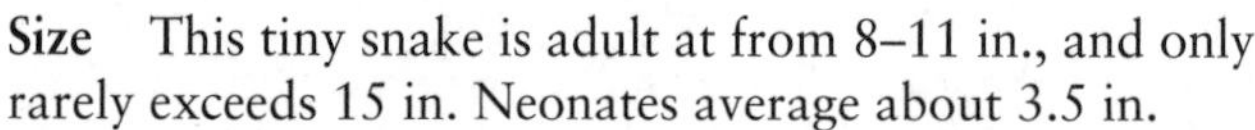

Size This tiny snake is adult at from 8–11 in., and only rarely exceeds 15 in. Neonates average about 3.5 in.

Range The Black Hills red-bellied snake is currently known to occur only in central-western South Dakota and adjacent Wyoming.

Habitat This snake seeks the seclusion of trash and natural cover in and near moist woodlands.

Prey Slugs and earthworms are the preferred prey, but this snake also consumes small snails, which it pulls from the shells as it swallows them.

Reproduction Like its conspecifics, the Black Hills red-bellied snake is viviparous. A clutch numbers from 5–12 (rarely a few more) neonates.

Coloring/scale form The dorsum is brown to gray. A lighter vertebral stripe and/or four narrow dark lines may be present. The ventral coloration may be yellowish, orange-red, or may, on occasion, be dark gray. This westernmost, and poorly differentiated subspecies, ostensibly lacks the nape and nuchal blotches and the light spot on the upper lip beneath the rear of the eye. However, neither of these characteristics are constant. The dorsal scales are keeled, in 15 rows, and the anal plate is divided.

Similar snakes Within its range, this is the only snake with a red belly and scales arranged in 15 rows.

Behavior The habits of the Black Hills red-bellied snake are not well known. It is reportedly active by day (especially following showers) and on warm nights. As would be expected, males seem most prone to leave cover and wander in the spring.

Comments Life history and taxonomic studies of this little snake are badly needed. It is one of the most poorly understood of North America's snake fauna.

Additional subspecies There are 2 additional subspecies of red-bellied snake in the eastern United States, and others in Mexico.

Garter and Ribbon Snakes

Genus Thamnophis

Garter snakes are among the few snake species able to coexist with humans. It may not always be easy for them, for humans often do not tolerate the presence of snakes well. But wherever they are not purposely persecuted (and sometimes even where they are), in many areas of our country, garter snakes continue to be easily found in dooryards, vacant fields, fencerows, gardens and commercial agricultural areas. Where irrigation canals draw frogs and toads, these colorful snakes may be actually abundant.

Garter snakes can be remarkably hard to identify to species. Geographic origin of the specimen can be important. Besides point of origin, such criteria as on which scale rows the lateral stripes occur (see next page), whether these stripes are straight edged or wavy, and head color, are important.

Garter snakes, as a group, are found in one form or another through most of the southern tier Canadian Provinces southward to northern Latin America.

These species are ovoviviparous, having large litters of live young.

When confronted, garter snakes may flatten their heads and strike savagely (ribbon snakes are more apt to just try to flee).

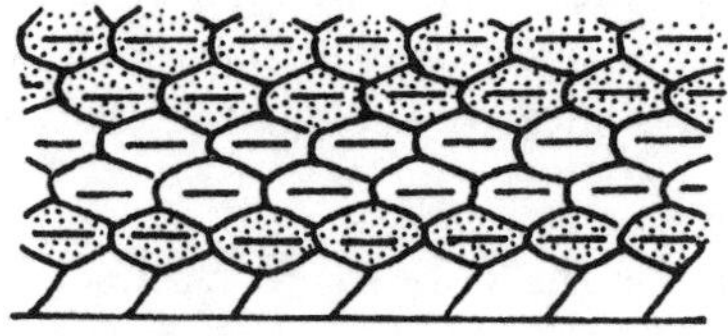

Light stripe on scale rows 2 & 3

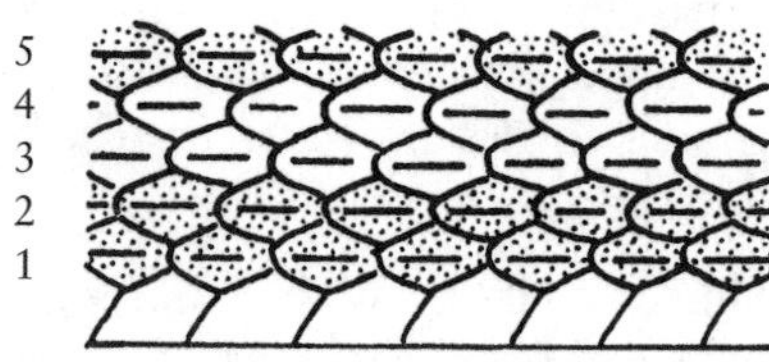

Light stripe on scale rows 3 & 4

97 SANTA CRUZ GARTER SNAKE

Thamnophis atratus atratus 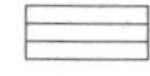

Nonvenomous This pretty garter snake does not hesitate to bite when frightened. Although there seems to be no published data on the effects from a bite, there is no reason to think that a bite would be of medical significance to a human.

Abundance *T. a. atratus* can be relatively common in areas of suitable habitat. Because of its affiliation for rocky streams, it cannot be considered a generally distributed species.

Size The Santa Cruz garter snake may near a yard in length, but most are noticeably smaller. Most specimens are 18–28 in. long, and are of reasonable girth. Neonates are 7–10 in. long.

Range This race ranges from the southern San Francisco Bay area to Santa Barbara County. It is absent from the Salinas Valley.

Habitat The Santa Cruz garter snake is highly aquatic, and is associated with rocky sections of creeks, streams, and ponds. It is a strong swimmer and if startled on shore will readily take to the water. It dives well and can remain submerged for some time.

Prey Like many other species in this genus, the principal prey of the Santa Cruz garter snake would appear to be amphibians and their larvae. However, some specimens will readily eat earthworms, and nestling rodents may also be accepted. Fish seem an important dietary item for baby garter snakes, and are for some adults as well.

Reproduction This snake has rather small clutches, with 12 apparently being the maximum recorded number, and 3–8 neonates being the more usual clutch size. Parturition occurs from midsummer to early autumn.

Coloring/scale form This garter snake has at least two color morphs—a three-striped and a one-striped. In both examples, the ground color is usually very dark (dark-brown to black—sometimes with a bluish or greenish overcast), with or without two rows of small, alternating dark (and, sometimes vaguely defined salmon), lateral spots. Short, lengthwise patches of white interstitial skin are often visible. Both phases also have a broad and precisely defined butter-yellow (occasionally orangish) vertebral stripe. The one-striped morph lacks lateral stripes; the three-striped morph has lateral stripes of variable intensity, but often paler than the vertebral stripe, on scale rows 2 and 3. The Santa Cruz garter snake often has a bright yellow throat. It has 8 upper and (usually) 11 lower labial scales which are narrowly barred with dark pigment along their vertical sutures. None of the labial scales are greatly enlarged. The belly is bluish or greenish and may bear pinkish or yellowish smudges. The keeled scales are in 19 rows at midbody; the anal plate is not divided.

Similar snakes The various races of the common garter snake have 7 upper labial scales. The 4 races of the western terrestrial garter snake have upper labials number 6 and 7 enlarged; these labial scales are also often higher than wide.

Behavior The Santa Cruz garter snake is diurnal during the cooler weather, but may also be active at dusk and after dark during the hottest weather. It is an active and alert species that is quick to plunge into the water and seek refuge beneath bottom debris when approached. They seem to prefer rocky-bottomed streams with a moderate to rapid current, but occasionally may be found in muddy pools and pond edges if there are sufficient rocks. Some populations show somewhat more terrestrial tendencies than others. If frightened, this snake flattens its head, inflates its body (but depresses the body from top to bottom) and strikes energetically. They will smear cloacal contents on a captor if carelessly grasped.

Comments This species was long considered a subspecies of the western aquatic garter snake, *T. couchii.* There is a broad zone of intergradation between this race and the Oregon garter snake in the northern San Francisco Bay region. The confusing animals in that zone were once called *T. a. aquaticus* (Rossman and Stewart, 1987).

98 OREGON GARTER SNAKE

Thamnophis atratus hydrophilus

Despite having a greater range in California than in its namesake state, the northern race of this species is often referred to as the Oregon garter snake. It ranges northward from the vicinity of northern Sonoma County, California, to Douglas County, Oregon.

This snake is less brightly colored and precisely marked than the Santa Cruz subspecies. The ground color of this race varies from a rather olive-tan or pale gray to olive-gray or olive-black. The lateral and vertebral stripes may be present or lacking. When present they may be quite well-defined, but often do not contrast sharply with the ground color. There are usually two rows of alternating dark spots present on each side. These are most visible on snakes with the lighter ground colors. Light interstitial skin may be visible both laterally and dorsally. The Oregon garter snake often has 21 rows of scales at midbody.

99 WESTERN AQUATIC GARTER SNAKE

Thamnophis couchii 

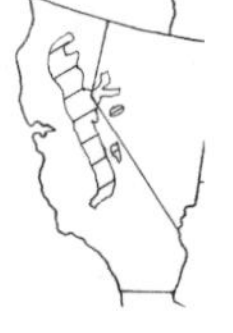

Nonvenomous There have been no problems associated with bites from this garter snake. However, it seems likely that the saliva has at least some toxic properties.

Abundance This is not an uncommon snake, but it is alert and may be difficult to approach.

Size Although it is usually considerably smaller, the western aquatic garter snake occasionally attains a 4-ft length. Most seen are 18–34 in., however. Neonates are comparatively small at birth, measuring 5–6.5 in. long.

Range *T. couchii* occurs in eastcentral California and western Nevada.

Habitat This is a snake that may be found in habitats as varied as cold mountain streams and pools, or warmer low elevation pond- and reservoir-edges. It prefers areas with vegetation on which it may bask, as well as jumbled rocks and boulders both at waterside and partially submerged. This snake occurs from near sea level to elevations of more than 7,500 ft in the Sierra Nevadas Mountains.

Prey Streamside and aquatic amphibians and their larvae and fish seem to be the principal dietary items of this garter snake. Earthworms, leeches, and fish eggs were also mentioned (Stebbins, 1985) but this was while numerous other species were thought to be subspecies of *T. couchii.*

Reproduction Female western aquatic garter snakes from low elevation populations may have their young up to a month earlier in the season (late July) than their counterparts from high elevations (August and September). Clutches usually number 7–20 babies, but up to 38 have been recorded.

Coloring/scale form The ground color of this dark garter snake varies from olive-gray, to olive-black, to olive brown. Rossman, Ford and Seigel (1996) have named three morphs—the northern, the southern, and the "plain," which actually has subdued markings. All have dark, elongate, neck blotches, but these may be difficult to see.

The northern morph has three poorly defined yellowish white stripes and two rows of small, alternating, dark spots on a ground color of olive-green. There is black mottling on the labial scales and chin shields, and usually on the venter.

The southern morph is basically a two-toned snake—olive-black dorsally and whitish ventrally. The vertebral stripe is barely visible, but is usually best defined anteriorly. The alternating black spots are present, but barely visible against the dark ground color. Much, or even all, of the black labial, chin, and ventral mottling is lacking.

The plain morph has very poorly defined stripes and spots on an olive-brown ground color. The venter is quite yellow. It is found near the central portion of the range. Melanism is rather common in this garter snake.

This is a small-eyed, narrow-snouted garter snake. It has 8 upper labial scales, with number 6 (counting backward along the lip from the snout) being the largest. The western aquatic garter snake usually has 21 rows of keeled scales at midbody, but southern specimens may have only 19 rows. The anal plate is not divided.

Similar snakes The fact that the western aquatic garter snake has a *very* poorly defined vertebral stripe (visible, but often barely so) will differentiate this species from other species of garter snakes in its range.

Behavior This is another of central California's (and western Nevada's) very aquatic (and quite defensive) garter snakes. It is often seen at least partially in the water. It forages both in the shallows and in rather deep water, and is quite adept at catching sizable fish. *T. couchii* is quite diurnal, basking extensively on emergent vegetational mats, streamside grasses, and the rocky banks of the streams, ponds, and other aquatic environs that it prefers. When temperatures allow, it may remain active through dusk, into the early evening. It occurs from virtually sea level to elevations of more than 7,500 ft. If threatened, the western aquatic garter snake will readily bite; if grasped it will not only bite but will thrash and smear cloacal contents on the captor.

Comments Until recently, this species and *T. ordinoides,* were repositories for many of our more poorly understood western garter snakes such as *T. atratus* ssp. and *T. hammondi.* Current research has removed all subspecies from *T. couchii,* which is now monotypic. This garter snake was once referred to as the "Sierra garter snake."

100 WESTERN BLACK-NECKED GARTER SNAKE, *Thamnophis cyrtopsis cyrtopsis*

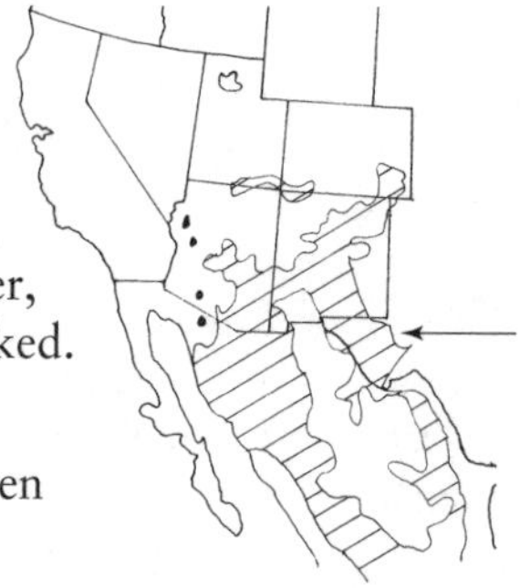

Nonvenomous There have been no adverse human reactions reported from the bites of this species.

Abundance This remains a rather common snake throughout much of its range. However, it is adept at hiding so may be easily overlooked.

Size Although most specimens found are 18–30 in. long, a specimen of 42.2 in. has been authenticated. Neonates are 7–8.5 in.

Range This pretty garter snake ranges westward from Texas' Big Bend region (intergrades between this and the eastern black-necked garter snake occur even further to the east) through much of New Mexico, southern Colorado, and parts of eastern and central Arizona. It also occurs far southward in Mexico.

Habitat The black-necked garter snake invades many semi-arid- and aridland habitats, but is usually associated with ponds, streams, rivers, or stock tanks. During the rainy season, it may wander far afield. It prefers rock-strewn hillsides, riverbeds, wooded canyons, and even cactus-succulent associations. Following the rains, as arid-land pools and ponds dry, this snake often follows the retreat of the waters to more permanent water sources.

Prey The preference of the western black-necked garter snake for anurans and their larvae, and for the aquatic larvae of salamanders, has aptly caused this snake to be termed an amphibian specialist. They feed heartily on stranded tadpoles and other such fare as the amphibians' home ponds dry. Occasionally, this snake will also eat fish, lizards, or earthworms.

Reproduction Clutches usually contain 4–18 babies. Up to 26 have been recorded. Parturition occurs in mid- to late summer. It is thought that females produce only a single brood each year.

Coloring/scale form This is a dark but pretty garter snake. The dorsal coloration is grayish brown, olive-brown, dark brown, or nearly black. The vertebral and lateral stripes (the latter are on scale rows 2 and 3) are well defined and of a whitish yellow to yellow or tan in color. All stripes are apt to be brightest anteriorly. Between the lateral and the vertebral stripes, there are two alternating rows of large black spots. These may contrast sharply with the ground color, or be barely discernible. A pair of black blotches are on the neck. These usually have rounded posterior margins. The top of the head is brownish gray or bluish gray. There are 7 or 8 upper labials. The vertical labial sutures are dark. The belly is pale blue, pale brown, or vaguely greenish. The dorsal scales are keeled, in 19 rows at midbody, and the anal plate is not divided.

Similar snakes The neck-blotches of the checkered garter snake, the species most similar to the black-necked, are often proportionately larger and more squared posteriorly than the more rounded ones of the black-necked. The checkered garter snake has a yellow crescent posterior to the corner of the mouth and 21 scale rows at midbody. Other sympatric garter snake species have a pale vertebral stripe, lack the neck blotches, or both. Patch-nosed snakes and whipsnakes have smooth scales and divided anal plates.

Behavior The western black-necked garter snake is active by day during the cool weather, but becomes night-active as well during the very hot days of summer. They are a rather mild-mannered garter snake that is usually reluctant to bite, and if handled gently, may not even indulge in the disconcerting (and normal) garter snake ploy of voiding and smearing the cloacal contents on their captor. Although they may be occasionally seen crossing some roadways, black-necked garter snakes are more apt to be encountered along the banks of streams, rivers, or even canyon-bottom rivulets. During the hot days of summer, the western black-necked garter snake becomes quite aquatic, and may be found floating on the water surface, or on floating plant mats. Despite its aquatic tendencies, this species does not frequently dive.

Comments Comparatively little is known about the reproductive biology of the western black-necked garter snake. This is surprising, for not only is it a common and widely distributed race, but it is often kept captive by hobbyists as well. Additional data would be welcome.

Additional subspecies An eastern and a Mexican race are also recognized.

101 Arizona Garter Snake

Thamnophis elegans arizonae 

Nonvenomous Redness, pain, and slight swelling have resulted from bites by this race and by other subspecies of this garter snake. Medical attention has not been needed, but we do suggest the use of care when handling any of the subspecies.

Abundance This snake may be uncommon in some areas, but relatively common in optimum habitat.

Size Although an occasional specimen may attain 3.5 ft in length, the more normal size is 16–30 in. Neonates are 6.5–8.5 in. long.

Range This pale-colored subspecies occurs in central western Arizona and central eastern New Mexico. It occurs from river-plains to elevations of about 9,000 ft. Its range is abutted on all sides but the south by the wide-ranging, and often similar appearing, wandering garter snake. Rely on range to help with identification.

Habitat Although it is often found in the proximity of water, the Arizona garter snake also wanders far afield. This is especially so during the rainy season. It is found from verdant mountain valleys to the proximity of aridland stock tanks, and in most habitats between, including elevations of about 9,000 ft. This snake prefers heavily vegetated areas, and can be common where pondside grasses and emergent rushes are thick. It uses vegetation and logs as natural cover, but also hides beneath human-generated debris.

Prey This garter snake accepts a broad array of prey. Amphibians and their larvae, fish, worms, insects, slugs, leeches, small rodents and small birds are all opportunistically accepted.

Reproduction The parturition season begins as early as late July in some populations, but extends well into September. Broods consist of 4–20 neonates, with 6–14 being the norm.

Coloring/scale form This is one of the more pallid races of this garter snake species. The ground color is often gray to grayish-brown, and the stripes may be well defined, or only poorly so. There are two rows of dark, alternating, spots between the lateral and the vertebral lines. The dark pigment from the upper row of these spots may encroach on the sides of the vertebral stripe, creating a wavy effect. There may be a pair of enlarged nuchal (nape) blotches, but even if present these may not be well defined. The vertical sutures of the (usually) 8 supralabial scales are dark. The anal plate is not divided. The body scales are keeled and usually in 21 rows at midbody.

Similar snakes The various races of the common garter snake have 7 upper labial scales. The checkered garter snake has bigger and better-defined dark body spots, and both it and the black-necked garter snake have proportionately large and well defined nuchal blotches. Patch-nosed and whipsnakes have smooth scales and a divided anal plate.

Behavior This snake is often diurnal. In fact, it is largely so during cool weather. However, crepuscular and nocturnal activity is the norm during hot weather. Although it is often found near water, it is more apt to seek a terrestrial, than an aquatic, path to safety if surprised. The Arizona garter snake may bask in the open, but is usually near ample cover to which it can gain rapid access.

Comments Collectively, the 6 races of *Thamnophis elegans* are referred to as the "western terrestrial garter snake." If taken literally, this common name is misleading, for, especially in the dryer portions of their ranges, these snakes are often associated with streamside or pondside habitats, are excellent swimmers, and are quite aquatic. Both the Arizona and the Upper Basin garter snakes are poorly differentiated subspecies.

102 Mountain Garter Snake

Thamnophis elegans elegans

intergrade

This is one of the prettier and more precisely patterned of this clan. The dorsum is usually olive-black to black, but may also be gray, or grayish brown. All three stripes are usually well defined (may be suffused by melanin in some very dark examples), but the lateral stripes may be somewhat paler than the vertebral stripe. Both vertebral and lateral stripes are about 2 scale rows wide (vertebral ½ + 1 + ½ rows; lateral 2 full scale rows). The stripe color is often whitish or butter yellow, but may be of some shade of orange. The belly is pale yellow, sometimes darker centrally, sometimes smudged with darker pigment. This race inhabits most of central California (excluding the coast) and immediately adjacent western Nevada.

The 8 upper labials and 3 prominent stripes and very dark ground color will differentiate the mountain garter snakes from many sympatric garter snake species and subspecies.

103 Coast Garter Snake

Thamnophis elegans terrestris 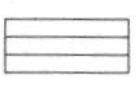

This subspecies is considerably more variable in color. The dorsal ground color may be russet, brown or black. There is a tendency for the more brightly colored examples to be from the San Francisco Bay area. Northern examples may vary between olive to russet; those from the southern part of the range have a black dorsum. Some examples have the white to yellow stripes well defined (this is especially so on the reddish specimens), but other specimens may have the lateral stripes less prominent than the vertebral stripe. There are usually two rows of alternating, but well-separated dark spots between the vertebral and the lateral lines. Some specimens may have red and black barred sides. Even dark specimens may have some orange scales on the side. The belly may have reddish spots or blotches on a field of pale yellow to bluish yellow. The throat is pale. This race ranges southward from the vicinity of Coos County, Oregon, to Santa Barbara County, California.

The Santa Cruz garter snake lacks red on the sides and venter. Other sympatric garter snakes often lack well developed stripes.

104 Wandering Garter Snake

Thamnophis elegans vagrans 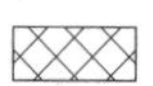

With a range larger than all other races combined, this subspecies occurs from Vancouver Island, British Columbia, in the northwest and southwestern Saskatchewan in the northeast, southward to central California, northern Arizona, and northern New Mexico. It is absent from eastern Utah (where it is replaced by *Thamnophis elegans vascotanneri*), and western central Arizona and adjacent New Mexico (where it is replaced by *Thamnophis elegans arizonae*). The wandering garter snake is a variably colored race, and may be black with well-defined striping in the northwestern part of their range, or gray or grayish brown further to the east and south. Lateral stripes may be well- or poorly defined. Because of intrusion of the dark pigment from the upper row of dark lateral spots, the vertebral stripe (which is narrow) may appear wavy, or be actually broken. The pattern definition may appear hazy. This is an abundant and commonly seen snake.

In western Washington and western British Columbia, the wandering garter snake is of very dark ground color. There the stripes tend to be narrow, have irregular edges, and to be suffused with some additional scattered scales or patches of dark pigment.

Because of its variability, this race can be problematic to identify. The various races of the common garter snake have 7, rather than 8 upper labials. Checkered and black-necked garter snakes have prominent nuchal blotches. The fact that the wandering garter snake often has a "hazy" pattern and/or a wavy vertebral stripe will differentiate it from many other forms.

105 UPPER BASIN GARTER SNAKE

Thamnophis elegans vascotanneri 

This subspecies is prominently checkered dorsally and laterally but often lacks the vertebral stripe. If the vertebral stripe is present, it may be incomplete and/or quite narrow. The lateral stripes may also be indistinct. The dorsal ground color is pale: olive-tan, olive-gray, grayish-brown, or pale gray. The two rows of alternating dark spots are quite evident, but are usually dark gray rather than black. This (usually) pallid race (which is largely restricted to Utah) occurs from southcentral Utah and immediately adjacent northcentral Arizona, northeastward to southwestern Wyoming and northwestern Colorado.

Besides the 5 races in the United States, a sixth race, *Thamnophis elegans hueyi,* occurs in northern Baja California.

106 NORTHERN MEXICAN GARTER SNAKE

Thamnophis eques megalops 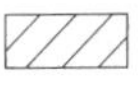

Nonvenomous Virtually nothing is known of the saliva composition of this snake. Since no adverse reports exist, we surmise that its bite is of no medical significance to humans.

Abundance This snake is of very restricted distribution in the United States, but, where found, it can be relatively common.

Size Most commonly seen at lengths of from 18–30 in., the Northern Mexican garter snake is known to reach 40 in. (Stebbins, 1985). Neonates are 7.5–11.5 in. long.

Range In the United States, this species occurs only in extreme southeastern Arizona and immediately adjacent New Mexico. Its range extends far southward into Mexico.

Habitat Like most garter snakes, this species is associated with aquatic habitats. Although in Mexico it is considered a species of montane canyons and woodlands, in the United States it seems more common at low elevations. It may be found near water in grasslands, mesquite thickets, and along desert watercourses. In some areas it seems most common in the environs of stock tanks, but prefers those surrounded by dense ground vegetation and having stands of emergents such as cattails growing near the shore.

Prey Amphibians—especially frogs—and their larvae are the preferred dietary items of this snake, but they also readily accept fish. Besides these garter snake staples, this species is known to eat leeches, worms, lizards, and small rodents.

Reproduction This, like other garter snakes, is a live-bearing species. Initial studies have indicated that this species produces young earlier in the year (June, July) than most other garter snake species. Clutches contain 4–16 babies.

Coloring/scale form This is a rather brightly colored, three-striped form of garter snake. The ground color is olive-gray to dark olive-brown or olive-black. There is a pair of moderately large dark nuchal blotches that may be distinct, or may blend almost imperceptibly posteriorly with the ground color. Three rows of black spots—2 alternating rows between the lateral and the vertebral stripes, and one beneath the lateral stripe—are present. They are easily visible on snakes with a light ground color, but less distinct on dark colored snakes. The vertebral stripe is often wide, involving the entire vertebral scale row and about ½ of each paravertebral row. The lateral stripe is on scale rows 3 and 4 anteriorly, and drops to rows 2 and 3 posteriorly. There is a short, but usually wide-based light crescent behind the mouth. The 8 supralabials have dark vertical sutures. The keeled dorsal scales are usually in 19 (more rarely 21) rows at midbody; the anal plate is not divided.

Similar snakes The placement of the lateral stripe on the Northern Mexican garter snake (3rd and 4th scale row anteriorly and 2nd and

3rd row posteriorly) and the limited USA range should adequately identify this species.

Behavior As with most reptiles and amphibians that are of peripheral range in the USA, the Northern Mexican garter snake is a protected species in its limited range north of the border. Like many natricines, the Mexican garter snake may react to threat by either flattening or inflating its body, flattening its head, and striking savagely and persistently at the offending object. If carelessly handled it will bite and smear its captor with the claocal contents. This snake readily enters water if frightened or pursued.

Comments Because it is of limited distribution in the the two states in which it occurs, this species is considered endangered by both Arizona and New Mexico. Habitat destruction continues to reduce populations.

Additional subspecies There are 2 additional Mexican subspecies.

107 GIANT GARTER SNAKE

Thamnophis gigas 

Nonvenomous Little has been reported about the significance of a bite by this garter snake. While some reaction to its toxic saliva would be likely, it seems improbable that the effects would be serious.

Abundance Because of habitat modifications, this interesting snake has dwindled in numbers. It may still be locally common, but has been extirpated over large sections of its range. It is now considered a threatened species by both the state of California and the federal government.

Size With a record size of more than 60 in., this is the largest species of garter snake. More typically, adults are 36–48 in. long. Neonates are 8.5–11.5 in. long.

Range This gargantuan garter snake is restricted in range to the San Joaquin and Sacramento valleys of the state of California. Because of habitat degradation, its historic continuous range has now been divided into a northern and a southern population. One has as its southernmost point San Francisco Bay area (San Joaquin County) and ranges from there northward to the vicinity of Butte County.

The second population ranges southward from the vicinity of Merced County to Kern County.

Habitat This is an extensively aquatic snake that is associated with wateredge habitats. It may be seen in marshes and along slow streams, and is most often found where emergent vegetation is thick and matted. The recumbent stems and leaves of these plants, as well as overhanging boughs of willows and other waterside shrubs, form basking sites for the giant garter snake.

Prey Amphibians, including their larvae, and fish are the principal dietary items of this snake.

Reproduction A live-bearing snake (as are all garter snakes), the giant garter snake has been known to give birth to more than 40 neonates in a single clutch. More normally, the brood size numbers 8–20 babies.

Coloring/scale form This snake occurs in 2 distinctly different color/pattern morphs, which are actually just variations of the same theme. One is olive-black striped with yellow. The other is a dark olive on light olive checkerboard pattern.

The striped morph has a deep olive-black ground color, but in good light, evidence of checkerboarding can still usually be seen. The vertebral and lateral stripes may be a rather bright yellow and well defined, or relatively pale and more poorly defined. The lateral stripe involves scale rows 2 and 3. The checkerboard pattern is more pronounced on snakes with paler ground color (the checkers remain dark) and striping. In some cases the stripes may be virtually absent. Both variations have a brown(ish) venter and a light throat.

There are usually 8 upper labial scales that are barred along their vertical sutures. And although a difficult to discern field characteristic, the 6th upper labial scale is shorter (from front suture to rear) than the 7th. There are between 21 and 23 scale rows. The anal plate is not divided.

Similar snakes Other garter snakes can be quite similar to the giant garter snake in appearance and may require close examination to differentiate. The subspecies of the common garter snake usually have 7 upper labial scales and proportionately large eyes. The western aquatic garter snake can be *very* similar to the giant garter snake in appearance. However, the 6th upper labial of the former is longer (from front suture to rear) than the 7th.

Behavior This is one of the most aquatic of the garter snakes. The big snakes are wary and quick to drop from their elevated perches, or to dive from their resting platforms, when approached.

The giant garter snake is essentially diurnal, but is also crepuscularly and nocturnally active when temperatures allow.

This is an alert and, if restrained, aggressive snake. They not only bite and chew, but smear cloacal contents on their captor as well.

Comments This snake was initially considered a race of *Thamnophis ordinoides,* the northwestern garter snake, and later of *T. couchii,* the western aquatic garter snake.

108 TWO-STRIPED GARTER SNAKE

Thamnophis hammondii 

Nonvenomous This snake will bite when unduly disturbed. Although there are no reports of irritation from the bite, it is reasonable to assume that the typical localized swelling, lividity, and tenderness would be experienced.

Abundance This garter snake is protected by the state of California. Many of its traditional habitats have been drained, or are suffering seriously reduced water flow, because of diversion for irrigation. This has resulted in the decline and/or extirpation of many populations of this snake.

Size This garter snake is of moderate size. Adults have been known to attain a yard in length, but are more often 18–30 in. long. Neonates are 7.5–9 in. long.

Range The home of this rather aquatic garter snake extends southward from Monterey Bay, California (largely west of the Diablo and Temblor ranges) to northern Baja California.

Habitat This is another of California's primarily aquatic garter snakes that, because of habitat modifications, is suffering population declines. It occurs along streams, flooded ditches, and in the vicinity of stock tanks and other permanent water. It is most frequently encountered where streamside (and streambed) rocks are prevalent where streams pass through chaparral, oak and pine woodlands.

Prey Amphibians and their larvae, fishes, and, perhaps very occasionally, other aquatic organisms form the diet of the two-striped garter snake.

Reproduction The largest recorded clutch produced by this species consisted of 36 babies, but usually 4–18 are born in mid- and late summer.

Coloring/scale form This is another of the garter snakes that occurs in two pattern morphs. Both morphs have an olive-drab to olive-brown, or gray dorsal color. Neither morph has a vertebral stripe; however, one has well to poorly developed yellowish to gray lateral stripes on scale rows 2 and 3, while the second lacks even vestiges of the lateral stripes. Although both variations have dark spots in 2 or 4 rows, the striped morph tends to have a more uniformly colored dorsum, while the non-striped variation has two rows of poorly defined dark spots on each side. The belly varies from a nearly unmarked pale yellow to butter yellow or even orange with dark smudging. The throat is light. The 8 supralabials (as well as the infralabials) are prominently barred along their vertical sutures. Supralabials 6 and 7 are roughly the same length. The keeled scales are usually in 19 rows at midbody; the anal plate is single.

Similar snakes The common garter snake usually has 7 supralabial scales. Other garter snakes usually have a vertebral stripe. See also the account for the giant garter snake (pages 155–157), a species which may lack the vertebral stripe.

Behavior This is a very aquatic garter snake which seems best adapted for life along rocky shorelines. It is alert and quick to dive and seek refuge amidst stream- or pond-bottom debris if frightened. It may be seen basking by day in cool weather, but is also active in the evening and at night when temperatures are suitably warm.

Comments Once considered a race of *T. couchii*, this garter snake is now recognized as a full species.

109 Northern Checkered Garter Snake

Thamnophis marcianus marcianus

Nonvenomous Although they will bite, checkered garter snakes are not especially prone to do so. The same cautions apply here as do to other garter and water snakes. Although the bite is probably not of medical significance to humans, the snakes should be handled with care.

Abundance Although there are no data to substantiate a cyclic fluctuation in numbers, the checkered garter snake seems more common some years than others. Most populations seem secure, and as irrigation stretches farther and farther into the desertlands, the range of the checkered garter snake does likewise.

Size With a normal length of 20–28 in., this species is an average-sized garter snake. Occasionally a specimen 3 ft long will be found, and the record size is a heavy-bodied 42.5 in. Males tend to be smaller and more slender than females. Neonates are 6.5–9.5 in. long.

Range In the United States this snake ranges westward continuously from central Texas and extreme southcentral Kansas to central New Mexico and southcentral Arizona. It is also found in southwestern Arizona and adjacent southeastern California, but seems absent from the harshest areas of the Sonoran Desert. Its range extends far southward into mainland Mexico.

Habitat This is a grassland, semi-aridland and aridland species. Although the checkered garter snake may wander rather far from water, especially during the monsoons, it is most often found in rather close proximity to irrigation canals, streams, stock tanks, ponds, and other water sources.

Prey Because it is more of a habitat generalist than certain other garter snakes, the checkered garter snake has a somewhat broader prey base than many. It readily accepts the traditional garter snake fare of amphibians and their larvae, and worms, but also preys upon lizards, and has been known to eat smaller snakes. Two captive checkered garter snakes readily ate newly born mice.

Reproduction The live babies normally number 5–15, but up to 31 in a single clutch have been recorded. Parturition occurs rather early in the year for a live-bearing snake. Newly born babies have been found as early as mid-May. The possibility that a given healthy female may double clutch has been broached, but not yet confirmed.

Coloring/scale form This is one of the prettiest of the garter snakes. The dorsal ground color is usually of some shade of tan, and both the lateral and vertebral stripes are usually well in evidence. The lateral stripe is usually restricted to scale row 3. Each side, between the lateral and the vertebral stripes, is prominently checkered with a double row of large, black spots. The top edge of the dorsalmost blotches encroaches slightly on the edges of the vertebral stripe, producing a slightly uneven appearance. There is a large, dark, neck blotch on each side, and a pale crescent is present at the rear of the mouth. The top of the head is olive-brown to brown. The belly is usually light (whitish or yellow) and can be either unmarked or smudged with darker pigment. The keeled dorsal scales are in 21 rows at midbody and the anal plate is undivided.

Similar snakes The large, black, neck blotches are shared in the United States only by the black-necked and by some Northern Mexican garter snakes. These, and the strongly checkered body pattern will eliminate most other garter snakes. The Northern Mexican garter snake has the lateral stripes on scale rows 3 and 4. The black-necked garter snake lacks a well-defined yellow crescent at the corner of the mouth.

Behavior Although considered a diurnal snake, checkered garter snakes are also active at dusk and well into the night during the hot nights of summer. They seem especially active during and following summer rains. On late spring and early summer evenings, large numbers of babies (perhaps dispersing?) may cross roadways that transect prime habitats. Many road casualties occur while these garter snakes are attempting to feed on amphibians and lizards previously killed by vehicles. The checkered garter snake can and does swim well and readily, and may dive when startled. They are often seen in the morning sunning or foraging along canal edges.

If startled, this snake will void and smear its cloacal contents on its captor, but seldom offers to bite.

Comments There is much yet to be learned about this common snake. Studies of its reproductive biology should be of considerable interest.

Additional subspecies There are 2 additional Mexican subspecies.

110 NORTHWESTERN GARTER SNAKE

Thamnophis ordinoides

Nonvenomous This is another of the garter snakes that is very reluctant to bite, no matter the provocation. However, the saliva has mild toxic properties. Despite the fact that a bite is of no significance to a human, we suggest that due care be used when handling this species.

Abundance The pretty and variable northwestern garter snake, *T. ordinoides,* is a common to abundant species of our Pacific states. It can be particularly abundant in suburban vacant lots. On an island in Puget

Sound, in one small building lot containing construction debris, we found more than 50 northwestern garter snakes (plus a dozen or more Puget Sound garter snakes).

Size Although exceptional specimens may exceed 3 ft in length, 20–24 in. is the more common adult size. Neonates are about 6 in. long at birth.

Range It ranges northward from northern California to, and including, Vancouver Island and the adjacent mainland of British Columbia, Canada.

Habitat This species is a damp meadow and woodland clearing snake. It continues to persist in the immediate proximity of humans, and can be particularly common in debris-laden vacant lots. It is adept at hiding beneath boards, roofing tins, logs, grass mats, and other surface cover. In these habitats it occurs sympatrically with other garter snake species. This snake is diurnally active, but may move at dusk or early evening when temperatures are suitable. This species may be found from sea level to elevations of 4,500 ft.

Prey Although it is said to eat frogs, specimens that I (RDB) have had have seemed to prefer worms and nightcrawlers above all else. Northwestern garter snakes are also known to eat slugs and salamanders.

Reproduction The neonates usually number between 5 and 10 and are born in midsummer. A very large captive female produced 16 babies.

Coloring/scale form The ground color may be tan, olive, brown or black and the middorsal stripe (lateral stripes are often absent) may vary from well defined along the entire length of the snake to entirely absent. If present, it is usually best defined anteriorly. The stripe color may vary from blue, to white, through yellow, to a rather bright orange. The lateral stripes are usually less well defined, and are often of much paler color than the vertebral stripe. There is often much white showing interstitially. Dark spots may be present, and if so, are often most visible just above the lateral stripe. Some northwestern garter snakes lack all vestiges of stripes. The belly is equally variable in color. It may be yellowish, gray, or brown, or any of numerous shades between. There are often reddish or dark spots present on the belly scutes. There are usually only 7 supralabial scales. The dorsal scales are keeled, most often in 17 rows, and the anal plate is not divided.

Similar snakes The small head—hardly wider than the neck—should aid in identifying this garter snake. Other snake species with which the northwestern garter snake might be confused have either a higher number of supralabial scales or a higher number of rows of body scales, and lack red markings on the belly.

Behavior Despite their reluctance to bite, northwestern garter snakes will readily smear voided feces on their captor if handled carelessly. This snake thermoregulates effectively, emerging from beneath cover to bask rather early in the morning. During the occasional particularly hot period, they may only protrude a coil or two from beneath an object under which they are hiding, or may be able to thermoregulate by merely bringing their back into contact with the underside of a sun-warmed board or sheet of tin. This garter snake seems more prone to avoid danger by darting into dense vegetation than by taking to the water.

Comments This small-headed garter snake is one of the most variably colored members of the genus.

111 ARIDLAND RIBBON SNAKE

Thamnophis proximus diabolicus

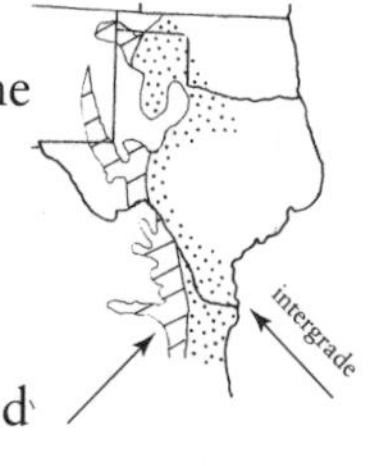

Nonvenomous This, like all garter snakes, has a Duvernoy's gland which may add a toxic element to the saliva. This slender snake is usually reluctant to bite a human, but bites have occurred. Bites have resulted in from no effects except a scratching of the skin to just lividity, or, in one case, a bite on the finger resulted in lividity, localized swelling and temporarily reduced mobility (Shockey, 1992).

Abundance While not an uncommon snake, neither, unless a brood of newly born and not yet dispersed, babies is encountered, is the aridland ribbon snake often found in any great numbers in a given area of habitat.

Size This race reaches the largest size of any of the subspecies of the western ribbon snake. Adult at 20–32 in., the largest authenticated specimen was 48.5 in. long. The tail comprises about one third of the snake's total length. Females tend to be longer and of greater girth than males. Neonates vary in size. They are most often 9–11 in. long and very slender.

Range This, the most westerly of the 4 races of the western ribbon snake, barely enters our coverage range. It occurs in 2 disjunct areas, one along the Pecos Drainage in New Mexico, the other in northeastern New Mexico. To the east of the scope of this book, this race intergrades widely with the other 3 subspecies, the western, the red-striped, and the Gulf Coast ribbon snakes.

Habitat Despite its aridland habitat, this ribbon snake (like the other races) is rather persistently aquatic. Although it may wander short distances from permanent and semi-permanent water sources, the aridland ribbon snake is most often found very close to surface water. Look for it along rivers, streams, stock tanks, irrigation canals, golf course water hazards, and in similar habitats.

Prey In keeping with their semiaquatic habits, the aridland ribbon snake preys almost exclusively upon amphibia (principally frogs and salamanders and their larvae) and small fishes. Some specimens, especially neonates, will also accept worms and aquatic insects. Ground skinks are occasionally eaten.

Reproduction Adult female aridland ribbon snakes have had up to 24 babies in a clutch. More normally the number is 5–14. There is little known with certainty about the reproductive biology of this snake. It is thought that specimens in North America produce only a single brood a year.

Coloring/scale form The aridland ribbon snake is a pretty snake race that is typified by an ochre, buff, or orange vertebral stripe and by well-developed yellow(ish) lateral stripes on scale rows 3 and 4. The lateral stripe is bordered ventrally by a dark field. The ground color is olive-gray, olive-brown, or nearly black. The venter is light and unmarked. There is often a small light spot on the top of the head, just anterior to the beginning of the vertebral stripe. The head is narrow, but moderately distinct from the neck. The 8 supralabial scales are *not* barred, an important fact when identification is in question.

The scales are keeled, usually in 19 rows at midbody, and the anal plate is not divided.

Similar snakes The lined snake has a double row of half-moons on its venter. Garter snakes are less attenuate, but can be difficult to distinguish. The Northern Mexican garter snake and the Plains garter snake have barred supralabial scales. The New Mexican garter snake and the wandering garter snake have the lateral stripe on scale rows 2 and 3. The western black-necked garter snake, the northern checkered garter snake, and the Northern Mexican garter snake all have conspicuous dark neck-blotches. Patch-nosed snakes and the various striped whipsnakes have smooth scales.

Behavior Ribbon snakes can and do climb opportunistically, but are primarily terrestrial and aquatic. The snakes often sit atop tangles of waterside vegetation, and may also be seen sunning on the vines that bedeck rock piles or on the stems of recumbent, ground-level vines near roadside canals.

Comments Ribbon snakes often cross roadways on warm, preferably damp, nights and should be searched for near standing or running surface water.

Additional subspecies Although there are none in our area, there are 3 additional forms in the eastern United States and 2 Mexican forms.

112 Plains Garter Snake

Thamnophis radix

Nonvenomous Similar to all members of this genus, bites from the Plains garter snake may result in virtually no symptoms more adverse than the slight scratches and punctures caused by the teeth, to lividity, numbness and slight swelling at the bite site.

Abundance In certain of the better habitats, where moisture is adequate, and food, in the form of worms and frogs, is abundant, *T. radix* can be an abundant species. In marginally acceptable areas the snakes may be absent or uncommon.

Size This is a relatively large and heavy-bodied garter snake. Adults can attain 3.5 ft. However, the more normal size is 18–28 in. Females are often the larger sex. Neonates are 6–7.5 in. long.

Range The range of the Plains garter snake extends from southcentral Canada in the north southward in a broad swath to northern Texas and northern New Mexico. There are 2 disjunct populations in Ohio and southern Illinois.

Habitat Although often referred to as a species of the wet central prairies, the Plains garter snake occurs in a vast array of habitats. It is found in backyards and wet mountain meadows, in drainage ditches and at marshedge, and in sloughs and the environs of ponds. It does wander from the immediate proximity of water during wet weather, but is less prone to stray far afield during dry periods.

Prey A robust species, *radix* is an opportunistic feeder that accepts both ectothermic and endothermic prey species. Earthworms figure prominently in the diet of this species, especially in more northerly areas and/or in the spring and autumn of the year. Mice, shrews, frogs, an occasional toad, and leeches are also eaten.

Reproduction There appears to be a geographic correlation with latitude and clutch size. Large northern females may produce up to 62 babies in a clutch, while a clutch size of 7–15 is the norm for females at the southern extreme of the range. Females produce their clutches in the mid- to late summer months.

Coloring/scale form This snake may be quite pretty or quite drab, but is usually in between. The ground color varies from olive brown to black to a rather bright red. No matter the ground color, the snake has a well-developed vertebral stripe that is orange(ish) anteriorly, shading to yellow posteriorly. The lateral stripes are more poorly defined and occupy the 3rd and 4th scale rows above the ventral scutes. Except on the black or nearly black specimens, a dark checkerboarding is also very visible in the dorsolateral dark field. A row of dark spots is usually present below the light lateral lines. There are a pair of large, dark, neck blotches (but these are not as conspicuous as in the black-necked, checkered, and northern Mexican garter snakes). The supralabial scales are vertically barred with dark pigment. *Thamnophis radix* may have 19 or 21 rows of keeled dorsal scales, and has a single anal scale.

Similar snakes The various striped whipsnakes and patch-nosed snakes lack checkers and have smooth scales. Terrestrial and common garter snakes have the stripes on the second and third scale rows.

Behavior This is one of the less excitable garter snakes. If grasped gently, they will often allow themselves to be lifted and handled with no show of temper. However, they can and will bite and void excrement if frightened. This snake is primarily diurnal in the north, but may be crepuscular and nocturnal during hot weather farther south in their range. They have a particularly long activity pattern, emerging from hibernation very early in the spring and being among the last species to enter hibernation.

Comments Although these snakes may wander some distance from water, they are seldom seen in areas devoid of plant cover. The fixed criteria that were once thought to distinguish an eastern and a western race of the Plains garter snake were found invalid.

113 Narrow-headed Garter Snake

Thamnophis rufipunctatus 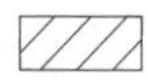

Nonvenomous There is nothing reported about effects from bites by this species. It is surmised that the effects would be similar to those from most other garter snakes, either no noted effects or some localized lividity, swelling, tenderness, and if on a digit, reduced mobility.

Abundance This distinctive garter snake is considered moderately rare to rare, and it is protected by law in Arizona and New Mexico.

Size This is a medium-sized garter snake. Most seen are 16–26 in. long, and the maximum recorded length is only 34 in. Neonates are 7–9.5 in. long.

Range The range of this snake in the United States is a rather narrow swath that extends eastward from eastcentral Arizona to westcentral New Mexico. It is more widely distributed in central northern Mexico.

Habitat Look for this garter snake in rocky stretches of streams and in lakeside rockpiles. It is almost always found in areas where cover is readily available.

Prey The diet of this snake consists primarily of fish, but frogs and aquatic salamander larvae are also accepted.

Reproduction Little is known about the reproductive biology of this species, but because of the harshness of the mountain winters in its range, it would almost assuredly require a period of complete hibernation to induce breeding readiness.

Coloring/scale form The narrow-headed garter snake looks and acts more like a water snake than a garter snake. Rather than being prominently striped (if stripes are present at all, they are weakly defined and only on the sides of the neck), this snake is prominently spotted. The ground color varies from a dingy olive to a reddish color. The pattern consists of narrow, dark, middorsal blotches and alternating dark lateral spots. It is dusky ventrally, but lightest on the throat and neck. The eyes are situated high on the sides of the rather narrow head. The colors and patterns blend remarkably well with the rocks, soil and vegetation of its streamside habitats. The keeled dorsal scales are in 21 rows and the anal plate is usually single (divided in about 10% of the snakes found).

Similar snakes In appearance, this snake is as dissimilar to other garter snakes as it is to other snakes in other genera. It is often thought to be a water snake but is not apt to be mistaken for any other species in its range.

Behavior This garter snake is associated with riverside or lakeside areas that are rock-strewn and overgrown. Besides basking on emergent rocks and boulders it may be found thermoregulating on flotsam and overhanging reeds and shrubs. It is an excellent swimmer that dives quickly and well when disturbed, and often takes shelter beneath submerged rocks and debris.

Comments It has long been debated by taxonomists whether this interesting snake is a garter snake or a water snake. The latest taxonomic conclusions place it in the genus *Thamnophis*. Unless it is the object of a specific search this is a snake that is more apt to be seen by a fisherman than the average reptile enthusiast.

114 RED-SPOTTED GARTER SNAKE

Thamnophis sirtalis concinnus 

Nonvenomous This pretty and common Pacific Coast snake does not seem to show much inclination to bite. However, it is fully capable of doing so, and swelling, redness, and some tenderness could occur at the bite site.

Abundance Although this remains one of the more commonly encountered snakes within its range, we are told it has become less so. This is not a surprising observation, for human encroachments on prime habitats, and intolerance of snakes—even pretty snakes—as neighbors, have taken a toll from populations of most snake species.

Size This snake is adult at 16–28 in. long, and seldom exceeds 36 in. Neonates are 7–9.5 in. long.

Range This Pacific Coast subspecies ranges northward from west-central Oregon to extreme southwestern Washington.

Habitat This snake may be encountered in a variety of habitats, ranging from woodlands to open damp meadows and rocky, open hillsides.

Prey Earthworms, leeches, slugs, fish, frogs, nestling rodents, and the nestlings of ground-dwelling birds, are all readily eaten by the red-spotted garter snake.

Reproduction Little is written regarding the reproductive biology of this race of the common garter snake. Some captives have bred annually, others biennially. The clutches have consistently been rather small, 4–9.

Coloring/scale form Like many garter snakes, this race is variable in coloration, but all are beautiful. Many have a ground color of ebony, with highlights of vermilion and lemon. The brilliant yellow vertebral stripe is well defined; the lateral stripes are poorly defined or lacking. The lower sides are patterned with regularly spaced, bright red spots. The top of the head is orange-red. The eyes are proportionately large. There are usually 7 upper labial scales and 10 lower labials. Some specimens are much paler (lacking much or all of the red), being ebony and butter-yellow instead.

The venter is bluish to blue-green along the midline, and darker along the sides. The throat is paler than the belly. There are usually 19 rows of keeled scales at midbody; the anal plate is undivided.

Similar snakes The wandering garter snake usually has 8 upper labial scales; the northwestern garter snake usually has 7 upper labials. Both have proportionately smaller eyes than the red-spotted (or other) race(s) of the common garter snake. Both the wandering and the northwestern garter snakes lack well-defined red spots on the sides.

Behavior This is an alert snake that may sometimes be surprised while sunning in open woodland glades or along meadow- or stream-edges. The snakes quickly retreat to the herbaceous understory or into rockpiles or other debris when startled. The red-spotted garter snake is primarily diurnal, but may be active in the evenings or at night during warm weather. Although this race of garter snake does not seem especially prone to bite, they are nervous and when restrained may whip about and smear excrement on a captor.

Comments In an excellent monograph of the genus *Thamnophis,* Rossman, Ford, and Seigel examined and realigned several taxa. We have followed their conclusions on all but this species. Because of certain taxonomic challenges, we have continued to use the taxonomy in vogue since 1951 in our accounts of the western races of the common garter snake. This includes the usage of *T. s. infernalis* for the wide-ranging red-sided garter snake of the Pacific Coast and *T. s. tetrataenia* for the federally protected form found on the San Francisco Peninsula. This usage restricts the distribution of the red-spotted garter snake, *T. s. concinnus,* to central and nothern western Oregon and immediately adjacent southwestern Washington. In future editions we may find the need to change this position, but for the moment will adhere to the conservative approach.

Additional subspecies In one or another of its 12 subspecies, the common garter snake is found from North America's Atlantic coast to the Pacific, and from southern Canada to the southernmost tip of the Florida Peninsula to just a few miles north of the U.S./Mexican border in California. The common garter snake is, however, absent from the American Southwest where it is replaced by aridland species. The common garter snake is also absent from a vast area of northern Montana, southern Saskatchewan and southern Alberta. Over most of that area it is replaced by the Plains, *T. radix,* and wandering, *T. elegans vagrans* garter snakes.

It is in western North America that the most strikingly colored subspecies of the common garter snake are found.

115 New Mexico Garter Snake

Thamnophis sirtalis dorsalis 

This subspecies is largely restricted to the Rio Grande Valley of New Mexico, but one disjunct population also occurs in the Pecos River Valley of that state and two additional populations exist in western Chihuahua, Mexico. This race often has red on the sides, but the red may be largely (or entirely) restricted to interstitial (between the scales) areas. The red is often quite dark, and does not contrast greatly with the black ground color. The vertebral and lateral stripes are very prominent and of a pretty butter yellow.

116 Valley Garter Snake

Thamnophis sirtalis fitchi 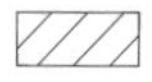

Another dark-colored subspecies, this snake lacks most, if not all, of the red on the sides, but both the yellow lateral and middorsal stripes are prominent. A gray morph exists in the vicinity of Crater Lake, Oregon. The valley garter snake occurs from extreme southern Alaska (the only snake to be found in that state) through British Columbia, Idaho, and southward into Utah and Nevada, and from there westward to northern and central California and eastern Oregon and Washington.

117 California Red-sided Garter Snake

Thamnophis sirtalis infernalis

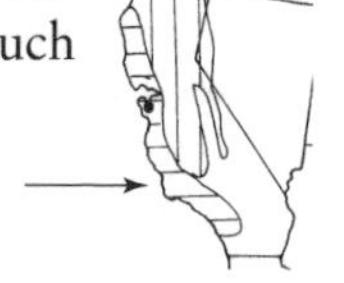

Another of the very pretty westerners, this subspecies is found over much of coastal California. It looks very much like the common red-sided garter snake (from which it is widely separated geographically) but has poorly defined lateral stripes and a red or orange(ish) head.

118 Red-sided Garter Snake

Thamnophis sirtalis parietalis

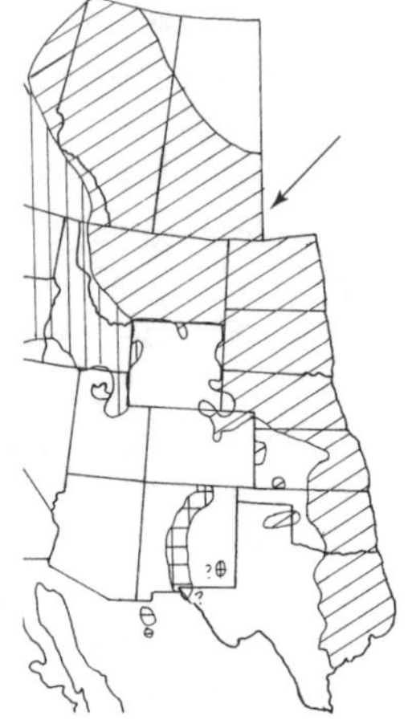

Another variably colored race, this common plains states and northwestern garter snake typically has discrete red bars extending upward from the well-defined lateral stripe, well into the black of the sides. Some specimens have the red extending in checkerboard-like squares from lateral to dorsal stripe. Other specimens may lack much of the red. The head of this race is black. This creature masses in incredibly high numbers for hibernation and for breeding (much of which is accomplished, both in autumn and spring, at the winter denning sites).

119 Puget Sound Garter Snake

Thamnophis sirtalis pickeringii

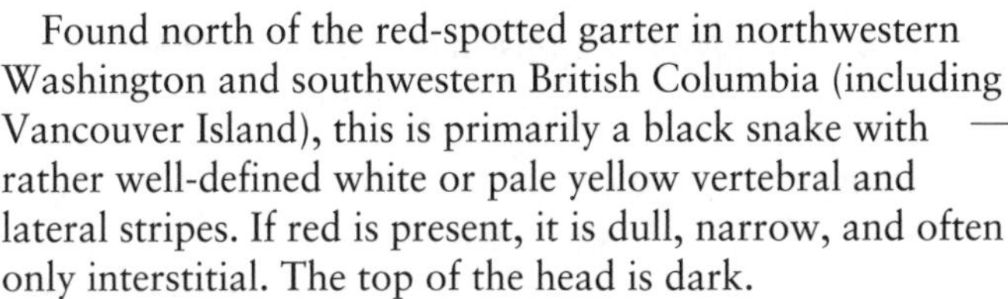

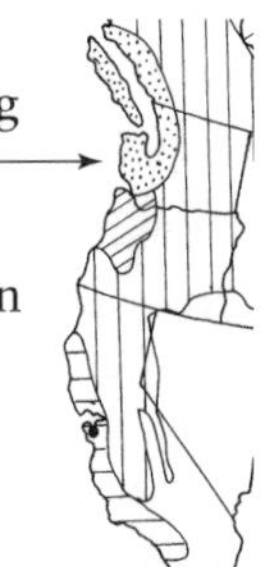

Found north of the red-spotted garter in northwestern Washington and southwestern British Columbia (including Vancouver Island), this is primarily a black snake with rather well-defined white or pale yellow vertebral and lateral stripes. If red is present, it is dull, narrow, and often only interstitial. The top of the head is dark.

120 San Francisco Garter Snake

Thamnophis sirtalis tetrataenia 

This is one of the world's most beautiful snakes. It occurs in reduced numbers in its ever-dwindling habitat on the western San Francisco Peninsula of central California. It is federally endangered and is entirely protected throughout its decreased range. Like many of the West Coast garter snakes, *tetrataenia* is an opportunistic feeder, accepting many aquatic organisms, nestlings of ground-dwelling birds and rodents, worms and slugs. The San Francisco garter snake is typified by a solid fire-orange to red-orange dorsolateral stripe along each side and a well-defined vertebral stripe of pale- to greenish-yellow. The lateral stripes are usually less intensely colored than the vertebral stripe. The belly is bluish-green.

Lined Snake

Genus Tropidoclonion

In gross appearance, the lined snake is much like a small garter snake and is, indeed, very closely allied to the snakes of the genus *Thamnophis*. From them, it may be immediately distinguished by the presence of the double row of bold half moons extending from the neck, virtually to the tail tip.

The lined snake is reluctant to bite. Its saliva composition is unknown. It is considered harmless to human.

This prairieland snake produces living young.

The 19 rows of scales are keeled; the anal plate is undivided.

LINED SNAKE, *Tropidoclonion lineatum*

Nonvenomous This is a tiny snake that is not known to bite. Even if it were so inclined, the snake is so small that its bite could be of no significance to humans.

Abundance Because of its need for moist habitats, the lined snake is found in local non-contiguous populations throughout most of its range. It may be moderately uncommon in some areas, abundant in others, and completely absent from still others. Because of its secretive habits, it is a difficult species to accurately census.

Size Normally, adult lined snakes are 8–12 in. long. A specimen of 15 in. is considered huge, and the 22-in.-long specimen reported by Tennant (1984) is Brobdignagian! Neonates are 4.5–5 in. long.

Range The principal range of the lined snake is east of our coverage area. However, several disjunct populations are found in southern and central New Mexico and in eastern Colorado.

Habitat There could hardly be a more adaptable snake than this species. Principally a species of the open grasslands, the lined snake has adapted well to the habitat degradation made by humans, continuing to exist in gardens, parks, the environs of drainage ditches, dumps, and many similar moisture-retaining habitats.

Prey The lined snake is an earthworm specialist. Although some insects and sow bugs have been mentioned as dietary components, most lined snakes will not accept these. A captive female reportedly ate her newly born brood but, again, this is the exception rather than the rule.

Reproduction This is a live-bearing snake. A single clutch of 4–10 babies is produced in mid-August. The largest documented clutch contained 17 babies.

Coloring/scale form Some examples of this little snake look like a cross between a dwarfed garter snake and a brown snake. The dorsal coloration is a warm brown to an olive-brown. This is divided by a whitish or tan vertebral stripe which is peppered along its outer edges with tiny dark markings. The dark dorsal color may be bordered ventrally by a narrow dark line, which is then bordered on scale rows 2 and 3 by tan a or whitish line. The dark line separating the dorsal ground color from the light lateral stripe may be absent. The belly is whitish to yellowish, but is patterned for its length by a double row of small, dark, half moons.

Similar snakes The double row of ventral half-moons should adequately identify the lined snake.

Behavior The lined snake is particularly active following warm rains. It is nocturnally active during the warm weather, but may occasionally emerge or partially emerge from beneath surface cover to thermoregulate in the morning sun. Because it is so secretive, it is very easy to overlook fairly sizable populations of this small snake. The lined snake not only uses even the smallest pieces of human-generated debris, but also secretes itself beneath plant material, rocks, and other such natural surface cover. The lined snake is also an accomplished burrower, often found even in urban fields, gardens, and parklands.

Comments There is a tendency today to consider this diminutive garter snake relative simply as a variable, monotypic species.

Problematic Colubrines; Uncertain Affinities

There are in the American West, three genera of snakes that are of problematic familial status. At the moment, Herndon Dowling refers to these three as "North American relicts (pers. comm., 1999)." Harry Greene states "several taxa are not yet confidently placed in subgroups . . . (Greene, 1997)" and includes the snakes in these three genera among them.

SHARP-TAILED SNAKE
Genus Contia

This monotypic genus occurs only from northern California northward to southern British Columbia. The single species is fossorial and is active at temperatures as low as 50°F—temperatures when many (if not most) other snakes would be inactive. The sharp-tailed snake is a slug-eating specialist that has proportionately long teeth to enable them to hold such slippery prey.

In many respects, the sharp-tailed snake is the ecological equivalent of the diminutive worm snakes of eastern United States. Both of these snakes have a tail tip scale that has modified into a sharp spine. Although totally harmless, the spine, when pushed against a captor, is sometimes so startling that the snake is dropped. Speculation has it that the spine may help position the slugs on which *Contia* feeds.

122 SHARP-TAILED SNAKE, *Contia tenuis*

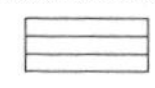

Nonvenomous The components of the saliva of this little snake are unknown, but it virtually never bites and, even if it should, it would be of no medical consequence to humans.

Abundance *Contia tenuis* is so secretive that census statistics are virtually impossible. It is probably not rare in suitable habitats, but is rather seldom seen. Life history studies of this snake are badly needed.

Size Although Stebbins (1985) states a maximum length of 18 in. for this snake, such a size is almost never seen. Most found are 8–12 in. long. Hatchlings are about 3 in. long.

Range Sharp-tailed snakes are found along both sides of Sacramento Valley in northern California, northward to northwestern Oregon (excluding the coastline), and in several disjunct colonies in the state of Washington, Vancouver Island, and South and North Pinder Island, British Columbia.

Habitat Soil moisture is mandatory for this snake. It occurs from sea level stream edges to foggy, mountaintop meadows. It is not only an accomplished burrower into damp substrates, but may be found behind the loosened bark of dead and decomposing trees (both fallen and standing), under rocks, and beneath moisture-retaining, human-generated debris. The sharp-tailed snake is occasionally surface-active, especially during or following rains.

Prey The principal food item of the sharp-tailed snake is slugs. The presence of the introduced European slug of the genus *Arion,* now an abundant species in the Pacific Northwest, has seemingly allowed the sharp-tailed snake to expand its range.

Reproduction Very little is known about the reproductive biology of the sharp-tailed snake. It is an oviparous snake species. Females lay 2–8 (normal clutch size is 3–5) eggs in late summer. The incubation period is unknown, but is thought to be about 60 days, with the hatchlings emerging in mid-autumn.

Coloring/scale form The dorsal coloration of this little snake may be gray, earthen red, or russet, but its sides are grayish. The dorsal coloration is often a little brighter posteriorly. Dorsal and lateral colors are delineated and separated by a reddish dorsolateral stripe on each side. The head is only slightly wider than the neck. The belly is white with a bar of black across each ventral plate from chin to vent. Black pigment sometimes occurs on the outermost edges of the subcaudal scales. The smooth dorsal scales are in 15 rows at midbody. The anal plate is divided. The terminal tail scale is modified into a spine. Hatchlings are reddish and have narrow dark lines on their sides. These are sometimes retained in faded version into adulthood.

Similar snakes The black and white barred venter and the tail tip spine are diagnostic.

Ring-necked snakes may occasionally lack a neck-ring and could then be mistaken for a sharp-tailed snake. However, ring-neckeds have an orange (not white) ventral ground color, and never have the terminal spine on the tail.

Behavior Besides being nocturnal, and/or active during rainstorms, this is a fossorial snake that is active at temperatures so cool that most other snake species would be inactive.

Ring-necked Snakes
Genus Diadophis

As currently described, this genus, restricted to the United States, Canada, and northern Mexico, contains only a single well subspeciated species. With but 2 exceptions in the United States, the members of this group are easily identified to genus by their brilliant orange to orange-red neck rings. The 2 exceptions are the Keys ring-necked snake, *Diadophis punctatus acricus,* of Florida's Big Pine Key, and the regal ring-necked snake, *D. p. regalis,* of the Southwest and northern Mexico on which the ring may be muted or absent. Dependent on subspecies, the western members of this genus of secretive snakes may be denizens of woodlands, plains, prairies, or even backyards. Most subspecies are absent from arid areas, but may be common wherever moisture occurs. Expect to find these snakes on mountain tops, in moist canyons, along riparian corridors, in the proximity of permanent or semi-permanent lakes and ponds, or along artificial water retention facilities, such as irrigation canals.

When startled, the subspecies that have bright red-orange subcaudal color, coil the tail tightly and elevate it. It is thought that this aposematic coloration may indicate to predators a degree of unpalatability. Some predators will eat, then regurgitate a ring-necked snake or will bite, then release the snake and wipe their mouths against grasses or sand as if trying to rid themselves of an unpleasant taste. However, other predators, coral snakes among them, readily eat ring-necked snakes with no sign of distress.

These snakes have 15–17 rows of smooth scales at mid body (often only 13 rows posteriorly) and divided anal plates.

Although a size of 30 in. is often quoted for this species, it is seldom that any race, other than the regal ring-necked, exceeds 18 in. The regal ring-necked may rather regularly attain 24 in. or more in total length and has a record size of 33.5 in.

Subspecific intergradation occurs where ranges abut. In appearance the intergrades can be intermediate and confusing. We suggest that you use range as a primary identification criterion.

Although it is difficult to count the scale rows on a living wriggling snake, these figure so prominently in the subspecific identification that we have included them here. If 2 figures (example, 15–13) are provided, the first figure indicates the number of scale rows on the neck, the second at midbody. If only a single figure is provided it is the scale count at midbody. Some races have enlarged teeth at the rear of the upper jaw and a toxic saliva.

R. W. VanDevender

1 **New Mexico Blind Snake,**
Leptotyphlops dulcis dissectus

R. D. Bartlett

2 **Desert Blind Snake,**
Leptotyphlops humilis cahuilae

3 **Southwestern Blind Snake,**
Leptotyphlops humilis humilis

4 **Trans-Pecos Blind Snake,**
Leptotyphlops humilis segregus

P. Medica

5 Utah Blind Snake,
Leptotyphlops humilis utahensis

R. D. Bartlett

6 Brahminy Blind Snake,
Ramphotyphlops braminus

7 Pacific Rubber Boa,
Charina bottae bottae (adult and juvenile)

R. D. Bartlett

8 Southern Rubber Boa,
Charina bottae umbraticus

9 Rocky Mountain Rubber Boa,
Charina bottae utahensis

10a Desert Rosy Boa,
Lichanura trivirgata gracia (Arizona)

10b Desert Rosy Boa,
Lichanura trivirgata gracia (California)

11 Coastal Rosy Boa,
Lichanura trivirgata roseofusca

12 **Mexican Rosy Boa,**
Lichanura trivirgata trivirgata

13 **Eastern Yellow-bellied Racer,**
Coluber constrictor flaviventris

R. D. Bartlett

14 Western Yellow-bellied Racer,
Coluber constrictor mormon

J. H. Harding

15 Smooth Green Snake,
Liochlorophis vernalis

16 Sonoran Mountain Whipsnake,
Masticophis bilineatus bilineatus

17 Ajo Mountain Whipsnake,
Masticophis bilineatus lineolatus

R. D. Bartlett

18a Sonoran Coachwhip,
Masticophis flagellum cingulum

R. D. Bartlett

18b Sonoran Coachwhip,
Masticophis flagellum cingulum (preying on a towhee nest)

19a Baja California Coachwhip,
Masticophis flagellum fuliginosus (dark phase)

19b Baja California Coachwhip,
Masticophis flagellum fuliginosus (light phase)

T. VanDevender, courtesy of R. W. VanDevender

20 Lined Coachwhip,
Masticophis flagellum lineatulus

R. D. Bartlett

21a Red Coachwhip,
Masticophis flagellum piceus (red phase)

21b Red Coachwhip,
Masticophis flagellum piceus (black phase)

R.W. Hansen

22 San Joaquin Coachwhip,
Masticophis flagellum ruddocki

23 Western Coachwhip,
Masticophis flagellum testaceus

K. Switak

24 Alameda Striped Racer,
Masticophis lateralis euryxanthus

R. D. Bartlett

25 California Striped Racer,
Masticophis lateralis lateralis

R. D. Bartlett

26 Desert Striped Whipsnake,
Masticophis taeniatus

27a Brown Vine Snake,
Oxybelis aeneus (aggressive stance)

27b Brown Vine Snake,
Oxybelis aeneus (interior of mouth)

R. D. Bartlett

28 Big Bend Patch-nosed Snake,
Salvadora deserticola

R. D. Bartlett

29 Mountain Patch-nosed Snake,
Salvadora grahamiae

30 **Desert Patch-nosed Snake,**
Salvadora hexalepis hexalepis

31 **Mojave Patch-nosed Snake,**
Salvadora hexalepis mojavensis

K.Switak

2 **Coastal Patch-nosed Snake,**
Salvadora hexalepis virgultea

R. D. Bartlett

3 **Sonoran Lyre Snake,**
Trimorphodon biscutatus lambda

34 **California Lyre Snake,**
Trimorphodon biscutatus vandenburghi

35a **Texas Lyre Snake,**
Trimorphodon biscutatus vilkinsonii

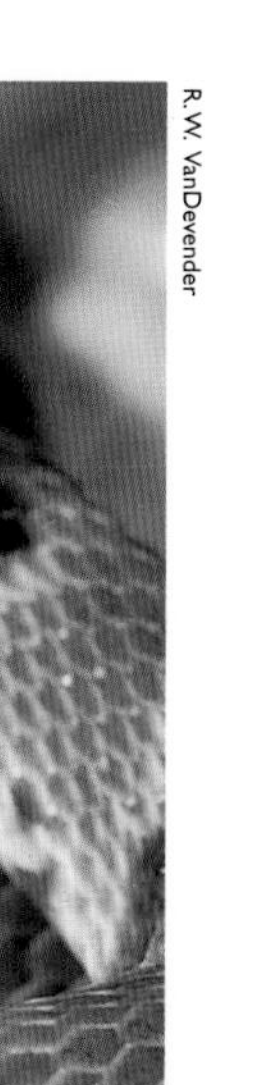

R.W. VanDevender

85b Texas Lyre Snake,
Trimorphodon biscutatus vilkinsonii

R. D. Bartlett

86 Banded Sand Snake,
Chilomeniscus cinctus cinctus

37 Colorado Desert Shovel-nosed Snake,
Chionactis occipitalis annulata

R.W. VanDevender

38 Tucson Shovel-nosed Snake,
Chionactis occipitalis klauberi

39 Mojave Desert Shovel-nosed Snake,
Chionactis occipitalis occipitalis

P. Medica

40 Nevada Shovel-nosed Snake,
Chionactis occipitalis talpina

R. W. VanDevender

41 Organ Pipe Shovel-nosed Snake,
Chionactis palarostris organica

R. D. Bartlett

42 Western Hook-nosed Snake,
Gyalopion canum

43 Desert Hook-nosed Snake,
Gyalopion quadrangulare

44a Pima Leaf-nosed Snake,
Phyllorhynchus browni browni

R. D. Bartlett

44b Pima Leaf-nosed Snake,
Phyllorhynchus browni browni

R. D. Bartlett

45 Maricopa Leaf-nosed Snake,
Phyllorhynchus browni lucidus

46 Clouded Leaf-nosed Snake,
Phyllorhynchus decurtatus nubilis

47 Western Leaf-nosed Snake,
Phyllorhynchus decurtatus perkinsi

R. D. Bartlett

8a Variable Ground Snake,
Sonora semiannulata (dorsally striped phase)

J. Harding

8b Variable Ground Snake,
Sonora semiannulata (banded phase)

48c Variable Ground Snake,
Sonora semiannulata (black-headed phase)

R. D. Bartlett

48d Variable Ground Snake,
Sonora semiannulata (red phase)

49 Southwestern Black-headed Snake,
Tantilla hobartsmithi

50 Plains Black-headed Snake,
Tantilla nigriceps

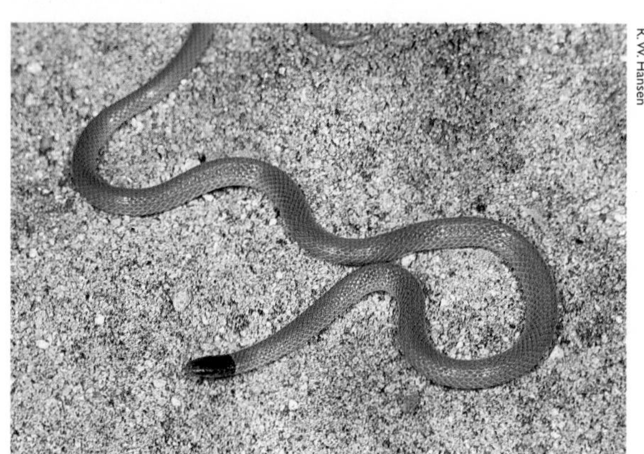

51 Western Black-headed Snake,
Tantilla planiceps

52 Huachuca Black-headed Snake,
Tantilla wilcoxi wilcoxi

53 Yaqui Black-headed Snake,
Tantilla yaquia

54 Desert Night Snake,
Hypsiglena torquata deserticola

R. D. Bartlett

Texas Night Snake,
Hypsiglena torquata jani

S. Zimmerman

San Diego Night Snake,
Hypsiglena torquata klauberi

57 Mesa Verde Night Snake,
Hypsiglena torquata loreala

58 California Night Snake,
Hypsiglena torquata nuchalata

R. D. Bartlett

9 **Spotted Night Snake,**
Hypsiglena torquata ochrorhyncha

R.W. VanDevender

0 **Mojave Glossy Snake,**
Arizona elegans candida

R.W. VanDevender

61 Desert Glossy Snake,
Arizona elegans eburnata

62 Kansas Glossy Snake,
Arizona elegans elegans

R. D. Bartlett

63 Arizona Glossy Snake,
Arizona elegans noctivaga

R. D. Bartlett

64 California Glossy Snake,
Arizona elegans occidentalis

R. D. Bartlett

65 Painted Desert Glossy Snake,
Arizona elegans philipi

R. W. VanDevender

66 Baja California Rat Snake,
Bogertophis rosaliae

67 Trans-Pecos Rat Snake,
Bogertophis subocularis subocularis

68a Great Plains Rat Snake,
Elaphe guttata emoryi

R. D. Bartlett

68b Great Plains Rat Snake,
Elaphe guttata emoryi (plain-bellied morph)

R. D. Bartlett

69a Gray-banded Kingsnake,
Lampropeltis alterna ("alterna" phase)

69b Gray-banded Kingsnake,
Lampropeltis alterna (dark Blair phase)

70a California Kingsnake,
Lampropeltis getula californiae (banded phase)

R. D. Bartlett

70b California Kingsnake,
Lampropeltis getula californiae (striped phase)

R. D. Bartlett

71 Desert Black Kingsnake,
Lampropeltis getula nigrita

72 Desert Kingsnake,
Lampropeltis getula splendida

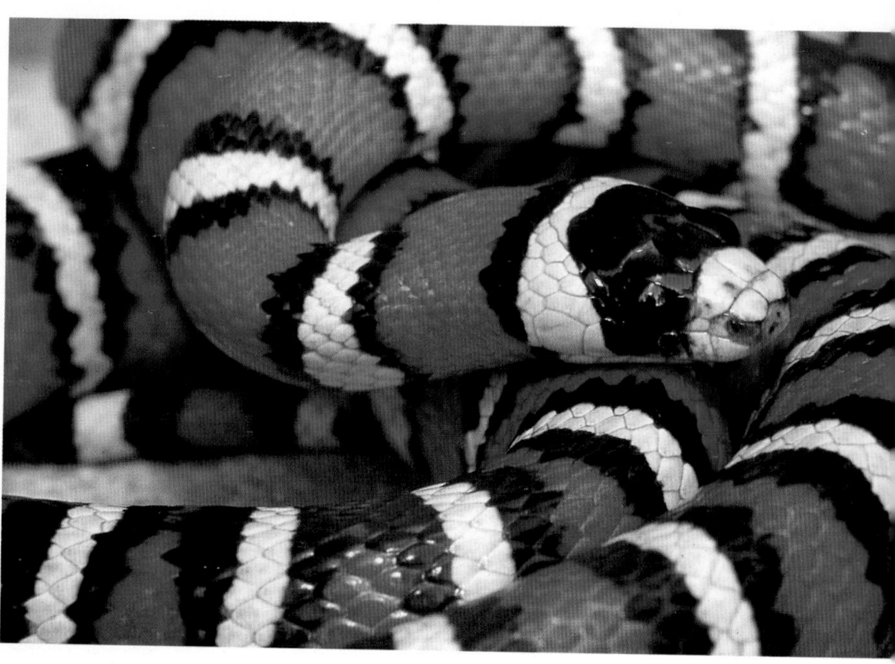

73 Utah Mountain Kingsnake,
Lampropeltis pyromelana infralabialis

R. D. Bartlett

74a **Arizona Mountain Kingsnake,**
Lampropeltis pyromelana pyromelana

S. Zimmerman

74b **Arizona Mountain Kingsnake,**
Lampropeltis pyromelana pyromelana (juvenile)

R. D. Bartlett

75 Huachuca Mountain Kingsnake,
Lampropeltis pyromelana woodini

76 New Mexico Milk Snake,
Lampropeltis triangulum celaenops

R. D. Bartlett

77 Central Plains Milk Snake,
Lampropeltis triangulum gentilis

R. D. Bartlett

78 **Pale Milk Snake,**
Lampropeltis triangulum multistrata

R. W. VanDevender

79 **Utah Milk Snake,**
Lampropeltis triangulum taylori

R. D. Bartlett

80 **Sierra Mountain Kingsnake,**
Lampropeltis zonata multicincta

81a Coastal Mountain Kingsnake,
Lampropeltis zonata multifasciata

81b Coastal Mountain Kingsnake,
Lampropeltis zonata multifasciata (Mt. Hamilton phase)

R. D. Bartlett

82 San Bernardino Mountain Kingsnake,
Lampropeltis zonata parvirubra

K. Switak

83 San Diego Mountain Kingsnake,
Lampropeltis zonata pulchra

84a St. Helena Mountain Kingsnake,
Lampropeltis zonata zonata (California)

W. P. Leonard

84b St. Helena Mountain Kingsnake,
Lampropeltis zonata intergrade (Washington)

85 Sonoran Gopher Snake,
Pituophis catenifer affinis

R. D. Bartlett

86 San Diego Gopher Snake,
Pituophis catenifer annectens

R. D. Bartlett

87a Pacific Gopher Snake,
Pituophis catenifer catenifer (saddled morph)

87b Pacific Gopher Snake,
Pituophis catenifer catenifer (striped morph)

R. D. Bartlett

88 Great Basin Gopher Snake,
Pituophis catenifer deserticola

89 Santa Cruz Gopher Snake,
Pituophis catenifer pumilus

R. D. Bartlett

90 **Bullsnake,**
Pituophis catenifer sayi

R. D. Bartlett

91a **Western Long-nosed Snake,**
Rhinochelius lecontei lecontei (black and yellow morph)

S. Zimmerman

91b **Western Long-nosed Snake,**
Rhinochelius lecontei lecontei (tricolored morph)

92 **Texas Long-nosed Snake,**
Rhinocheilus lecontei tessellatus

93 **Green Rat Snake,**
Senticolis triaspis intermedia

R. W. VanDevender

94 Blotched Water Snake,
Nerodia erythrogaster transversa

R. D. Bartlett

95 Northern Water Snake,
Nerodia sipedon sipedon

96 Black Hills Red-bellied Snake,
Storeria occipitomaculata pahasapae

97 Santa Cruz Garter Snake,
Thamnophis atratus atratus

W.P. Leonard

98 Oregon Garter Snake,
Thamnophis atratus hydrophilis

R.W. VanDevender

99 Western Aquatic Garter Snake,
Thamnophis couchii

100 Western Black-necked Garter Snake,
Thamnophis cyrtopsis cyrtopsis

101 Arizona Garter Snake,
Thamnophis elegans arizonae

R.W. VanDevender

102 Mountain Garter Snake,
Thamnophis elegans elegans

R. D. Bartlett

103 Coast Garter Snake,
Thamnophis elegans terrestris

R. D. Bartlett

104 Wandering Garter Snake,
Thamnophis elegans vagrans

105 Upper Basin Garter Snake,
Thamnophis elegans vascotanneri

R. D. Bartlett

106 Northern Mexican Garter Snake,
Thamnophis eques megalops

R. W. Hansen

107 Giant Garter Snake,
Thamnophis giga

R. D. Bartlett

108 Two-striped Garter Snake,
Thamnophis hammondi

R. D. Bartlett

109 Northern Checkered Garter Snake,
Thamnophis marcianus marcianus

110a Northwestern Garter Snake,
Thamnophis ordinoides (blue morph)

110b Northwestern Garter Snake,
Thamnophis ordinoides (orange-striped morph)

R. D. Bartlett

111 Aridland Ribbon Snake,
Thamnophis proximus diabolicus

R. D. Bartlett

112 Plains Garter Snake,
Thamnophis radix

113 Narrow-headed Garter Snake,
Thamnophis rufipunctatus

114a Red-spotted Garter Snake,
Thamnophis sirtalis concinnus (normal morph)

R. D. Bartlett

114b Red-spotted Garter Snake,
Thamnophis sirtalis concinnus (no-red morph)

R.W. VanDevender

115 New Mexican Garter Snake,
Thamnophis sirtalis dorsalis

116a Valley Garter Snake,
Thamnophis sirtalis fitchi (dark morph)

116b Valley Garter Snake,
Thamnophis sirtalis fitchi (red morph)

B. Griswold

117 **California Red-sided Garter Snake,**
Thamnophis sirtalis infernalis

R. D. Bartlett

118 **Red-sided Garter Snake,**
Thamnophis sirtalis paretalis

R. D. Bartlett

119 Puget Sound Garter Snake,
Thamnophis sirtalis pickeringii

120 San Francisco Garter Snake,
Thamnophis sirtalis tetrataenia

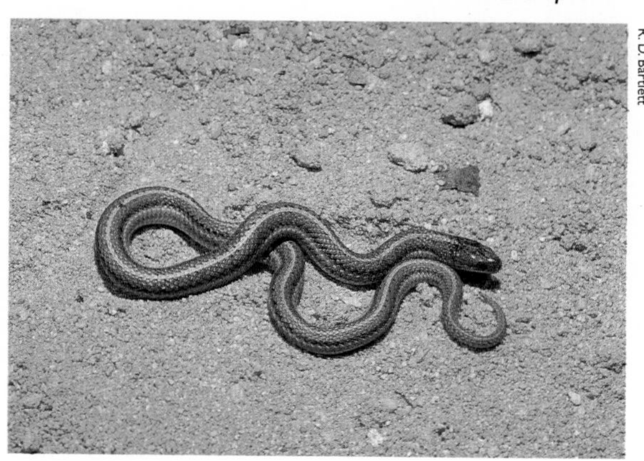
R. D. Bartlett

121a Lined Snake,
Tropidoclonion lineatum

R. D. Bartlett

121b Lined Snake,
Tropidoclonion lineatum

R. D. Bartlett

122a Sharp-tailed Snake,
Contia tenuis (gray morph)

J. H. Harding

122b Sharp-tailed Snake,
Contia tenuis (red morph)

123 Pacific Ring-necked Snake,
Diadophis punctatus amabilis

R. W. VanDevender

124 Prairie Ring-necked Snake,
Diadophis punctatus arnyi

125 San Bernardino Ring-necked Snake,
Diadophis punctatus modestus

J. H. Harding

126 Northwestern Ring-necked Snake,
Diadophis punctatus occidentalis

K. Switak

127 Coral-bellied Ring-necked Snake,
Diadophis punctatus pulchellus

R. W. VanDevender

128a Regal Ring-necked Snake,
Diadophis punctatus regalis (non-ringed morph)

128b Regal Ring-necked Snake
Diadophis punctatus regalis (ringed morph)

129 San Diego Ring-necked Snake,
Diadophis punctatus similis

R. W. VanDevender

130 Monterey Ring-necked Snake,
Diadophis punctatus vandenburghi

R. D. Bartlett

131 Mexican Hog-nosed Snake,
Heterodon nasicus kennerlyi

R. D. Bartlett

132 Plains Hog-nosed Snake,
Heterodon nasicus nasicus

R. W. VanDevender

133 Arizona Coral Snake,
Micruroides euryxanthus euryxanthus

R. D. Bartlett

134 Yellow-bellied Sea Snake,
Pelamis platurus

R. D. Bartlett

135a Western Diamond-backed Rattlesnake,
Crotalus atrox

B. Griswold

135b Western Diamond-backed Rattlesnake,
Crotalus atrox (defensive position)

R. D. Bartlett

136 Mojave Desert Sidewinder,
Crotalus cerastes cerastes

R. D. Bartlett

137 Sonoran Sidewinder,
Crotalus cerastes cercobombus

R. D. Bartlett

138 Colorado Desert Sidewinder,
Crotalus cerastes laterorepens

R. D. Bartlett

139 Northern Red Diamond Rattlesnake,
Crotalus exsul ruber

R. D. Bartlett

140a Banded Rock Rattlesnake,
Crotalus lepidus klauberi (New Mexico)

S. Zimmerman

140b Banded Rock Rattlesnake,
Crotalus lepidus klauberi (Arizona)

R. D. Bartlett

141 Mottled Rock Rattlesnake,
Crotalus lepidus lepidus

142 Southwestern Speckled Rattlesnake,
Crotalus mitchellii pyrrhus

143 Panamint Rattlesnake,
Crotalus mitchellii stephensi

R. D. Bartlett

144a Northern Black-tailed Rattlesnake,
Crotalus molossus molossus

R. D. Bartlett

144b Northern Black-tailed Rattlesnake,
Crotalus molossus molossus (Harcuvar Mountains color variant)

145 Twin-spotted Rattlesnake,
Crotalus pricei pricei

R. D. Bartlett

146 Mojave Rattlesnake,
Crotalus scutulatus scutulatus

147 Tiger Rattlesnake,
Crotalus tigris

C. R. Schwalbe

48 Grand Canyon Rattlesnake,
Crotalus viridis abyssus

R. D. Bartlett

149a Arizona Black Rattlesnake,
Crotalus viridis cerberus (black morph)

R. D. Bartlett

49b Arizona Black Rattlesnake,
Crotalus viridis cerberus (patterned morph)

150 Midget Faded Rattlesnake,
Crotalus viridis concolor

151 Southern Pacific Rattlesnake,
Crotalus viridis helleri

S. Zimmerman

52 **Great Basin Rattlesnake,**
Crotalus viridis lutosus

R. D. Bartlett

53 **Hopi Rattlesnake,**
Crotalus viridis nuntius

154 Northern Pacific Rattlesnake,
Crotalus viridis oreganus

155 Prairie Rattlesnake,
Crotalus viridis viridis

R. D. Bartlett, courtesy of B. Tomberlin

156 **New Mexico Ridge-nosed Rattlesnake,** *Crotalus willardi obscurus*

R. D. Bartlett

157a **Arizona Ridge-nosed Rattlesnake,** *Crotalus willardi willardi*

157b Arizona Ridge-nosed Rattlesnake,
Crotalus willardi willardi (neonate)

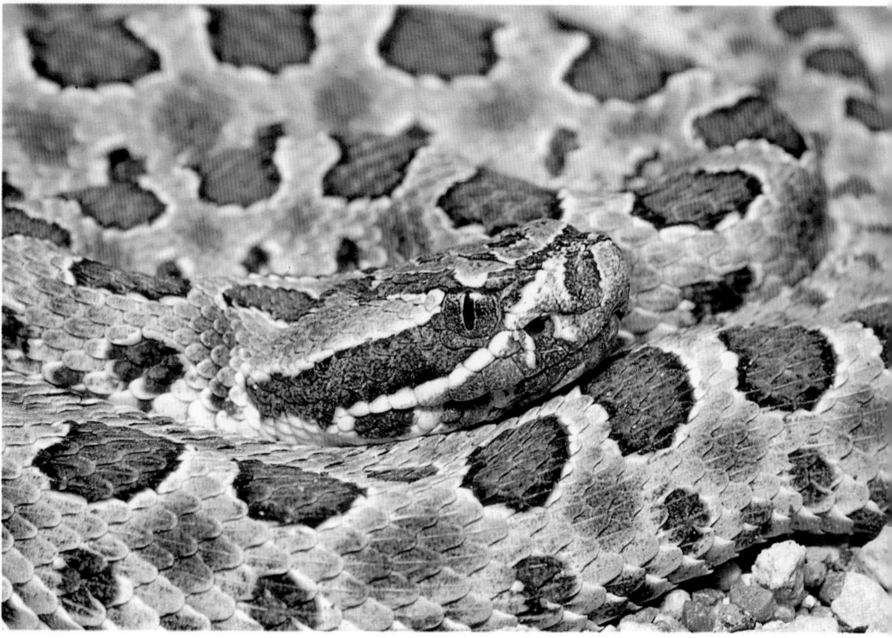

158 Desert Massasauga,
Sistrurus catenatus edwardsi

123 Pacific Ring-necked Snake

Diadophis punctatus amabilis 

Mildly venomous Although it is difficult to induce these small snakes to bite, they do have enlarged teeth in the rear of the upper jaw and are mildly venomous. The bite of even a large individual is not dangerous to humans.

Abundance These can be common snakes, but are often overlooked if not specifically sought. Ring-neckeds may occasionally be surface-active on rainy or foggy days or at dusk. Heavy rains may force these snakes from areas of seclusion which they would otherwise seldom leave.

Size This is a small and slender species. It is adult at 10.5–16 in.

Range This race of ring-necked snake, restricted to the coastal mountain ranges and their adjacent regions, ranges southward from just north of San Francisco Bay to the vicinity of Monterey Bay, California.

Habitat This is a snake of damp meadows, canyons, rocky hillsides, fallow fields, backyard gardens, and irrigated agricultural areas. When habitats are sufficiently moist, the Pacific ring-necked snake is often encountered beneath both natural and human-generated surface debris such as flat rocks, dried cow-patties, or discarded boards. The spaces behind bark-shards on both standing and fallen trees are favored hiding areas. As an area dries the snake will nudge its way into moisture retaining decomposing logs, or, where soil conditions allow, may burrow rather deeply.

Prey Ring-necked snakes may weakly constrict their prey. These snakes eat small ectothermic vertebrates and invertebrates. Most seem particularly fond of small salamanders (especially slender salamanders, *Batrachoseps,* and woodland salamanders (*Plethodon*), but may eat tadpoles, small frogs, smaller snakes, tiny lizards, earthworms, slugs, and, perhaps, certain insects. The mild venom may not only help the snakes subdue struggling prey, but may also serve as a weak predigestant.

Reproduction Although they are considered an oviparous form, viviparity has been recorded in southeastern females. Clutches normally contain 2–5 eggs. Large females may produce up to 10 eggs. Incubation durations are variable, but probably average about 7 weeks. The hatchlings are about 5 in. long. Occasional females may double-clutch.

Coloring/scale form Typically, the dorsal color of this snake is steel-gray, occasionally with fawn or olive overtones. Blue-gray to nearly black are common color variations. The yellowish orange to range belly is rather sparsely speckled with black. The subcaudal scales are bright red. The ventral color ascends onto the sides for one half to one and a half scale rows. The orange neck band is narrow, being only one to one and one half scale rows wide. The rows of smooth dorsal scales rows are usually 15–15.

Similar snakes Black-headed snakes have white(ish) neck rings. Brown and red-bellied snakes have keeled scales.

Behavior Ring-neckeds of all races are among the more persistently secretive snakes. Although the snakes may not burrow deeply, they are adept at using fallen leaves and conifer-needles, moss-beds, and patches of loose soil to their advantage. Flat surface stones and fallen logs are also favorite covers.

If disturbed, ring-necked snakes often coil, hide their head, and elevate their corkscrewed tail. This latter ploy is used most extensively by snakes in populations with particularly brightly colored subcaudal scales, and seldom or not at all by snakes in populations having subcaudal scales that do not differ markedly in color from the orange belly scales. When handled, or otherwise frightened, ring-necked snakes will smear musk and cloacal contents on captor or surroundings.

Comments As previously mentioned, these snakes can be difficult to identify to subspecies. Careful consideration of the range in which the snake has been found and counting the scale rows should help in subspecies determination.

124 Prairie Ring-necked Snake

Diadophis punctatus arnyi 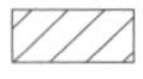

Wide-spread in the central states, it occurs from southcentral Texas, northward to northern Iowa and westward to central New Mexico and southeastern Colorado. Adult at 10–13 in., the record size is 16.5 in. The neck-ring is wide and well-defined, but may be discontinuous vertebrally. The dorsum can vary from olive-gray to olive. Scale rows, 17–15. The belly is orange and patterned with (often) paired, but well separated, black half-moons. The orange of the venter seldom extends upwards onto even the lowest row of lateral scales. The subcaudal scales are bright red.

125 San Bernardino Ring-necked Snake

Diadophis punctatus modestus

Found in coastal areas from the vicinity of Santa Barbara, California to the Los Angeles area, this is a rather dark race of ring-necked and the (often) narrow neckband (½–2 scales wide) does not always strongly contrast with the body color. The belly color is a bright orange to orange-red. Most ventral scutes have four conspicuous black spots, one at each outer edge and two more centrally. The orange ventral coloration extends upwards, encompassing the bottom half of the lowermost row of lateral scales. The subcaudal scales are bright red. Scales are in 17–15 rows.

126 Northwestern Ring-necked Snake

Diadophis punctatus occidentalis 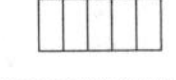

In the states of Oregon and Washington, where it is the only race of ring-necked snake to occur, subspecific identification of this snake is a simple matter. From the Cascade Range of Washington, this snake ranges southward to Sonoma County, California. The 15 rows of dorsal scales are grayish green to olive. The chin is heavily speckled. The neck ring is from 1 to 3 scales wide, the venter is reddish orange venter, and the subcaudals are brilliant red. Each ventral scute bears one (or two) prominent black spot. The bright ventral color extends upwards onto the sides for from one half to two full scale rows. Black flecks may also occur on these lowermost scale rows. Although it is known to attain a full two feet in length, most northwestern ring-necked snakes are adult at 11–18 inches.

127 Coral-bellied Ring-necked Snake

Diadophis punctatus pulchellus 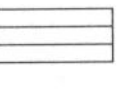

One of the more brilliantly colored races, this snake occurs on the western slopes of California's Sierra Nevadas. It does not range eastward to the coastal ranges. It is quite similar in appearance to the Northwestern ring-necked snake, but has a reduced amount of black on the ventral scales and lacks black flecks on the lowermost two rows of lateral scales. The adult size seems to be 11–16 in.

128 Regal Ring-necked Snake

Diadophis punctatus regalis 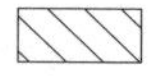

This is the largest, palest, and most arid-adapted subspecies. Although it can attain sexual maturity at 10–16 in., this pretty snake often exceeds 18 in., occasionally exceeds 24 in., and has a record size of 33.5 in. It seeks the dampest areas (riparian corridors, the environs of stock tanks, etc.) in semiarid grasslands and thornscrub. The regal ring-necked snake ranges widely in our interior western states. Although found from southeastern Idaho southward to central Texas and Mexico, and from central-eastern Nevada to western Arizona, there are vast tracts of truly arid land within its range from which this snake is absent. Check the range map carefully. This is one of the most distinctively colored of the ring-neckeds. The dorsal color is pale ash-gray, olive-gray, or olive. The belly is yellowish to pale orange. There are 4 rows of well-defined dark black spots on each ventral scute. The central 2 rows are the most prominent. The yellow ventral color often includes the lowest of the lateral scale rows. The underside of the tail is quite a bright red. The neck ring may be well-defined, poorly defined, or entirely absent. There are 17 scale rows.

129 San Diego Ring-necked Snake

Diadophis punctatus similis 

This subspecies has a rather small range, occurring primarily in San Diego County, California and adjacent Baja California. It is also known from southwestern San Bernardino County, California. It has 15 scale rows, has heavy dark markings at the outermost edge of each ventral scute, and more poorly defined central ventral spotting. The central spots may join the outermost ones to form a single prominent row along each side of the venter. The orange of the venter includes at least part of the first row of lateral scales. The subcaudal scales are bright red. Each chin and lower labial scale bears a dark spot. The neck ring may be well-defined or rather pale, and is one and a half to three scales wide. The dorsum may vary from olive to a rather dark gray, and be darker laterally than middorsally.

130 Monterey Ring-necked Snake

Diadophis punctatus vandenburghi 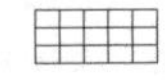

The last of the western races of the ring-necked snakes, this snake is restricted to the coastal ranges and adjacent habitats, from Santa Cruz County, California, southward to Ventura County. The neck ring is one and a half to two and a half scale rows wide. The back can vary from yellowish-green to olive-gray. The ventral color is brighter than that of many subspecies, being red anteriorly and an even brighter red posteriorly and beneath the tail. The ventral color extends upward, including all of the first row of scales and the lower half of the second row. The dark ventral spotting is poorly defined.

Hog-nosed Snakes

Genus Heterodon

There are 3 species in this genus, only one of which, the western hognosed snake, is subspeciated. Two of its 3 subspecies, the Mexican and the Plains hog-noseds, range westward into the area covered by this guide.

Hog-nosed snakes are famous for their impressive suite of defensive actions, which include huffing, puffing, writhing, and bluffing. The snakes spread a hood, flatten their head, may strike, and when all else fails, writhe, open their mouth, loll their tongues out to the fullest extent, roll onto their back and play possum. They then show life only by immediately again rolling upside down if righted.

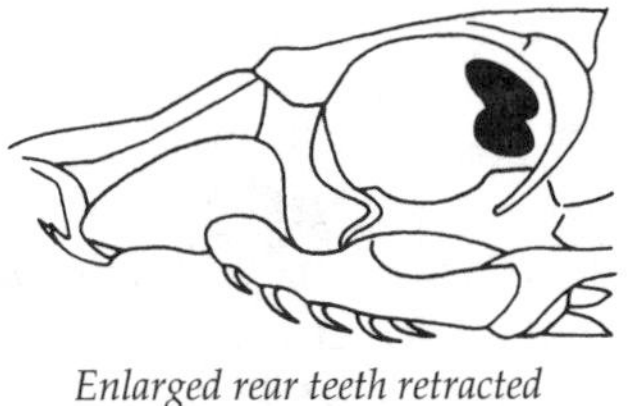

Enlarged rear teeth retracted

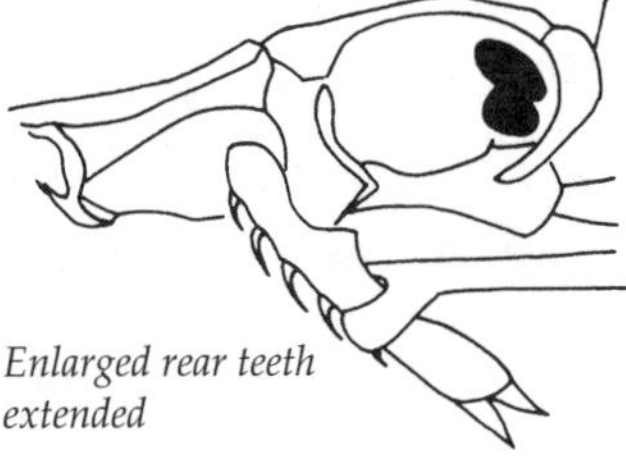

Enlarged rear teeth extended

Unlike the 2 eastern species of hog-nosed snakes, which are specialist feeders on toads, the three races of the western hog-nosed snake routinely accept, besides toads, lizards and small rodents.

Hog-nosed snakes have enlarged teeth in the rear of the upper jaw, but seldom bite. However, their saliva does contain toxins. Humans who have been bitten by these snakes, have experienced lividity, tenderness and quite considerable swelling at the bite site. Despite their tendency to not bite, wild hog-nosed snakes should be handled with care.

These snakes are egg-layers that tend to be active by day, but during the hottest weather, the western hog-nosed adopts crepuscular or nocturnal behavior patterns.

The hog-nosed snakes are stout for their length, have a moderately to prominently upturned and dorsally keeled rostral scale, from 23–25 rows of keeled body scales, and a divided anal plate.

131 MEXICAN HOG-NOSED SNAKE

Heterodon nasicus kennerlyi

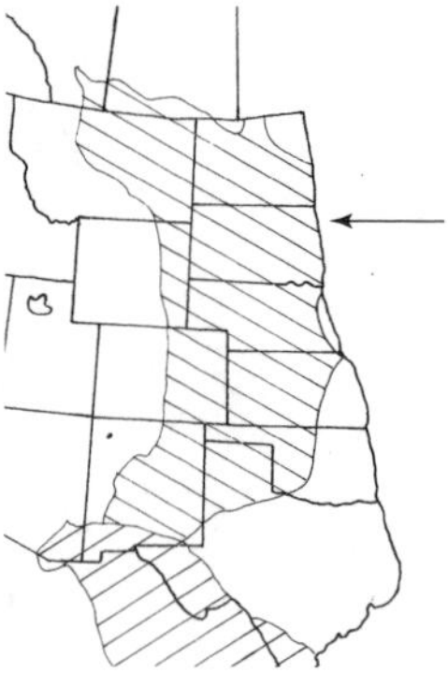

Nonvenomous Although they seldom bite, hog-nosed snakes have complex proteins and enzymes in their saliva and very elongate rear teeth in the upper jaw. Humans who have been bitten have developed tenderness, discoloration, and swelling at the bite site. These snakes should be handled carefully.

Abundance The Mexican hog-nosed snake is a rather generally distributed snake, but does not seem to be particularly common in any given area. These snakes are often most abundant, in floodplains or in other such areas, where amphibians are common.

Size While Mexican hog-nosed snakes of 20–26 in. can be considered adult, occasional specimens attain, or slightly exceed 3 ft in length.

Range This is primarily a Mexican race of the western hog-nosed snake. In the United States it occurs only in southeastern Arizona, southern New Mexico, and western Texas.

Habitat This is a snake of sand or gravel-covered, arid- and semiaridland areas, both near, and well away from temporary or permanent water sources. It occurs in areas of desert scrub, but is also found in relatively barren regions where it takes refuge from the desert sun amid boulders, pack-rat nests, in burrows, or in other such areas of seclusion.

Prey Although toads remain a favored prey item, the various races of the western hog-nosed snake actually consume a rather wide range of prey. Frogs, lizards, smaller snakes, and nestling rodents and birds are all eaten when encountered. Hatchling hog-nosed snakes also eat crickets, grasshoppers, and cicadas.

Reproduction This is an oviparous snake that can lay up to 25 eggs in a clutch. However, clutches are usually considerably smaller, and may contain as few as three (normally 6–15) eggs. Incubation varies from about 50 to more than 70 days. Hatchlings emerge as 7″ long replicas of the adult.

Coloring/scale form The dorsal and lateral ground color is variable, always subdued, but usually blends well with the substrate in which a given example is found. The dorsal and lateral surfaces are usually tan, olive-tan, light brown, or gray. The darker middorsal blotches are rather irregular, usually well-defined, but not outlined with dark pigment. The uppermost row of lateral blotches are often round(ish), may be somewhat darker than the dorsal series, but are not outlined with darker pigment. Lower rows of lateral blotches are paler and less well-defined. Six or fewer small (azygous) scales are present on the top of the snout. These are positioned posterior to the rostral scale and between the prefrontal scales. The top of the head is primarily dark. A poorly defined light mark outlines a dark interorbital bar, which then extends diagonally down, through the rear of each eye, to the jawline. A second dark teardrop shaped marking extends diagonally downward from the rear of the head to the nape. The rostral scale is sharply upturned, pointed anteriorly, and keeled dorsally. The tail is short and stout. The belly is primarily dark, but bears scattered white and/or yellow-orange spots. The subcaudal scales (the scales beneath the tail) are black. The keeled scales are in 23 rows. The anal plate is divided.

Similar snakes Hook-nosed snakes have smooth (non-keeled) scales and lack a keel on the dorsal surface of the upturned rostral scale. Eastern hog-nosed snakes do not have black subcaudal scales.

Behavior Hog-nosed snakes are particularly adept at scenting and excavating buried amphibians. Hog-nosed snakes are diurnal during cool weather, but become crepuscular, and even nocturnal, when the weather becomes uncomfortably hot.

Additional subspecies The dusty hog-nosed snake, *Heterodon nasicus gloydi,* is an extralimital Texas race.

132 Plains Hog-nosed Snake

Heterodon nasicus nasicus

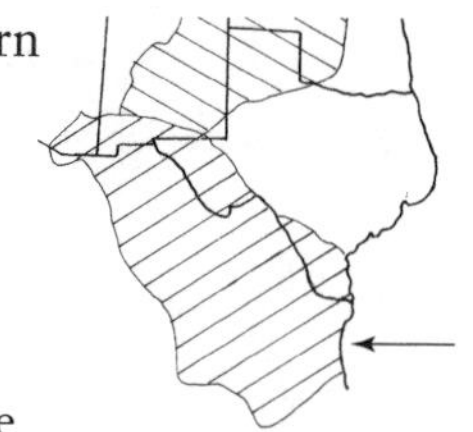

This subspecies ranges northward from southern New Mexico and northern Texas to southern Saskatchewan and southwestern Alberta. There are many narrow eastward range projections and disjunct populations both to the east and west of the main range. This is the most widely-ranging of the 3 races of western hog-nosed snake in the United States. Subtle dimorphic differences are present. Males have a dark dorsal-body-blotch count of 35 or more while females have 40, or more, blotches. The blotches contrast strongly and sharply with the tan to gray dorsal and lateral ground color, but may be somewhat paler than the alternating lateral blotches. There are 9 or more small (azygous) scales grouped on the snout immediately posterior to the rostral scale and between the prefrontals (the Mexican hog-nosed snake has 6 or fewer of these scales). The belly is predominantly black but bears scattered patches of white and/or yellow-orange. This race's natural history is very similar to that of the Mexican hog-nosed.

Comments Despite the fact that hog-nosed snakes of all species are popular as pets and are legally considered nonvenomous serpents, respect and care should be used when handling them. Bites can be uncomfortable and result in frightening symptoms.

Coral Snakes

Family Elapidae

This family contains the deadly cobras, mambas, kraits, and their allies (all of which have fixed front fangs), and is of primarily Old World distribution. Only the micrurine elapines—the coral snakes—occur in the New World. In the North American west, only a single species, the small Arizona coral snake, occurs. It is clad in rings of red, yellow, and black, with the two caution colors, yellow and red, touching.

A familiar ditty, "red to yellow, kill a fellow, red to black, venom lack," is often used to remember the color sequence that identifies the 2 coral snake species of the United States. However, we have found that, for some reason, school children have difficulty with the rhyme. We have gone, therefore, to using the sequence of lights on a traffic signal, an icon with which even very young children are familiar, to illustrate the color sequence of the coral snake—the two caution colors, red and yellow, touch.

The elapine snakes have short, fixed (immovable) fangs, are dangerously venomous, and should not be handled. Any bite by a coral snake should have medical attention. The venom is predominantly neurotoxic and a bite can be fatal.

133 ARIZONA CORAL SNAKE

Micruroides euryxanthus euryxanthus

Venomous The Arizona coral snake is nervous and "twitchy" when frightened or touched. It seems more prone to hide its head beneath its body coils than to try to bite. However, the neurotoxic venom of the Arizona coral snake is dangerously toxic and the snake should be considered a species with lethal potential.

Abundance *Micruroides* is seldom seen, but because it is so persistently fossorial, accurate population estimates seem impossible to accrue. Although this snake may actually be no more common than the very occasionally found surface-active specimen would indicate, it may, in fact, be far more common.

Size The Arizona coral snake is a small species. Most specimens seen are 15 in. or less in length; 21 in. is thought to be this snake's maximum size.

Range In the United States the Arizona coral snake occurs westward from extreme southwestern New Mexico to central Arizona. It also may be found south of our border to central Sonora, Mexico.

Habitat This small and beautiful snake occurs in myriad habitats in Arizona. It may be occasionally encountered in manicured, irrigated, yards, crossing suburban roadways (especially following a substantial rain), traversing unpopulated deserts, or on rock-strewn plains and meadows. This snake seems most common (a comparison only) on mesquite flats in river valleys. It seeks seclusion beneath rocks and other surface debris, but is also an accomplished burrower.

Prey Despite mention in the literature of this snake eating insects, it would seem likely that its diet is actually restricted entirely to small reptiles—mostly smooth-scaled snakes, with a strong preference for blind snakes of the genus *Leptotyphlops*. Besides blind snakes, ring-necked snakes, black-headed snakes, night snakes, and small skinks are also occasionally eaten.

Reproduction This is an oviparous snake species. Clutches are small, consisting of 1–3 relatively large, elongate, eggs. In Arizona, eggs are laid during the summer months, apparently in conjunction with the monsoon season. Depending on soil temperature and moisture, the incubation duration seems to last for from 55–65 days. Hatchlings are about 7.5 in. long.

Coloring/scale form The Arizona coral snake is of slender build and is colored in what Americans have come to think of as the characteristic coral snake colors and pattern. Broad bands of black, red, and yellow (the red and yellow touch) encircle the body. We hasten to mention that neither this pattern nor the colors hold true on many neotropical species.

The coral snake has a narrow head, that it may flatten when frightened. The snout is bluntly rounded. A loreal scale is lacking. The tail, ringed in black and yellow, and is quite blunt. The scales are non-keeled, quite shiny, and in 15 rows at mid body. The anal plate is divided.

Similar snakes The various king- and milk snakes have the 2 caution colors separated by bands of black. The banded phase of the ground snake usually lacks yellow bands. Both the shovel-nosed snake and the banded sand snake are saddled, not ringed, and have immaculate cream-colored bellies.

Behavior The Arizona coral snake would seem to be primarily crepuscular and nocturnal, but it may also be surface-active on cloudy or, especially, rainy days. A frightened snake may curl and elevate its tail tip, waving this to and fro, perhaps to decoy attention from its head. A curious habit of everting and withdrawing the vent lining is also indulged in. This makes a characteristic popping sound and is termed cloacal popping (this habit is shared with other desert snakes, among which are the hook-nosed snakes).

Comments Because of its secretive habits, the Arizona coral snake continues to persist even in suburban areas. It has a reputation for seldom biting, and is often handled with relative impunity. However, like many members of the cobra family, it has an unpredictable disposition and it may bite at any time. It should be considered a very dangerous snake. Despite the erroneous belief that this snake can bite only small extremities, it is capable of biting almost any exposed body part.

Sea Snakes

Family Hydrophiidae

Despite being assigned to a separate family, the sea snakes are essentially oceangoing cobras. Many genera and many more species are present in the tropical oceans of the world. Only a single species, the pelagic sea snake, *Pelamis platurus,* enters our waters, and then only by accident. All have fixed (immovable) front fangs, and all are dangerously toxic. Most are reluctant to bite unless carelessly restrained. Some apparently display increased aggression during the breeding season. All eat fish; some specialize in eels.

Sea snakes have flattened, oar-like tails, and swim with a typical side-to-side undulation. They lack enlarged belly scutes. Many are rather helpless when out of the water. Both egg-laying and live-bearing species are known.

134 Yellow-bellied Sea Snake

Pelamis platurus

Venomous Although it is seldom encountered in the United States, and seldom bites, this is a dangerously venomous snake that should be treated with extreme caution. The strongly neurotoxic venom quickly overcomes the fish on which this species feeds.

Abundance The yellow-bellied sea snake is common to abundant in many areas of the Pacific. It occurs only rarely in waters of California, but is more common in Hawaiian waters.

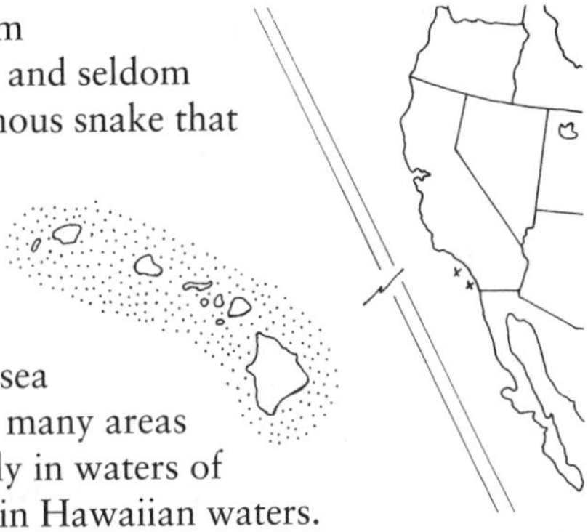

Size Although most specimens seen in the eastern Pacific are in the 18–25-in. range, in Australian waters specimens of slightly more than 3.5 ft long have been found. Neonates are 8–10 in. long.

Range This snake is, perhaps, the most widely distributed snake in the world. It is known from most areas of the Indian and Pacific oceans (including Hawaiian waters), and can be common along the pacific coasts of most Central American countries. It occurs also along Mexico's Pacific Coast (including the Baja Peninsula) and is accidental in American waters, where it has been found as far north on the California coast as southern Orange County.

Habitat Perhaps the most widely distributed snake in the world, this fully aquatic snake is entirely at home in warm ocean waters, but just as entirely out of its element when washed ashore. Movement on land is all but impossible. This snake most often occurs in the quiet slicks that are formed by converging ocean currents. It is alert, and may dive deeply at the approach of a boat.

Prey Small, surface-dwelling fish are the principal prey of this marine serpent.

Reproduction Although little is known about the breeding biology of this snake, pairs have been found knotted together and what have been thought to be large breeding congregations have been seen. It is speculated that breeding occurs only in the parts of its range where mean water temperatures attain or exceed 68°F (Dunson and Ehlert, 1971). *Pelamis* is a live-bearing sea snake. In coastal Central America, 1–6 neonates are produced.

Coloring/scale form The yellow-bellied sea snake is aptly named. It is a very dark brown to black dorsally, has bright yellow lower sides, and is often an equally bright yellow below. In some cases, the mid-ventral area may be olive-yellow. The amount of yellow may vary. In Costa Rican waters we found a snake of this species that had only a narrow vertebral stripe of black; the remainder of the snake was bright yellow. Solid yellow examples are well documented. Only typically colored specimens have been found in California. The delineation of the 2 colors is precise. The flattened, oar-like, yellow tail bears a variable black pattern. It may be barred, spotted, and/or scalloped. The snout is long and the head is distinctly triangular both in profile and when viewed from above. The gape is considerably wider than in most of the short-nosed species of sea snakes. Both the eyes and nostrils of the yellow-bellied sea snake are set high on the sides of the head. The nostrils are valvular and can be closed when the snake dives. The scales are nonimbricate (do not overlap) and although nonkeeled, are rough to the touch. Neonates are similar to the adults in color and pattern.

Similar snakes None in American waters.

Behavior The yellow-bellied sea snake is among the most extensively aquatic of any snake species. Although it is most commonly seen within a few miles of shore, it is of pelagic habits, and drifts with the ocean currents, often accumulating in some numbers where ocean currents and debris converge. This is fortuitous, for small surface-dwelling fishes, the primary dietary item of this species, also accumulate in such areas. The fish shelter, not only beneath the debris, but beneath the floating snakes themselves. The fish are captured with a lateral snap of the head (often as the snakes scull backward), and are very quickly swallowed.

Ecdysis (shedding) is facilitated by the snake forming one or more knots in its body and crawling through these. The roughened scales assist in removing the skin. It is thought that crawling through a tightly knotted body also removes such clinging creatures as barnacles.

This snake species has a reputation for being nonaggressive. This may be so, but if carelessly restrained, *Pelamis* will most definitely attempt to bite its captor.

Comments Because these sea snakes are abundant along the Pacific coast of Panama, speculation has long existed that the creatures will eventually work their way through the Panama Canal and become established in the Caribbean. This is not yet known to have happened.

RATTLESNAKES
Genus Crotalus

The genus *Crotalus* is of New World distribution. The various species occur from the southernmost of the western Canadian Provinces in the west and central New Hampshire in the east, southward through South America to Argentina. In the United States the genus is best represented west of the Mississippi River. East of the Mississippi, only two species occur, the timber and the eastern dia-

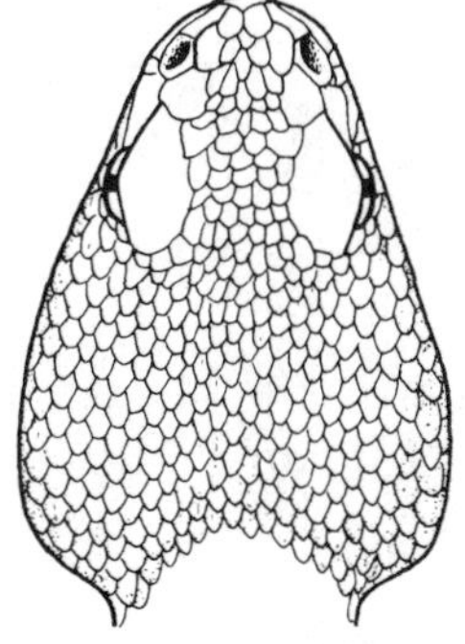

Crotalus *rattlesnake*

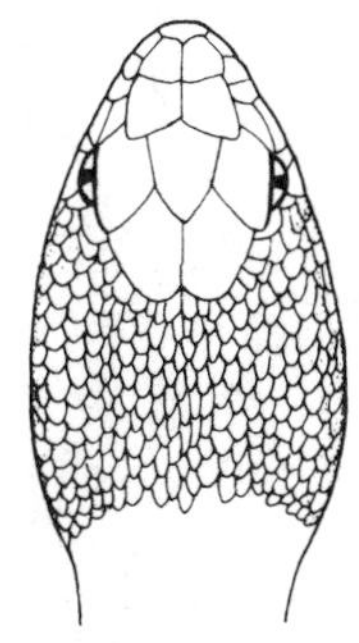

Sistrurus *rattlesnake*

mond-backed rattlesnake. However, east of the Mississippi, two smaller rattlesnakes of the genus *Sistrurus* are also widely distributed.

The rattlesnakes of the genus *Crotalus* have finely fragmented crown scales. This alone will allow easy differentiation from the rattlers in the genus *Sistrurus* which, like most harmless snakes, have 9 large plates on the top of their head.

The rattlesnakes, along with the copperheads and cottonmouths, also of eastern United States, belong to the subfamily Crotalinae, which is contained in the family Viperidae. Because of the presence of a heat (infrared) sensory pit on each side of their face, the crotalines are referred to as pit vipers. The pit permits these snakes to detect and ascertain the position of warm-blooded prey (such as mice, rats, squirrels, or rabbits) and to strike, delivering a venomous bite, unerringly, even in complete darkness.

The pit vipers have a long hollow fang attached to a rotable maxillary bone on each side of the upper jaw. The maxilla can be rotated posteriorly to fold the fangs against the roof of the mouth when the mouth is closed, or rotated anteriorly to direct the fangs almost straight forward when the snake is indulging in a gaping, lunging, forward strike. If a fang breaks it is quickly replaced. The fangs are ducted to venom glands at the rear of the head. It is these glands, and the controlling muscles that surround them, that cause the posterior enlargement so typical of the head of the viperine snakes. A pit viper can regulate the amount of venom expended during a bite. Some bites are "dry"; no venom is injected during the strike. During other bites a full complement of venom is injected. Secondary infections can be caused by any bite.

The venom, a complex combination of proteins and enzymes, has been developed primarily for food procurement and secondarily as a defense mechanism. The drop-for-drop toxicity of pit viper venom varies species by species, and even within a species.

Rattlesnakes are wait-and-ambush hunters that, by chemosensory testing, are able to unerringly position themselves along active rodent trails. Most strike and immediately release their prey, allowing the venom a chance to immobilize the stricken animal before trailing it. It has been shown that rattlesnakes are able to differentiate between the trail of a non-envenomated animal and an envenomated one, even if of the same species.

Many of the rattlesnake subspecies are only subtly different from each other. Such things as uneven, or smooth, edges to the supraocular scales or the number of internasal scales in contact with the rostral scale are identifying criteria. We hasten to advise you that if you are close enough to a living specimen to see many of these characteristic differences *you are much too close for your safety.*

When fully adult, male rattlesnakes of a given species are often larger than the females—sometimes quite considerably so.

The males of many species are known to indulge in stylized "combat rituals" or fights. These occur most often during the breeding season, and usually involve reproductively ready males. In this, the males approach each other and by pressing, venter against venter, elevate the anteriors of their body until the head is high above the ground. Eventually they may entwine necks and forebodies, and the heavier snake will topple and dominate the lighter one. No biting occurs during these bouts, and the subordinate male will usually disengage from the combat and leave the scene after sustaining several body slams.

All rattlesnakes of both genera have vertically elliptical pupils that dilate widely in the dark.

The rattle is present at birth as a single segment button. A basal segment is added at each shed. It is not until at least 2 segments are present that the rattle can produce the characteristic whirring sound.

135 Western Diamond-backed Rattlesnake, *Crotalus atrox*

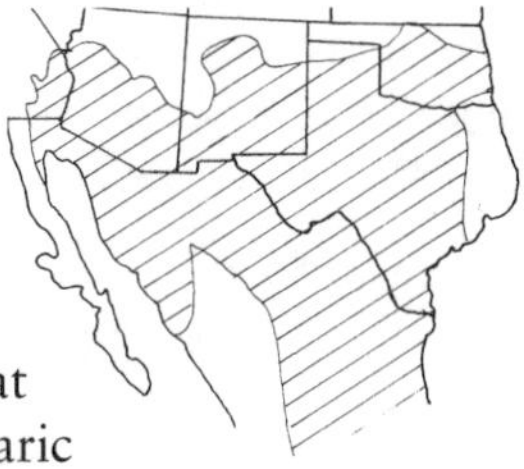

Venomous This abundant rattlesnake, which is often defensive but less often aggressive, has highly toxic venom. It should be considered very dangerous and given a wide berth.

Abundance Despite decades of persecution at the hands of humans, now including the barbaric practices of rattlesnake roundups, the western diamond-back remains abundant over most, if not all of its range. Although it may be absent from many urban areas, it continues to persist in suburban habitats and may follow canals, ditches, and riverbeds well into rather heavily populated areas. Babies may be seen in late summer and early autumn, often by the dozens, as they seek secure areas in which they may overwinter safely. They may be especially abundant on grassy or scrubby rangelands.

Size The western diamond-back is the largest of the western rattlers, and second only to the eastern diamond-back in size. Although those seen are often between one and four feet in length, specimens of five feet or more are still seen with regularity. The record size is only ⅛ in. less than 7 ft in length! Neonates vary from as small as 8.5 in. to about a foot in length.

Range This rattlesnake ranges westward and southward from central Arkansas to southeastern California and central Mexico.

Habitat This is one of the most ubiquitous of arid- and semiarid-land rattlesnakes. It occurs in sparsely vegetated desert, on rocky plains, in lushly grassed lomas, as well as in all areas between, and is the rattlesnake most commonly seen in suburban areas and crossing roadways in the evening.

Prey Neonate western diamond-backs seem to be more opportunistic feeders than the adults. Amphibians, lizards, nestling birds, and small rodents—even an occasional cicada or locust—are eaten by babies. Larger examples consume ground birds, rabbits, and rodents, but do not seem to as readily accept ectothermic (cold-blooded) prey. This species is an effective ambush hunter, positioning itself near a rodent or rabbit runway when hungry. The virulent venom quickly overcomes virtually any small mammal struck.

Reproduction Clutch size of this live-bearing snake numbers 4–25 babies. It seems that 6–10 is the usual number. Females first reproduce when they are about a yard in length and three years of age. It is probable that most females breed biennially, but some may reproduce only every third year. Males indulge in ritualistic combat (shoving and body pinning) that may be associated with the breeding biology or territoriality.

Coloring/scale form The western diamond-backed rattlesnake is one of the more variably colored species both in ground color and in pattern intensity. Typically the diamond pattern is dusty appearing but very apparent. Conversely, on some examples the pattern is pale and difficult to discern. The diamonds are outlined in shades of gray (often ash) bordered on the inside by light to very dark brown. The ground color usually blends well with the soils on which this snake is found. It may vary from pale gray through dark gray, to a deep red. The face has a prominent light diagonal preocular bar and a somewhat less prominent diagonal postocular bar. The posterior stripe touches the jawline well anterior to the rear of the mouth (do not get close enough to a living snake to ascertain this!). The tail is prominently patterned with black and white (or light gray) rings of roughly equal width. Some of these may be broken and offset middorsally. Because males have a longer tail, they often have a higher ring count, but this is far from an infallible method of determining sex. The scales are keeled, in 23 to 25 rows, and the anal plate is not divided.

Similar snakes The red diamond rattlesnake is of quite similar appearance but has scales in 29 rows, is redder than most diamond-backs and occurs in the United States only in southwestern California. The Mojave rattlesnake is also rather similar and occurs over much of the range of the western diamond-back, but has *narrow* and often broken dark tail-rings on a gray ground, often a greenish ground color, usually a stronger dorsal pattern, and the posterior facial stripe either touches the corner of the mouth or passes behind it. Other rattlesnake species are either prominently speckled, have bars rather than dorsal diamonds, or have the dorsal markings widely separated.

Behavior Although some western diamond-backs will surprise you with their comparative docility, the attitude of most examples of this big snake can be summed up in a single word: aggressive. When disturbed, the western diamond-back often stands its ground, neck raised high in an effective striking coil, head slightly lowered, and rattles madly. In fact, many specimens would remain unseen were it not for their tendency to loudly rattle at the slightest disturbance. If pressed too closely, western diamond-backs will strike repeatedly, occasionally advancing toward their antagonist, but usually either merely standing ground or backing slowly away.

The western diamond-back is active by day and evening when temperatures allow, but becomes largely nocturnal during the searing heat of an aridland summer. Rocky escarpments, earthen fissures, trash piles, and other such areas serve as denning and hiding areas.

Comments This remains one of the most common of rattlesnakes. Dozens of babies may often be seen crossing roadways on late summer and autumn evenings. During the hottest months large examples may often be seen actively crossing roadways from 11 p.m.–4 a.m. They may be especially active on the night following a rainfall. This rattlesnake can cause human fatalities. Use extreme caution when handling or photographing western diamond-backeds.

136 MOJAVE DESERT SIDEWINDER

Crotalus cerastes cerastes 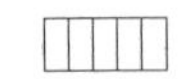

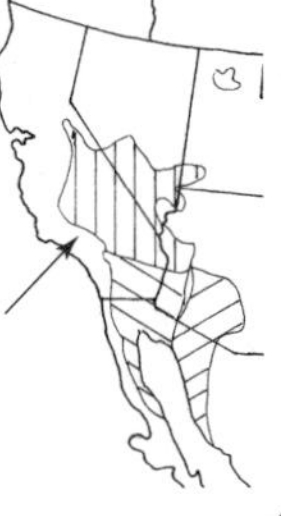

Venomous Despite the small size of this snake, relatively long fangs, a rather virulent venom, and a readiness to bite if molested, dictate that bites by this rattlesnake should be avoided. Since the venom yield is rather small, envenomation is probably not life-threatening. Envenomation will, however, be sufficiently painful to induce you to use greater future care.

Abundance In suitable habitats, this is a common rattlesnake. It is secretive and primarily nocturnal, hence easily overlooked.

Size Although most specimens seen are 12–18 in. long, sidewinders are known to attain an overall length of 33 in. Neonates are about 7 in. long at birth.

Range This is the northernmost of the 3 subspecies of sidewinder. It occurs in desert regions from extreme southwestern Utah to east-central California and southward to westcentral Arizona and adjacent California.

Habitat The northernmost of the three subspecies of sidewinder, this subspecies is typically associated with areas of fine, shifting, wind-blown sands, but it also inhabits desert areas with somewhat more stable soil characteristics. It seems particularly common in areas vegetated by creosote bushes and may often be found near kangaroo rat warrens.

Prey While young, the sidewinder feeds primarily on lizards, but also accepts nestling rodents and birds. The size and diversity of the prey increases with the growth of the sidewinder.

Reproduction It is not known with certainty whether the sidewinder is an annual or biennial breeder. From 2 to 18 live babies are produced from late summer to mid-autumn. The usual number of young is 4–10. As would be expected, smaller females produce smaller clutches.

Coloring/scale form There are few snake species that blend any better with their backgrounds than the sidewinder. Light colored specimens are usually associated with light colored soils while darker specimens often occur in regions of darker soil. The ground color of this subspecies is often darkest middorsally. There are about 40 lighter middorsal blotches that are well-defined anteriorly and posteriorly but which often blend almost imperceptibly with the ground color laterally. The light blotches are often wider than the dark interspaces. There is usually a pair of dark spots on the rear of the head. A dark, diagonal facial bar is present. The diagnostic supraocular horns are a feature shared only with the other two races of sidewinder. The Mojave sidewinder has keeled body scales in 21 rows and the basal segment of the rattle is brown. The anal plate is not divided.

Similar snakes There are several rattlesnakes of similar coloration, but only the sidewinder has supraorbital horns. In northern Baja, the Baja California rattlesnake, *Crotalus enyo*, may be encountered. Although the supraocular scales of this latter species are tipped upward, they do not extend into "horns."

Behavior The curious "sidewinding," the throwing of raised body loops to the side, is a mode of locomotion used by no other rattlesnake of North America. The sidewinder is a wait-and-ambush species which buries itself just beneath the surface of the desert sand, often in the proximity of kangaroo rat warrens, but sometimes along pocket mouse or lizard trails. In such a position, often with only the top of its head visible, the snake is easily overlooked by both prey and humans. The sidewinder is feared by humans, and summarily dispatched whenever seen. The sidewinder may be active by day in cool weather, but is crepuscular and nocturnal during the hottest months. Although easily overlooked in its desert habitat, its light body color renders the snake prominently visible when it crosses paved desert roads.

Comments The 3 subspecies of sidewinder are poorly differentiated and difficult to identify visually. Use range as a primary criterion. The sidewinder is often referred to as the horned rattlesnake.

137 SONORAN SIDEWINDER

Crotalus cerastes cercobombus 

Ranging over much of arid southcentral Arizona and northwestern mainland Mexico, this subspecies of the sidewinder is often considerably redder than the others, with the middorsal ground color being the darkest. The (approximately) 40 light dorsal blotches are often poorly defined and are usually narrower than the areas of ground color that separate them. This pretty sidewinder has 21 rows of scales and a black basal rattle segment.

138 COLORADO DESERT SIDEWINDER

Crotalus cerastes laterorepens 

This subspecies occurs in southeastern California, southwestern Arizona, northwestern Sonora, and eastern Baja California Norte. It is a pallid race on which the 40 (plus or minus a few) pale dorsal blotches are often wider than the dark interspaces. The scales are in 23 rows and the basal rattle segment is black (often brown(ish) on immature specimens).

139 NORTHERN RED DIAMOND RATTLESNAKE, *Crotalus exsul ruber*

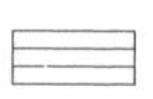

Venomous Although the venom of this rattlesnake is not as high in drop-for-drop toxicity as that of some others, the large size of adult red rattlesnakes allows a large venom-yield. Despite a reluctance of many red diamond rattlesnakes to strike, the snake should be considered dangerous and either avoided altogether or approached with caution.

Abundance The red diamond rattlesnake can be relatively common in areas of prime habitat. Despite decades of persecution in San Diego County, it continues to persist, even in the vicinity of some of the smaller cities.

Size This is a large and heavy-bodied rattlesnake. While those seen are typically 2–4.5 ft long, occasional examples attain 5 ft in length. The largest recorded specimen was 5 ft 5 in. long. Neonates are about a foot long.

Range In the United States the range of this Baja species extends only into southwestern California.

Habitat Boulder-strewn grasslands, aridland scrub, thick chaparral, and open oak and pine woodlands, are among the habitats utilized by this impressive and pretty rattlesnake. It is also occasionally encountered in agricultural districts bordered by undeveloped land.

Prey Adults feed primarily on endothermic prey species such as rabbits, ground squirrels, and wood rats. Besides nestling rodents and birds, and smaller species of mice, juvenile red diamond rattlers opportunistically feed upon lizards such as swifts and whiptails. Although it may prowl extensively in search of prey, this rattlesnake is often seen coiled in wait near a rodent trail.

Reproduction Typical clutches contain 5–12 babies. Clutches containing from 3–20 neonates have been documented.

Coloring/scale form Although variable in ground color and pattern, the reddest red diamond rattlesnakes are beautiful animals indeed. From what has come to be thought of as the typical red coloration, this snake grades downward through pink to a rather dull-reddish-tan. The diamonds are also variable in intensity and definition. Even on those specimens with the best defined, white out-lined, diamonds, these markings are paler anteriorly and posteriorly than at midbody. Some snakes have the diamonds defined only on the anterior and posterior margins, with the lateral areas merging almost imperceptibly with the lateral ground color. The tail is boldly ringed with black and white. A light, diagonal, preocular and postocular line is present. The first lower labial is divided (do not try to check this on a living snake). Neonates are much duller than the adults, often exhibiting a ground color of gray. This usually becomes suffused with red after only a shed or two. The keeled scales are in 29 rows and the anal plate is undivided.

Similar snakes Red-phase western diamond-backs can closely approximate the color of the red diamond rattlesnake. However, the ranges of the 2 species barely abut (and do not overlap).

Behavior This is a spectacular rattlesnake that usually displays a quiet non-rattling, non-aggressive demeanor. However, the occasional aggressive specimen will quickly swing into an impressively hostile striking position, neck held in a high loop, lowered head facing its antagonist, and shows every indication of being well able to defend itself. Even non-aggressive specimens may strike suddenly and without additional provocation.

Red diamond rattlers may be at least partially diurnal through even the hottest weather. This is especially so when they are in the comparative coolness of heavily shadowed boulder fields. However, the snakes certainly are also crepuscular and nocturnal during hot weather. Male to male combat is well documented. This rattlesnake occasionally partially ascends trees, shrubs, or may lie atop thick vertical grasses a foot or two above the ground.

Comments It is only recently that the red diamond rattlesnake has been considered conspecific with the Cedros Island rattlesnake, *Crotalus exsul*. Previously it was known as *Crotalus ruber ruber*.

140 BANDED ROCK RATTLESNAKE

Crotalus lepidus klauberi 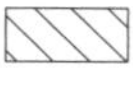

Venomous The comparatively short fangs of this little rattlesnake deliver a venom that is strongly hemorrhagic in its composition. Although probably not life-threatening to a normally healthy human, the swelling and pain associated with an envenomation would be a decidedly unpleasant experience.

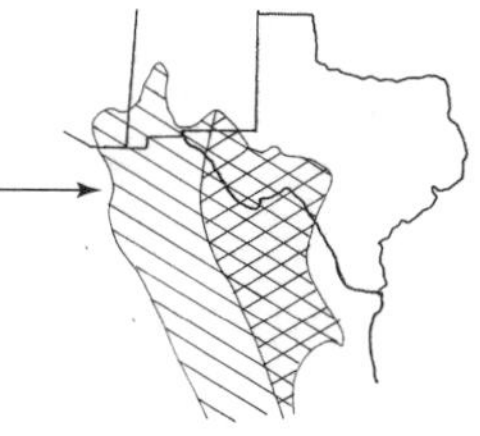

Abundance It is difficult to accurately assess populations of retiring snakes, but the banded rock rattlesnake appears to be fairly common in regions of suitable habitat. It is a species that is often more easily heard than seen.

Size The normal size range of this small rattlesnake is 12–18 in. The record size is just over 32 in. Neonates are about 7 in. long.

Range The banded rock rattlesnake is the westernmost representative of this species. It may be found in rocky, isolated canyons and mountain refuges westward from the Franklin Mountains of western Texas to several of the mountain ranges of southeastern Arizona, and southward to Jalisco, Mexico.

Habitat The habitat of this little rattler is always associated with rocks—rocky hillsides and mountain slopes, canyonside fissures, rocky dry stream- and riverbeds, and other such areas. The banded rock rattlesnake basks by day, but often hunts and seeks new territory at dusk or after darkness.

Prey Adult banded rock rattlers seem to prey preferentially on lizards, but will accept small rodents, and an occasional snake, as well. Neonates and juveniles may add invertebrates such as crickets, centipedes, and locusts to their predominantly lizard diet. Lizards are caught as they dart about the rocks and fissures this little rattlesnake calls home. Cannibalism has been documented.

Reproduction This live-bearing rattlesnake usually gives birth in July or August, but the actual parameters seem to be from mid-April (rare) to mid-September. It seems probable that the banded rock rattlesnake is a biennial breeder. Clutches number 1–8, with the usual number being 2–4.

Coloring/scale form This race has a cleaner, less busy, pattern than the mottled rock rattlesnake. In fact, many specimens of the banded rock rattlesnake lack even vestiges of secondary markings between the primary bands. There is a tendency toward sexual dimorphism, with many males having a ground color of green (moss-green to bluish-green) while that of the females is grayish to bluish. The bands are deep brown to black. This race either has no facial markings, or they are faded. The tail tip of hatchlings is bright yellow to yellow-orange. This fades, but is often not entirely lost, as the snakes mature.

Similar snakes Compare the mottled rock rattlesnake, next account. The twin-spotted rattlesnake (restricted to a few mountain tops in southeastern Arizona (and then southward into Mexico) is grayish to brownish with twinned dorsal spots and a prominently banded tail.

The massasauga prefers grassland habitats, and has 9 large scales and prominent dark bars on the top of its head. The speckled rattlesnake occurs far to the west of the mottled rock rattler.

Behavior This is a feisty little rattler that is quick to buzz if disturbed, quick to bite if restrained, and quick to seek seclusion in horizontal fissures or amongst jumbles of rocks if approached. It often continues to rattle long after it has retreated out of sight to safety. When cool, the banded rock rattlesnake often thermoregulates from the comparative safety of a fissure by extending a body coil out into the warming sunlight. As its body temperature nears optimum more and more of the coil is drawn back into the shade. This little snake is active principally by day, but when temperatures become very hot it may remain active until long after nightfall.

Comments This race is less often seen on roadways than the mottled rock rattlesnake, but may occasionally be encountered on hot summer nights following an afternoon shower.

141 MOTTLED ROCK RATTLESNAKE

Crotalus lepidus lepidus 

Also a snake of rocky mountain sides, cliff-faces, escarpments and outcroppings, and fissured canyon walls, this more easterly subspecies occasionally wanders quite far afield and may be encountered considerable distances from typical habitat.

In the United States, the mottled rock rattlesnake is largely restricted to western Texas, from the Edwards Plateau to Hudspeth County. It also occurs in Eddy and Otero counties, New Mexico. It ranges southward to the vicinity of San Luis Potosi, Mexico.

Despite coming from a relatively small range, the mottled rock rattlesnake is quite variable in color. The ground color typically blends well with the color of the rocks among which the snake is found. The ground color can vary from pinkish, to russet, to gray, to bluish-gray, to a chalky white (and all colors between these). The primary bands are usually at least faintly visible (sometimes vividly so), and the secondary mottling is somewhat less contrasting. This snake is capable of quite considerable day to night color changes. The top of the head is weakly mottled or plain. A diagonal dark bar is present from beneath each eye to the corner of the mouth. The weakly banded tail is a rather bright yellow to orange at birth, but darkens somewhat as the snake ages. The keeled body scales are arranged in 23 rows. The anal plate is not divided.

The normal size range of this small rattlesnake is 12–18 in. The record size is just over 30 in. Neonates are about 7 in. long.

142 SOUTHWESTERN SPECKLED RATTLESNAKE

Crotalus mitchellii pyrrhus 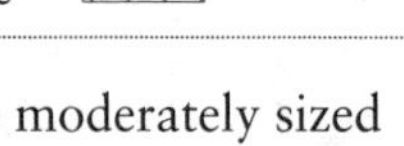

Venomous This is another of the moderately sized rattlesnake species with a formidably potent venom and, often, with a nervous, ready-to-bite, demeanor. It should be either studiously avoided or approached with extreme caution.

Abundance This rattlesnake can be relatively abundant in suitably rocky habitats. Because of its nearly perfect camouflage, it can be easily overlooked unless the snake is moving or becomes defensive, when it then may rattle furiously.

Size This rattlesnake attains 2–3.5—occasionally 4—ft in length. The head is rather small, but body girth is considerable. Neonates are 8.5–10.5 in. long.

Range This race ranges northward from southern Baja California (Norte) and northern Sonora to the vicinity of Riverside County, California, extreme southern Nevada, and western Arizona.

Habitat Rock- and boulder-strewn areas are favored habitats of this aridland rattlesnake. It occurs in open, sparsely vegetated, and succulent desert. Look for it also near the sides of buttes and mesas, and near desert outcroppings and escarpments.

Prey Warm-blooded prey seems favored by adults of this rattlesnake, but neonates and juveniles readily accept lizards. Like most other rattlesnakes, prey is sometimes found while the snakes are actively prowling. However, wait-and-ambush techniques, with the snakes quietly coiled along rodent or lizard trails, or in the proximity of an entry-exit from a kangaroo rat warren, are often successfully employed.

Reproduction This rattlesnake is seen breeding, often partially secluded by boulders, soon after emergence from the denning site. It is not known whether this snake produces young annually or biennially, but it seems likely that it is the latter, especially in cool regions. Clutches contain between 2 and 11 neonates, but normally between

3 and 8 are produced. It seems probable that gravid females of this rattlesnake give birth well prior to their return to the denning site.

Coloring/scale form The southwestern speckled rattlesnake displays a great variety of ground colors and a far less precise pattern than most rattlesnakes. In fact, it is the most variable and intricately colored of the rattlesnakes of the United States.

The ground color may vary from off-white to yellowish, from tan to gray, or from pinkish to orange. The darker crossbands are hazy and have imprecise edges. Speckles of dark pigment in the light areas, and vice versa, are the norm in this race. Some individuals from regions of dark rocks and/or ancient lava beds may be almost black. The tail is usually rather conspicuously banded, and darkest near the tip. A light triangle, bordered by a darker bar fore and aft, is usually present beneath each eye. The supraocular scales are not wrinkled and there is a row of small scales separating the prenasals from the rostral scale. Neonates look pretty much like the adults, but may be just a bit more precisely patterned.

Similar snakes Sidewinders move in a characteristic mode, oblique to the direction in which their head is pointing. They also have raised supraoculars ("horns"). Western diamond-backs have a coon's tail of black and white rings. Mojave rattlers have enlarged scales on top of the head and black and gray rings of uneven width on their tail. The southern Pacific and the northern Pacific rattlesnakes tend to have distinctly diamond-shaped dorsal blotches at midbody. The related Panamint rattlesnake (next account) has wrinkling on the supraocular scales, and no row of small scales between the rostral and the prenasal scales, and, usually, a far more precise pattern.

Behavior The southwestern speckled rattlesnake seldom shows the tolerance for approach displayed by the more northerly Panamint rattlesnake. The speckled is almost invariably irascible, and usually rattles loudly and strikes furiously if closely approached. Cool weather induces diurnal activity in the spring, autumn, and throughout its period of activity in naturally cool habitats. However, the southwestern speckled rattlesnake becomes crepuscular and nocturnal wherever in its range truly hot summer daytime temperatures prevail.

Comments During the summer months, speckled rattlesnakes often utilize the unused burrows of ground squirrels, kangaroo rats, or the middens of wood rats for seclusion. *Crotalus mitchellii* is considered a Baja species by biologists. Both Lilliputian and Brobdignagian races occur on Baja islands.

143 PANAMINT RATTLESNAKE

Crotalus mitchellii stephensi

Found in eastern central California and western southern Nevada, the Panamint rattlesnake is primarily associated with rocky, aridland foothill, escarpment and outcropping habitats, but may also be encountered in sandy creosote bush and cactus-studded desert settings, and even in open coniferous woodlands. It is often seen crossing transdesert roadways in the early to late evening. Because of its solitary and secretive summer habits, and camouflage coloration, Panamint rattlesnakes may be thought to be uncommon where such is not actually the case. A better idea of area populations can often be gotten in the autumn, when the snakes gather at traditional denning sites—fissured escarpments and ledges, abandoned mines, caves, and other such settings. At some dens, 20, 50, or even more snakes will congregate.

This is a rather small-headed, heavy-bodied, large-rattled rattlesnake that can be difficult to positively identify. The ground color of this interesting rattlesnake is variable, tending to blend well with the color of the sand and rocks amongst which the snakes dwell. The ground color can be buff, tan, yellowish, or grayish, and the darker bands, which are usually rather well defined and margined with lighter pigment, may also be diamond-shaped. The head often lacks any well-defined pattern, but frequently bears a diffuse, gray or tan, diagonally oriented, subocular triangle. The dorsal surface of each supraocular scale is often greaved (puckered), pitted, or has weakly uneven outer edges. The tail is narrowly, but evenly and distinctly banded, blackens distally, and the dark color also encompasses the basal rattle segment. Neonates are very similar to the adults, but may be somewhat more precisely marked. There are 23–27 rows of keeled scales and the anal plate is not divided.

Although other subspecies may exceed 4 ft in length, most specimens of the Panamint rattlesnake are considerably smaller; 2–3 ft seems the more usual size. Neonates average 10 in.

This snake varies somewhat in temperament, some specimens lying quietly until actually prodded, while others will assume a striking coil and rattle loudly while a disturbing object is still some distance away.

144 Northern Black-tailed Rattlesnake

Crotalus molossus molossus 

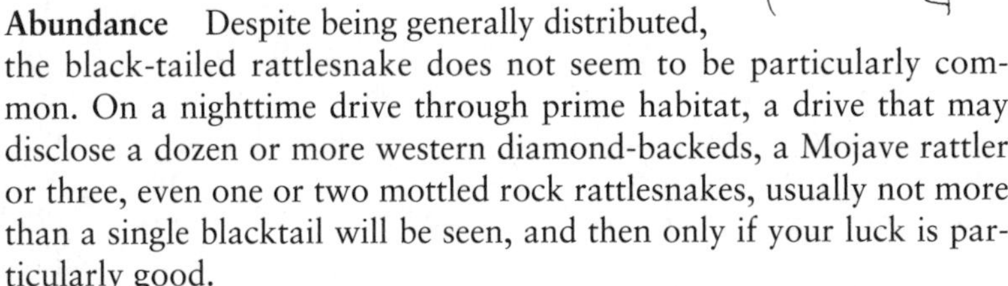

Venomous This is a large rattlesnake with a dangerously toxic venom, but is a species that is nowhere nearly as apt to bite as some of its aridland counterparts.

Abundance Despite being generally distributed, the black-tailed rattlesnake does not seem to be particularly common. On a nighttime drive through prime habitat, a drive that may disclose a dozen or more western diamond-backeds, a Mojave rattler or three, even one or two mottled rock rattlesnakes, usually not more than a single blacktail will be seen, and then only if your luck is particularly good.

Size Although occasional specimens may attain just over 4.5 ft long, most specimens seen are 1.5–3.5 ft long. Neonates are about 10.5 in. long.

Range The range of the black-tailed rattlesnake extends westward from Texas' Edwards Plateau to western Arizona and from southern Sonora to northern Arizona and northwestern New Mexico.

Habitat In the minds of many, the presence of a black-tailed rattlesnake signifies open country, and rugged open country at that. It is a rattlesnake of rocky canyons and mountains, of talus and lava beds, of desert arroyos, rocky plains and floodplains. It has been found in arid dunelands, in boulder-strewn flatlands, in creosote-opuntia desertlands and in coniferous and mixed woodlands. It is a habitat generalist, yet a monument to the now rapidly developing deserts that were considered wastelands in the days of yore. It is the rattlesnake of the western states that is more apt than other species to ascend into trees and shrubs to forage and bask.

Prey Ground squirrels, rabbits, wood rats and other desert mammals, and ground-dwelling or low-nesting birds, comprise the diet of larger individuals, but smaller black-tailed rattlesnakes accept nestling rodents and birds, as well as pocket and piñon mice and lizards.

Reproduction Other than clutch size and parturition dates, the reproductive biology of this large rattlesnake remains pretty much unknown. Male to male combat has been reported both in the wild and in captivity. Copulation has been seen in February, March, May, June and July. It is not known whether females produce young annually, biennially, or even less frequently. Parturition has occurred in late July, throughout August, and in early September. Clutches have contained from 3 to 16 neonates, with 4 to 9 being the norm.

Coloring/scale form The black-tailed rattlesnake shows a considerable east to west color change. In Texas, the ground color varies from greenish brown to silvery-green. The dorsal color is alternating black and silver or silver-gray blotches which become less contrasting and more poorly defined, posteriorly. The neck tends to bear black stripes. The black dorsal blotches, variable and uneven in outline, usually contain light centers (which may break the dark blotch laterally), or at least a few light scales. These blotches narrow laterally and often continue to the venter as a thin irregular dark bar. The nose, from above the eyes to the tip, is suffused with dark pigment. A broad, diagonal, dark bar extends from the crown, through the eye, to the angle of the mouth. It is bordered anteriorly by a broad, rather well-defined, light bar, and posteriorly, by a more poorly defined light bar. The tail is black.

In New Mexico, the ground color may be rather similar, but somewhat more intense than that of specimens from Texas. Arizona specimens may have a grayish or gray-green ground color, or may be a greenish yellow to deep gold. The light dorsal areas of yellow specimens are also correspondingly brighter.

Examples from the Harcuvar Mountains (central western Arizona) may have black only on the tail, being otherwise patterned in gray-green and yellow-green, with a light nose.

Neonates of Texas specimens are rather similar to the adults, but a degree of barring is visible on the tail. Neonates of the yellow Arizona examples tend to be paler than the adults, but barring is still visible on the tail.

Similar snakes The (usually) dark nose, black tail, and light-spotted dark blotches present a diagnostic suite of characteristics.

Behavior Many black-tailed rattlesnakes are quiet and disinclined to strike unless seriously threatened or injured. Others, if startled, may immediately swing into a striking coil, neck high and head lower, hiss, and strike if approached.

This is a cold-tolerant rattlesnake, and, except on very cool days, it may forage throughout most of the winter. It may be active either by day or night, but during the hottest weather, is primarily nocturnal.

Comments Despite its reputation of being a reluctant striker, a full envenomation by a large black-tailed rattlesnake can have very serious consequences. Whether quiet or feisty, every specimen should be treated with the same respect and caution.

145 TWIN-SPOTTED RATTLESNAKE

Crotalus pricei pricei 

Venomous Because few studies have been done, the drop-for-drop toxicity of the venom of this species is unknown. Ernst (1992) states "The venom is probably highly toxic, but the yields are low." While Lowe, Schwalbe, and Johnson (1986) agree that the yield is low, they state "The few studies indicate a venom of moderate to very low toxicity." Despite these discrepancies, the small size of the snake, and the low venom yield, we feel that due care should be used by researchers and others who have occasion to handle a twin-spotted rattlesnake.

Abundance While not uncommon in suitable habitat, neither could this protected, secretive, rattlesnake be called truly common. Because it is so retiring, it is difficult to assess the viability of most populations with any great accuracy.

Size Although this little rattlesnake is known to attain 26 in. in length, most seen are 12–18 in. Neonates are 6–8 in. long.

Range In the United States this little rattlesnake is restricted in distribution to sub-summit and summit areas of several rugged mountain chains in the southeastern corner of Arizona. From this restricted United States range, it occurs in suitable mountain habitats at least as far south as southern Durango, Mexico

Habitat This is a high-elevation species. The lowest elevation at which this species occurs in Arizona is about 6,200 ft. From this it ranges upward to 10,700 ft. It is a species well adapted to life in rocky montane meadows, fissured outcroppings, and extensive slopes of talus.

Prey The twin-spot is primarily a lizard eater, feeding extensively on mountain (Yarrow's) spiny lizard. Small rodents are also accepted by some, but apparently not all, specimens.

Reproduction Details of breeding in the wild seem unknown. Captive snakes have bred both in the late autumn (immediately prior to artificial induced hibernation) and in the spring and early summer. In keeping with the small size of this snake, clutches are also small; 2–9 babies are born in midsummer, coinciding with the birth of mountain spiny lizards. One captive female produced 3 young on each of 2 successive years. It is not known whether the twin-spot is an annual, biennial, or triennial breeder in the coolness of its mountain homelands.

Coloring/scale form This is a small, slender, rattlesnake with a relatively narrow head and a small rattle. It has grayish ground color (occasionally with the vaguest blush of pink dorsally) and paired dark paravertebral spots, which are occasionally connected dorsally to form a short, dumbbell-shaped blotch. A nearly horizontal, dark, postorbital marking is often present. The crown of the head may bear several dark spots, and the banded tail is yellowish at the tip. Neonates are so dark that their dorsal markings are largely obscured.

Similar snakes None.

Behavior Ready to rattle, but retiring, and not particularly feisty would describe the attitude of most specimens of this quietly colored rattlesnake. It is one of the several montane forms that would be discovered far less frequently if it were not so prone to rattle. These snakes are often encountered coiled quietly in patches of sun along hiking paths, or basking atop talus following a summer rain. In the wild they seem active primarily by day, but captive specimens also forage after darkness has fallen.

Comments Unless you make a concerted effort to find this little rattler in its Sky Island home, it is unlikely that it will cross your path, either literally or figuratively. Mountain hikes through rocky meadows and along the base of talus may bring you into the realm of the twin-spotted rattler.

146 MOJAVE RATTLESNAKE

Crotalus scutulatus scutulatus

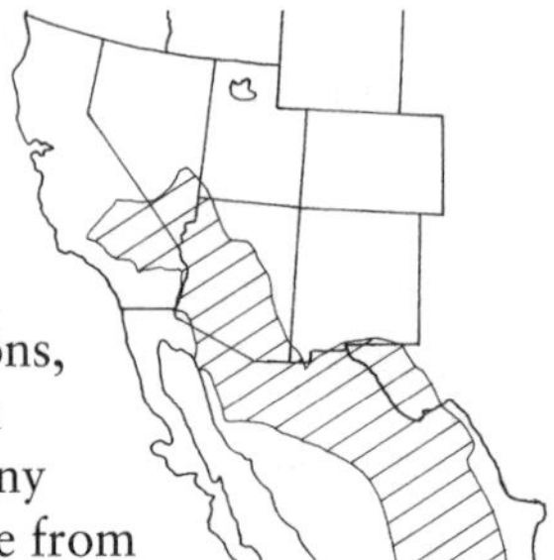

Venomous The potent neurotoxic property of the venom of this rattlesnake is legend—but the legend is not always deserved. In reality, the venom is populationally variable, being extremely virulent and highly neurotoxic in some regions, and largely without neurotoxic properties in other regions. However, envenomation by any snake is not a pleasant experience, and a bite from even a non-neurotoxic Mojave rattler will have you wondering exactly why you were careless enough to get within striking distance. The legendary neurotoxin is identifiable, and is now called Mojave-toxin.

Abundance The Mojave rattlesnake is a relatively common species but in many areas its true population statistics are skewed because it is often mistaken for the even more abundant, and often sympatric, western diamond-backed. It is, perhaps, more uncommon in its eastern (Texas) segment of range than it is in Arizona and California.

Size The Mojave rattlesnake is not a particularly large species, nor is it quite as proportionately heavy-bodied as some other rattlers. Most seen are in the 18–40 in. range and the largest recorded specimen measured only 4.25 ft in length. Neonates are about 10.5 in. long.

Range In the United States the Mojave rattler is present in two northward extending populations, disjunct in the U.S., but fully contiguous in northern Mexico. One U.S. population occurs in western Texas and immediately adjacent southcentral New Mexico. The other population extends westward from southwestern New Mexico to southern California. The main range of this snake is in northern and central mainland Mexico. This rattler does not occur along the Mexican boundary in California.

Habitat This rattlesnake is essentially a species of rock-strewn grasslands, desert scrub areas, and rocky, vegetated mountain slopes. Plant communities with which it is associated include mesquite, Joshua tree, cholla and prickly pear, and creosote bush.

Prey Even when a neonate, this rattlesnake shows a preference for endothermic prey. Necessarily varying according to the size of the snake, the prey animals favored include various species of mice, rats, ground squirrels, rabbits and hares. Lizards, other snakes, toads, and an occasional invertebrate may also be accepted by a hungry snake.

Reproduction As with several other rattlesnake species, little is known with certainty about the breeding biology of the Mojave rattlesnake in the wild. Based on examination of male gonads, it is suspected that copulation may occur both in the autumn and the spring. Neonates are most commonly found in mid-August, but have been found from mid-July to September. Clutch size numbers 2–13, with the normal number being 3–7.

Coloring/scale form Because of the irregular, very well defined, dark, diamond- or rhomboid-shaped markings on its back, the Mojave rattlesnake was long referred to as the Mojave diamondback. The dorsal markings have light centers and are usually rather broadly margined with dark brown pigment. The ground color may vary from greenish yellow, through tan, to brownish, or olive. Of the two rows of lateral blotches, the uppermost is only faintly defined, but the lower row contrasts strongly with the ground color. There are two light, diagonal, facial stripes. The aft stripe passes downward behind the angle of the jaws. The tail is ringed, the dark rings being irregular, often offset vertebrally, and less than half as wide as the white to light-gray ones.

Typically, the Mojave has a characteristic crown scalation. Rather than being fully fragmented, there are usually 2 or 3 rather large scales between the supraoculars. These are followed by numerous crown scales that are proportionately, but variably, larger than those on the heads of all rattlesnakes, other than those in the genus *Sistrurus*. This seems a good, but difficult to ascertain field mark in specimens from the western populations. However, it is less constant on specimens from Texas, many of which have nearly fully fragmented crown scales. Neonates are very similar to the adults in appearance. The scales are in 25 rows and the anal plate is undivided.

Similar snakes The western diamond-back has well-defined black and white tail rings of equal width. The red diamond rattlesnake also has a more precise coontail pattern, and, even the duller examples have a redder ground color than the Mojave.

Behavior Despite having the ability to put on a very impressive defensive display, the Mojave is often a quiet rattlesnake that would rather avoid, than confront a threat. When frightened, it often lowers (rather than elevates) its head and raises its tail which is then flicked slowly from side to side, producing a very minimal, but quite audible, "tick-tick-ticking" sound. However, once enraged, *C. s. scutulatus* can become an animated and formidable adversary, rattling loudly, and striking with such force that its entire body may slide forward.

This snake species spends considerable periods in the unused burrows of small mammals, and does not, apparently, congregate in any great numbers to hibernate.

These snakes bask, and even forage, diurnally during cool weather. However, during the heat of summer they are extensively nocturnal.

Comments Because of its superficially similar pattern and coloration, the Mojave rattlesnake is often confused with the western diamond-backed rattlesnake. However, the Mojave rattlesnake does not indulge in the impressive defensive displays of the western diamond-back and seems less prone to stand its ground when confronted with a perceived threat.

147 TIGER RATTLESNAKE, *Crotalus tigris*

Venomous Studies indicate that the tiger rattlesnake has a very virulent venom (containing a high percentage of neurotoxins) but, because of its small head, a relatively low venom yield. Despite the low yield, this rattlesnake should be treated with a great amount of respect and caution.

Abundance Although seemingly not present in any great concentrations, the tiger rattlesnake has been found in a great many locations in Arizona. For this reason it is not considered a rare species.

Size This is a rather small but heavy-bodied rattlesnake. Most seen are between 18–26 in. long, but occasional males near or attain 36 in. Neonates are about 9 in. long.

Range The range of this small but impressive rattlesnake extends northward from southern Sonora, Mexico to southcentral Arizona.

Habitat The tiger rattlesnake is firmly associated with rocky hillsides, canyons, escarpments, outcroppings, and cliff-faces in thornscrub desert. Plant associations include saguaro-ocotillo, as well as mesquite-creosote bush. The snake seldom roams far from rocky terrain. It occurs upward on some rock-strewn, vegetated, desert slopes to the lowest level of the evergreen hardwoods.

Prey Lizards and small rodents comprise the prey items of the tiger rattlesnake. It seems probable that neonate and juvenile tiger rattlesnakes are quite dependent on lizards as prey.

Reproduction There have been few observations made regarding the reproductive biology of the tiger rattler. It is speculated that breeding occurs when the snakes emerge from winter dormancy (April). Successfully bred captive females have produced young annually. Clutch sizes are 1–6, with 2–4 (often 3) being the normal number.

Coloring/scale form A small head, a heavy body, and a proportionately huge rattle, typify this interesting and variably colored rattlesnake. The ground color varies from almost black, through gray, to buff, yellow, and orange. The bands, which are most prominently dorsally (or, if you prefer, most diffuse laterally) are gray, through brown, to lava black, and extend from neck to tail tip. The head is either vaguely patterned or unpatterned. The scales are keeled and in 23 rows. The anal plate is undivided.

Similar snakes Except for the southwestern speckled rattlesnake which has a proportionately larger head and a row of small scales between the rostral and the prenasal scales, other rattlesnake species have diamonds, rhombi, or blotches, rather than bands.

Behavior Many examples of this unique rattlesnake are reluctant to rattle or strike. Others may be a little more feisty. Occasionally basking by day, the tiger rattlesnake seems more inclined to nocturnal activities than many other members of the genus. This is true even in relatively cool weather. It seems to be seen with the greatest frequency in August and September, late in Arizona's annual cycle of rains (monsoons).

Comments It has been suggested that the very small head of this snake is an adaptation that allows the extraction of immobilized, envenomated prey from narrow crevices in the rocky escarpments and canyonsides that this snake inhabits.

148 Grand Canyon Rattlesnake

Crotalus viridis abyssus 

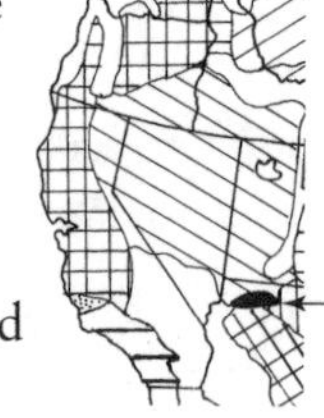

Venomous Because of the small range of this race, the composition of its primarily hemorrhagic venom is more uniform than that of some other subspecies, and because of its relatively small size, smaller quantities are delivered during a bite. However, this should be considered a dangerously venomous snake, and it should be approached with extreme caution.

Abundance This is the most distribution-restricted of the many races of western rattlesnake. Although it is not frequently seen, neither is this subspecies thought to be particularly rare.

Size The usual size of this rattlesnake is 18–32 in. In rare instances 36 in. (record, 39 in.) is attained. Neonates are about 9.5 in. long.

Range The Grand Canyon of northwestern Arizona is the sole range of this subspecies.

Habitat The Grand Canyon rattler, in its purest form, is known only from well within the interior of the canyon. It inhabits piñon-juniper woodlands as well as desert- and mesquite- scrublands.

Prey Lizards, amphibians, small mammals and ground nesting birds are all known to be included in the diet of *Crotalus viridis abyssus.* Neonate specimens also include non-noxious insects in the diet.

Reproduction As are all rattlesnakes, the many races of the western rattlesnake are live-bearing. The clutch size of the Grand Canyon rattler varies between 2–13, with 6–8 being the norm. Parturition apparently occurs biennially.

Coloring/scale form Despite the color reference in both the scientific and common names of the midget faded rattlesnake, in lacking a contrasting pattern, the Grand Canyon rattler should share equal honors. Individual snakes are capable of limited color change. The ground color of this pretty rattler is often of some shade of pink, but may vary from nearly cream to salmon. The ground color is lightest dorsally. The darker, narrow, dorsal blotches, often barely visible and occasionally absent, are, when present, best defined anteriorly and posteriorly, usually blending almost imperceptibly with the ground color laterally. The upper row of lateral blotches, usually rather readily discernible on other races, is often poorly defined. There is a tendency for the ventrolateral row of blotches to be somewhat better defined, but they usually lack a light border. The head is weakly patterned, but vestiges of a diagonal preocular and a postocular stripes may remain. Neonates are much more strongly patterned than the adults. Usually more than two internasal scales touch the rostral scale. The tail is banded, most distinctly distally. The basal segment of the rattle is dark (often black). The keeled scales are usually in 25 (23–27) rows and the anal plate is undivided.

Similar snakes Although, admittedly, almost impossible to ascertain on a living snake, the presence of more than two internasal scales is diagnostic of the many subspecies of the western rattlesnake. Use range and body color to separate the Grand Canyon rattler from the other races of the western rattlesnake and from other rattlesnake species.

Behavior This snake may either rattle furiously or lay quietly when approached. Its demeanor is not normally as adversarial as that of some other races. The Grand Canyon rattler is largely diurnal in its activity patterns, but may also be crepuscular and nocturnal when temperatures allow. This seems particularly true when the snake is hungry and lying quietly in wait at the edge of a rodent or lizard trail.

Comments Collectively, the subspecies of this snake are called "western rattlesnakes." There is a marked difference in attitudes among the subspecies, with the prairie, and the northern Pacific rattlesnakes being most defensive—actually aggressive at times—and the Arizona black rattlesnake being relatively complacent. Do remember that these are merely comparisons.

"Pure" Grand Canyon rattlesnakes occur only within the confines of the Grand Canyon. Those examples near the rim are considered intergrades. The Grand Canyon rattlesnake is known to intergrade with the Great Basin rattlesnake, the Hopi rattlesnake, and the midget faded rattlesnake.

149 Arizona Black Rattlesnake

Crotalus viridis cerberus 

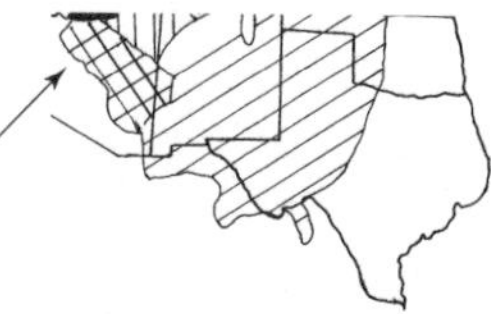

This is a montane subspecies found in a west-east swath across central Arizona and in adjacent western New Mexico. Although dangerously venomous, it tends to be less irascible than many other races. Adults are of moderate size, attaining 28–36 in. Occasional specimens may reach a length of 42 in. This, the darkest of the western rattlesnake group, is capable of considerable color change. By day, the snakes are the darkest, some having both a ground and a blotch color of jet black. On these, the blotches are discernible only because they are narrowly outlined with yellow. The ground color of the same snake may lighten to olive- or blackish gray by night, at which time the light-outlined, darker blotches are readily visible. Other examples are lighter, varying from a dark-blotched, rather light gray to brownish gray. The blotches are best defined on the posterior two-thirds of the body. The facial pattern of a diagonal, light, preorbital and postorbital bar may be rather strongly apparent or, as is often the case, virtually indiscernible. Narrow light bands are visible on the tail of light-colored examples. Neonates, which number from 3–12 (usually 5–8), and which are about 10 in. long, are much lighter and more boldly patterned than even the lightest colored adults.

The keeled scales are usually in 25 (23–27) rows and the anal plate is undivided.

150 Midget Faded Rattlesnake

Crotalus viridis concolor 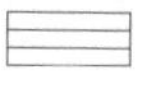

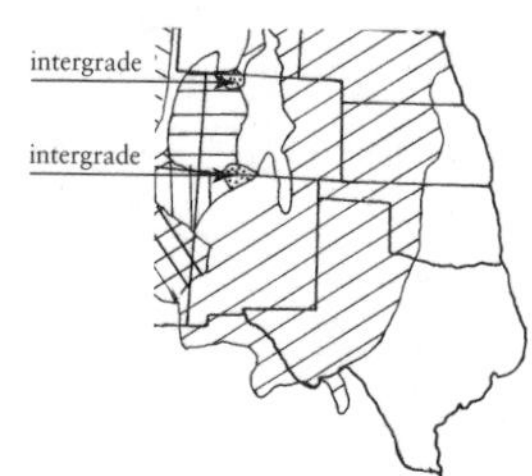

Quite similar in appearance to the Grand Canyon rattler, this subspecies is clad in scales of tan, cream, or yellow-brown and has rather well-defined to virtually indiscernible darker dorsal blotches. If present, the dorsal blotches may be defined by darker pigment along their anterior and posterior margins. The dorsal surface of the head is largely unpatterned and the 2 typical facial stripes are obscure. The basal segment of the rattle is dark. Neonate midget faded rattlesnakes are about 7.5 in. long, number from 2–10 (normally 3–6) in each clutch, and are more prominently patterned than the adult snakes. The keeled scales are usually in 25 rows and the anal plate is undivided. In drop-for-drop toxicity, the venom of this race surpasses that of other subspecies. Despite its small size (18–24 in., rarely a little more) the midget faded rattlesnake, which can be moderately aggressive, should be considered a dangerously venomous snake. This race ranges in suitable rocky desert and plains habitats over much of eastern Utah, immediately adjacent southwestern Wyoming, and western Colorado. It is considered uncommon by many researchers.

151 SOUTHERN PACIFIC RATTLESNAKE

Crotalus viridis helleri 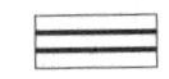

One of the larger subspecies, adults are 30–44 in long; occasional specimens may attain a length of 4.5 ft. This southern California and Baja race is very similar to the Arizona black rattlesnake, but has a brown to olive-brown ground color and deeper brown, dorsal blotches that are completely outlined by light (cream to yellowish) pigment. The blotches are obscure anteriorly, and in the form of bars on the posterior fifth or so of the body. Between these the markings are well-defined diamonds. The two light facial markings are diffuse, and may do little more than to outline the dark uborbital triangle between them. The tail is ringed, and the terminal dark tail-ring is more than twice the width of the more anterior rings. The keeled scales are usually in 25 rows and the anal plate is undivided. This attractive and moderately aggressive rattlesnake is pretty much a habitat generalist. It may be encountered in areas as diverse as seaside habitats, grassy plains, scrubby deserts, rocky hillsides, agricultural areas, and open woodlands. Neonates average about 10 in. in length, about 7 (between 3 and 14 are birthed) per clutch, and are vividly patterned.

152 Great Basin Rattlesnake

Crotalus viridis lutosus

This subspecies ranges widely over much of the west, from northwestern California eastward and northward to western Utah, southern Wyoming, and southeastern Oregon. Rocky hillsides, buttes, mesas, grassy plains, meadows, barren alkali flats and agricultural areas are all readily colonized by these abundant, 3–4-ft-long, snakes.

The Great Basin rattler has an ash-gray, tan, yellowish, or buff ground color. The dorsal pattern consists of well-separated, light centered, deep brown, bars, that are wider anteriorly than posteriorly. These may be imprecisely edged and light-centered, or rather well defined and lack light centers. Vestiges of light pigment may further define the bars on the anterior two-thirds of the snake's body. The tail is barred and the terminal dark bar is very wide and often almost black in color. The 2 light facial stripes vary from well defined to virtually nonexistent. When the snake is young, the top of the head bears an intricate pattern of dark blotching separated by light lines, and a light line from eye to eye. This also diffuses with advancing age. Females produce young biennially or triennially, depending on how fast they can replace their body fat content. The precisely patterned neonates number 3–14 (normally 5–8) per clutch, and are about 10 in. long. The scales are keeled, usually in 25 rows and the anal plate is undivided.

153 Hopi Rattlesnake

Crotalus viridis nuntius 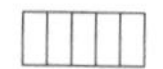

This race tends to be rather slender, with a ground color of reddish gray, reddish brown, pink, or pale orange. This small snake figures rominently in the ceremonial dances of the Hopi (and other) Indians where it is handled with relative impunity. Despite this, it can be short-tempered and is capable of producing a rather serious envenomation. It should be considered dangerous. It is adult at from 18–24 in. in length, but may occasionally attain a full 27 in. The dorsal markings are widest anteriorly, in the form of light-margined, well-defined blotches or wide-bars centrally, but are paler, not as prominent, and lack light edging posteriorly. The tail is barred; the basal rattle segment is black. The facial stripes are well defined; the anterior bars and the dark suborbital marking often meet on top of the snout. Posteriorly, the dorsal surface of the head tends to be entirely or largely, unpatterned. The Hopi rattler tends to feed largely on lizards, a prey lacking the potential to replace the snake's body fat quickly. Because of this, female Hopi rattlesnakes probably reproduce either biennially or triennially. The neonates are strongly patterned, about 7 in. long at birth, and number up to 10 (normally 3–6) per clutch.

The Hopi rattlesnake occurs in northwestern Arizona and immediately adjacent Utah and New Mexico, and perhaps the immediate southwestern corner of Colorado. It is associated with arid and semi-arid plains and grasslands, but it may be encountered in open coniferous woodlands as well. This rattlesnake is diurnal in the spring, but as temperatures warm, becomes more crepuscular and nocturnal. As with the other races, the scales are keeled, usually in 25 rows, and the anal plate is undivided.

154 NORTHERN PACIFIC RATTLESNAKE

Crotalus viridis oreganus

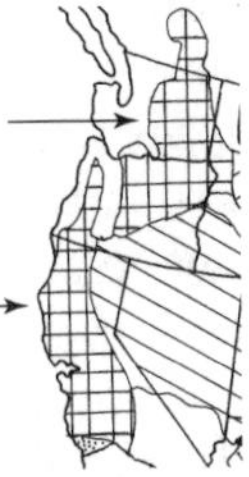

Abundant in many areas, and potentially quite aggressive if hard-pressed, this subspecies will turn and rapidly flee if given an opportunity.

The northern Pacific rattlesnake is strongly and precisely patterned when young, but the pattern tends to become more diffuse with advancing age. Although some adults can be strongly melanistic, most retain greenish brown to grayish brown sides and dorsal ground color. The dorsal markings are in the form of well-defined blotches on the anterior two-thirds of the snake, but in the form of dark bars posteriorly. The tail is strongly barred, but the terminal dark bar is not noticeably wider than those that precede it. The facial stripes may be well defined or obscure, and the top of the head is not usually boldly patterned. This race probably does not breed any more often than every second year at the southern extreme of its range, and may reproduce only every third or fourth year in more northerly, or normally cold, regions. From 3–15 (normally 4–9) neonates, measuring about 10.5 in. are produced.

This, the northwestern representative of the species, occurs southward from southcentral British Columbia to central western Idaho and central California. Because of prevailing cool temperatures, it is largely diurnal in habits, but on hot evenings may remain active until well after dark. It is associated with rocky escarpments and outcroppings, rocky hillsides, rocky areas in grasslands and pastures, and other similar habitats. The scales are keeled, usually in 25 (23–27) rows, and the anal plate is undivided.

155 Prairie Rattlesnake

Crotalus viridis viridis

The easternmost representative of the species, it ranges southward from southeastern Alberta and adjacent Saskatchewan to southern Texas and northern Mexico. It is opportunistically active, being diurnal much of the time, but crepuscular and nocturnal when warm temperatures permit.

The redundant specific name indicates that this is the nominotypical race of the species. The specific name refers to the greenish ground color of some examples, but the ground color may also be brownish or grayish. The dorsal blotches are usually well defined, and on the anterior two-thirds of the body, edged anteriorly and posteriorly with darker pigment, and completely margined with light pigment. Posterior blotches are less well defined. The 2 light facial stripes are usually well defined, and a light bar crosses the dorsal surface of the head from supraocular scale to supraocular scale. The tail is strongly, but narrowly, barred and the distalmost bar and basal segment of rattle are black. Neonates are more precisely patterned than adults.

The prairie rattler is an irascible, grassland-prairie race, that has been extirpated in populated areas, but persists in some numbers elsewhere. It hibernates in rocky outcroppings, escarpments, and mountainside dens. It attains a length of more than 4.5 ft, but is considered adult at 2.5–4 ft in length. Reproduction probably occurs no more frequently than biennially in the south, and only every third or fourth year in the north. The clutch of 10-in.-long babies can number from 3–21, but is normally 6–12.

Contrary to popular belief, the prairie rattler probably does not cohabit peacefully with prairie dogs, burrowing owls, or other endotherms. Rather, these are known to be on the list of prey species.

The keeled scales are usually in 25 (23–27) rows and the anal plate is undivided.

156 NEW MEXICO RIDGE-NOSED RATTLESNAKE, *Crotalus willardi obscurus* 

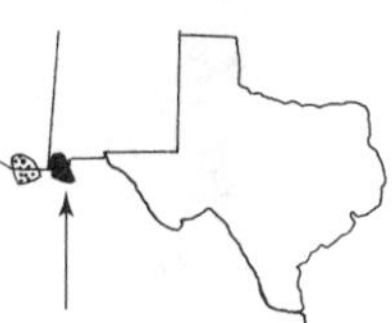

Venomous The venom yield is known to be low, and the toxicity is suspected to be low. If this is actually the case, while envenomation would be unpleasant, it would certainly not be life-threatening to a human in normally good health.

Abundance While not rare at the moment, this rattlesnake is so restricted in distribution that it is possible that its numbers could be sent into an irreversible decline by just a few seasons of indiscriminate exploitation. Currently it is considered federally threatened, and state endangered.

Size This is one of the smallest of the rattlesnakes. Adults are normally 16–20 in. long, and only rarely attain a size of 24 in. Neonates are about 7 in. long.

Range This small rattlesnake is known from the Animas and the Peloncillo mountains of extreme southwestern New Mexico. It is now known to occur as far west as virtually on the Arizona-New Mexico border. It also occurs south of the international boundary in the Sierra San Luis of Chihuahua, Mexico.

Habitat This is a secretive rattlesnake of montane meadows and open woodland. It occurs in suitable habitats, such as at the base of talus slopes or in brushy montane canyons having intermittent streams, between the altitudes of 5,000 and 9,000 ft. Characteristic vegetation of the habitat is pine, fir, oak, and juniper.

Prey The ridge-nosed rattlesnakes are truly opportunistic hunters. They will readily accept insects and other arthropods (including scorpions and centipedes), lizards, smaller snakes, nestling birds, and small mammals.

Reproduction The New Mexico ridge-nosed rattlesnake produces from 1–8 babies per clutch. Despite living at high altitudes, healthy females may breed annually. Breeding may occur either or both in the autumn as the snakes gather in small numbers to hibernate, or in the spring as they emerge from hibernation. The babies are born in the early to midsummer months.

Coloring/scale form Adults are grayish snakes, with a peppered appearance in addition to faint, but apparent, dorsal barring. The barring is somewhat lighter than the ground color, and margined fore and aft with darker gray pigment. A prominent ridge follows the dorsal contour of the snout. Facial markings are obscure or absent. There are two rows of lateral spots, both equally obscure. The gray tail bears a dorsal stripe. Neonates are brown to reddish brown, have light lips, and usually a dark tail. The scales are keeled, usually in 23–27 rows, and the anal plate is not divided.

The New Mexico ridge-nosed rattlesnake is by far the less colorful of the 2 races that occur in North America.

Similar snakes None within its range. The nose-ridge, lack of facial markings, and rattle are diagnostic.

Behavior This is a snake that will usually rattle and flee, rather than coil and strike. If in talus it will virtually dart from sight if disturbed, but will often continue to rattle for some time.

157 Arizona Ridge-nosed Rattlesnake

Crotalus willardi willardi

In contrast to its dusty-appearing, drab New Mexico relative, this is one of the prettiest rattlesnakes. It has attractive, crisp, colors that blend well with the fallen leaves of its montane canyonland-stream bottom habitat. The ground color is an attractive russet, and the dorsal crossbarring is a very light gray, bordered anteriorly and posteriorly by darker reddish-brown pigment. The face is prominently striped with white, and a vertical white bar appears on the rostral scale. The tail is grayish with russet dorsal striping. Neonates are grayer than the adults and often have yellow-orange tails for the first few weeks of their lives. This race, too, seldom exceeds 20 in. in total length. It is restricted to the Patagonia, Santa Rita, and Huachuca mountains of southeastern Arizona and occurs also on the northernmost peaks of the Sierra Madre Occidental of Sonora, Mexico.

Captives breed in the autumn and the spring, and continue to breed on into the early summer months. A breeding in the wild was observed in July. Parturition occurs in August and early September. The clutch size varies from 1–9, with 2–5 seeming to be the norm. Babies indulge in caudal luring, continuing to utilize this method of prey procurement even after the tail color fades. Neonates are about 7.5 in. long.

Massasaugas and Pygmy Rattlesnakes

Genus Sistrurus

Of the three species of primitive rattlesnakes in this genus, only one race (plus one population of intergrades) of one species, the massasauga, occurs in the American West. The snakes of this genus have 9 large scales (similar to those of most harmless snakes) on top of the head, rather than the fragmented scales borne by the snakes of the genus *Crotalus*. Massasaugas have a relatively slender tail and a small rattle that can be difficult to hear.

Besides the massasauga, the Mexican massasauga and the pygmy rattlesnake of the eastern United States are contained in the genus.

158 Desert Massasauga

Sistrurus catenatus edwardsi 

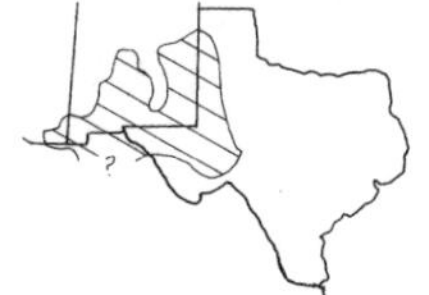

Venomous Although the potency of the venom of the massasauga is thought to be nearly as great as that of the more dangerously venomous populations of the Mojave rattlesnake, the overall venom yield of the massasauga is relatively low. Despite this the massasauga should be considered a dangerously venomous species and treated with infinite respect.

Abundance This rattlesnake varies in abundance from being rather uncommon in Texas to being quite rare in Arizona. It is protected in the latter state. Rather than occurring generally throughout its range, the desert massasauga occurs in numerous well-separated, disjunct populations.

Size This, the smallest race of the massasauga, is adult at 14–18 in. The largest documented size of this relatively slender snake is about 21.5 in. Neonates are a slender 6.5–7 in. in length.

Range The range of this little rattlesnake extends westward from southern and central Texas to the little remaining grassland habitat in the extreme southeastern corner of Arizona. It also occurs in immediately adjacent areas south of the international boundary in Mexico.

Habitat This is an arid-grassland species, but where the grasslands have been destroyed, it continues to persist (at least temporarily) in marginally suitable opuntia-agave habitats. It has been eradicated from many historic sites by agricultural development.

Prey Lizards, frogs, and mice are all prey items of the desert massasauga. Of the lizards, earless and side-blotched lizards and whiptails seem to figure the most prominently in the diet of this snake. It seems probable that because of their tiny size, neonate massasaugas prey almost entirely on lizards but will accept nestling mice.

Reproduction Like all others, this is a live-bearing rattlesnake. Breeding occurs both in the autumn and in the spring of the year. Parturition occurs in mid- to late summer. Brood size varies from 2–10 (3–6 is normal) babies.

Coloring/scale form The desert massasauga is a pretty, but quietly colored little snake. Eastern specimens tend to be a little more deeply colored than the pale specimens from the Cochise County, Arizona grasslands. The ground color is a sandy tan that usually blends well with the substrate on which the snake is found. There are about 35 (27–41) dorsal saddles of darker brown (sometimes with an orangish blush) that are narrowly edged with even darker pigment. A dark diagonal eye stripe (often the darkest marking on the snake) covers most of each cheek and extends upward over the snout anterior to the eye. On the face, this is bordered above and below by a narrow white line. An irregular elongate bar, beginning on each supraocular, extends back onto the nape. The tail is prominently banded. The scales are keeled, usually in 23 rows, and the anal plate is undivided.

Similar snakes Although similarly sized, the twin-spotted rattlesnake of southeastern Arizona has twinned dorsal markings, fragmented head scales, and is a montane species. The Great Plains rat snake is quite similar in color, but lacks a rattle.

Behavior This is a nervous little snake that would rather flee than stay. However, if hard-pressed, and escape is thwarted, they will coil, rattle, and may strike repeatedly. Besides being very secretive, the massasauga is largely nocturnal. They are particularly active during the summer rains.

Comments The desert massasauga seems nowhere common, and because of habitat modifications may actually be rapidly declining in some areas.

Additional subspecies Although 2 additional subspecies are recognized, both occur to the east of the scope of this book. However, a population of intergrade massasaugas exists in southeastern Colorado. The parent races were the desert and the western massasaugas. The snakes in the Colorado population attain an adult size of about 2 ft and bear intermediate characteristics.

GLOSSARY

aestivation: A period of warm weather inactivity; often triggered by excessive heat or drouth.

ambient temperature: The temperature of the surrounding environment.

anterior: Toward the front.

anus: The external opening of the cloaca; the vent.

arboreal: Tree-dwelling.

brille: The transparent "spectacle" covering the eyes of a snake.

caudal: Pertaining to the tail.

cloaca: The common chamber into which digestive, urinary and reproductive systems empty and which itself opens exteriorly through the vent or anus.

constricting: To wrap tightly in coils and squeeze.

convergent evolution: Evolution of two unrelated species as the result of environmental (or other) conditions.

crepuscular: Active at dusk and/or dawn.

deposition: As used here, the laying of the eggs or birthing of young.

deposition site: The spot chosen by the female to lay her eggs or have young.

dimorphic: A difference in form, build, or coloration involving the same species; often sex-linked.

diurnal: Active in the daytime.

dorsal: Pertaining to the back; upper surface.

dorsolateral: Pertaining to the upper sides.

dorsum: The upper surface.

ecological niche: The precise habitat of a species.

ectothermic: "Cold-blooded."

endothermic: "Warm-blooded."

form: An identifiable species or subspecies.

fossorial: Adapted for burrowing. A burrowing species.

genus: A taxonomic classification of a group of species having similar characteristics. The genus falls between the next higher designation of "family" and the next lower designation of "species." Genera is the plural of genus. The genus is always capitalized when written.

glottis: The opening of the windpipe.

gravid: The reptilian equivalent of mammalian pregnancy.

gular: Pertaining to the throat.

heliothermic: Pertaining to a species which basks in the sun to thermoregulate.

hemipenes: The dual copulatory organs of male lizards and snakes.

hemipenis: The singular form of hemipenes.

herpetology: The study (often scientifically oriented) of reptiles and amphibians.

hibernacula: Winter dens.

hybrid: Offspring resulting from the breeding of two species.

insular: As used here, island-dwelling.

intergrade: Offspring resulting from the breeding of two subspecies.

Jacobson's organs: Highly enervated olfactory pits in the palate of` snakes and lizards.

juvenile: A young or immature specimen.

keel: A ridge (along the center of a scale).

labial: Pertaining to the lips.

lateral: Pertaining to the side.

melanism: A profusion of black pigment.

mental: The scale at the tip of the lower lip.

middorsal: Pertaining to the middle of the back.

midventral: Pertaining to the center of the belly or abdomen.

monotypic: Containing but one type.

nocturnal: Active at night.

ontogenetic: Age related (color) changes.

oviparous: Reproducing by means of eggs that hatch after laying.

ovoviviparous: Reproducing by means of shelled or membrane-contained eggs that hatch prior to, or at deposition.

photoperiod: The daily/seasonally variable length of the hours of daylight.

postocular: To the rear of the eye.

race: A subspecies.

rostral: The (often modified) scale on the tip of the snout.

rugose: Not smooth. Wrinkled or tuberculate.

saxicolous: Rock-dwelling.

scute: Scale.

species: A group of similar creatures that produces viable young when breeding. The taxonomic designation that falls beneath genus and above subspecies. Abbreviation, "sp."

subspecies: The subdivision of a species. A race that may differ slightly in color, size, scalation, or other criteria. Abbreviation, "ssp."

sympatric: Occurring together.

taxonomy: The science of classification of plants and animals.

terrestrial: Land-dwelling.

thermoreceptive: Sensitive to heat.

thermoregulate: To regulate (body) temperature by choosing a warmer or cooler environment.

triad: As used here a series of three body rings (often black-red-black), the count of which is often used to help differentiate the subspecies of tricolored kingsnakes and milk snakes.

vent: The external opening of the cloaca; the anus.

venter: The underside of a creature; the belly.

ventral: Pertaining to the undersurface or belly.

ventrolateral: Pertaining to the sides of the venter (=belly).

Bibliography

Bartlett, Richard D. 1988. *In Search of Reptiles and Amphibians.* Leiden: E. J. Brill.

Baxter, George T. and Michael D. Stone. 1980. *Amphibians and Reptiles of Wyoming.* Cheyenne: Wyoming Game and Fish Dept.

Behler, John L. and F. Wayne King. 1979. *National Audubon Society Field Guide to North American Reptiles and Amphibians.* New York: Alfred A. Knopf.

Brown, Philip. 1997. *A Field Guide to Snakes of California.* Houston: Gulf Publishing Co.

Brown, Vinson. 1974. *Reptiles & Amphibians of the West.* Happy Camp, Calif.: Naturegraph Pub.

Collins, Joseph T. 1982. *Amphibians and Reptiles in Kansas.* Lawrence: Univ of Kansas.

_______. 1997. *Standard Common and Current Scientific Names for North American Amphibians and Reptiles.* Lawrence. Soc. for Study of Amphib. and Rep.

Conant, Roger and Joseph T. Collins. 1991. *A Field Guide to Reptiles and Amphibians; Eastern and Central North America.* Boston: Houghton Mifflin Co.

Degenhardt, William G., Charles W. Painter, and Andrew H. Price. 1996. *Amphibians and Reptiles of New Mexico.* Albuquerque: Univ. of New Mexico Press.

Dowling, Herndon G. 1957. "A Taxonomic Study of the Rat Snakes, Genus *Elaphe Fitzinger.*" V. The Rosaliae Section. Ann Arbor: Univ. of Michigan.

_______. 1960. "A Taxonomic Study of the Rat Snakes, Genus *Elaphe Fitzinger.*" VII. The Triaspis Section. *Zoologica* 45:53–80.

_______ and William E. Duellman. 1974–1978. *Systematic Herpetology: A Synopsis of Families and Higher Categories.* New York: HISS Publications.

Ernst. Carl H. 1992. *Venomous Reptiles of North America.* Washington: Smithsonian.

Fowlie, Jack A., M.D. 1965. *The Snakes of Arizona.* Fallbrook, Calif.: Azul Quinta Press.

Funk, Richard S. 1967. "A New Colubrid Snake of the Genus *Chionactis* from Arizona." *The Southwestern Naturalist* 12 (2): 180–188.

Greene, Harry W. 1997. *Snakes: The Evolution of Mystery in Nature.* Berkeley: Univ. of Calif. Press.

Halliday, Tim R. and Kraig Adler (eds.). 1987. *The Encyclopedia of Reptiles and Amphibians.* New York: Facts on File.

Hammerson, Geoffrey A., 1986. *Amphibians and Reptiles in Colorado.* Denver: Colorado Div. of Wildlife.

Lowe, Charles H., Cecil R. Schwalbe, and Terry B. Johnson. 1986. *The Venomous Reptiles of Arizona.* Phoenix: Arizona Fish and Game Department.

McKeown, Sean. 1996. *A Field Guide to Reptiles and Amphibians in the Hawaiian Islands.* Los Osos, Calif.: Diamond Head Pub.

Mehrtens, John M. 1987. *Living Snakes of the World in Color.* New York: Sterling Publishing.

Rossman, Douglas A., Neil B. Ford, and Richard A. Seigel. 1996. *The Garter Snakes, Evolution and Ecology,* Norman, Okla.: Univ. of Oklahoma Press.

Shaw, Charles E. and Sheldon Campbell. 1974. *Snakes of the American West.* New York: Alfred A. Knopf.

Stebbins, Robert C. 1966. *A Field Guide to Western Reptiles and Amphibians.* Boston: Houghton Mifflin Co.

________. 1985. *A Field Guide to Western Reptiles and Amphibians.* Boston: Houghton Mifflin Co.

Storm, Robert M. and William P. Leonard (eds.) 1995. *Reptiles of Washington and Oregon.* Seattle: Seattle Audubon Soc.

Tennant, Alan. 1998. *A Field Guide to Texas Snakes,* 2nd ed. Houston: Gulf Publishing Co.

Tennant, Alan and R. D. Bartlett. 1999. *Snakes of North America: Eastern and Central Regions.* Houston: Gulf Publishing Co.

Wright, Albert H. and A. A. Wright. 1957. *Handbook of Snakes,* Vols. 1 & 2. Ithaca, N.Y.: Comstock.

Index

Bold face page numbers indicate photo(s).

About the Authors

Richard D. Bartlett is a veteran herpetologist/herpetoculturist with 40 years' experience in studying, photographing, and educating people about reptiles and amphibians. He is the author of more than 425 articles and the author of numerous books, including Gulf's *Field Guide to Texas Reptiles and Amphibians* and *Field Guide to Reptiles and Amphibians of Florida.* Mr. Bartlett is the founder of the Reptilian Breeding and Research Institute, a private facility dedicated to herpetofauna study and support.

Alan Tennant is an award-winning writer, wildlife lecturer, wilderness guide, and herpetologist. He is the author of many articles and books including Gulf's *Field Guide to Texas Snakes, Second Edition,* and *Field Guide to Snakes of Florida* is a National Outdoor Book Award winner.